3800 13 005

KT-151-850

High Life Highland

'Ben Hatch makes me laugh more and more' – John Cleese

'Ben Hatch is a very funny writer. His work is fresh and heartfelt' – David Jason

'A French odyssey to rival the greatest aventures in history – if you like jokes, and a car full of ... touching as an overfriendly clown' – Danny Wallace

'Magnifique! Honest, warm and written with feeling and flair' – Terry Wogan

'Just did the kind of laugh that made me snot down my own face. Highly recommended to anyone holidaying in France this year. Or to anyone holidaying anywhere. Or to anyone holidaying with kids. Or to anyone with kids but no holiday plans. Basically to anyone with a sense of humour' – Charlotte Heathcote, *Daily Express*

'Parents will either roar with laughter or roll their eyes with recognition at this family road-trip memoir' – *Metro*

'I am going to shout this very loudly. YOU MUST READ THIS BOOK. The funniest travel memoir you will read this year. Ben Hatch is a genius. The funny bits were so funny. The sad bits were so sad' – Lisa Jewell

HIGHLAND
LIBRARIES

WITHDRAWN

'I loved Ben Hatch's funny, honest, touching memoir' – Jenny Colgan

'Goes from one hilarious situation to another. Very entertaining. The author is naturally funny' – *The Sun*

'Haven't laughed as much in ages' – Mike Gayle

'An Epic French odyssey' – *Daily Express*

'Fantastically funny and touching. I laughed and winced and will never look at baguettes in the same way again' – Sophie Kinsella

Ben Hatch was born in London and grew up there, in Manchester and Buckinghamshire, where he lived in a windmill which meant he was called Windy Miller at school for years, though he's not been scarred by this experience at all. He now lives in Brighton with his tiny wife Dinah, and two children, in a normal house. He likes cheese and is balding although he disguises this fact by spiking his hair to a great height to distract people he wishes to impress. You can follow him on Twitter @BenHatch.

ROAD TO ROUEN

A 10,000-mile journey in a cheese-filled Passat

Ben Hatch

HIGH LIFE HIGHLAND

3800 13 0058512 6	
Askews & Holts	Nov-2013
914.4048	£8.99

headline

Copyright © 2013 Ben Hatch

The right of Ben Hatch to be identified as the Author of
the Work has been asserted by him in accordance with the
Copyright, Designs and Patents Act 1988.

Lyric from 'Hot Hot Hot' by Arrow © Alphonsus Cassell 1982
Warner/Chappell Music Ltd
Lyric from 'Thunder Road' by Bruce Springsteen © Bruce Springsteen
1975 Columbia Records/Sony
Lyric from 'Homeward Bound' © Paul Simon 1965 Columbia

First published in 2013 by HEADLINE PUBLISHING GROUP

1

Apart from any use permitted under UK copyright law, this publication
may only be reproduced, stored, or transmitted, in any form, or by any
means, with prior permission in writing of the publishers or, in the case
of reprographic production, in accordance with the terms of licences
issued by the Copyright Licensing Agency.

Every effort has been made to fulfil requirements with regard to
reproducing copyright material. The author and publisher will
be glad to rectify any omissions at the earliest opportunity.

Cataloguing in Publication Data is available from the British Library

ISBN 978 07553 6456 5

Typeset in Sabon by Avon DataSet Ltd, Bidford-on-Avon, Warwickshire

Printed and bound in Great Britain by Clays Ltd, St Ives plc

This book is based on true events, but some names of characters
and places have been changed.

Headline's policy is to use papers that are natural, renewable and
recyclable products and made from wood grown in sustainable forests.
The logging and manufacturing processes are expected to conform to the
environmental regulations of the country of origin.

HEADLINE PUBLISHING GROUP
An Hachette UK Company
338 Euston Road
London NW1 3BH

www.headline.co.uk
www.hachette.co.uk

This book is dedicated to my wife Dinah

CHAPTER 1

'I have a new packing system.'

'Have you, love?' says Dinah.

The study windows are obscured with lining paper, like we're expecting a Luftwaffe raid, and the kitchen's so full of teetering piles of boxes it resembles the deck of a cargo freighter.

'Do you want to know what it is?'

'No. But I expect you'll tell me anyway.'

'Squishy bags!'

I look at my wife. She's wrapping wine glasses in old newspaper on the sideboard.

'We're not taking suitcases this year. We're taking squishy bags.'

The idea came to me last night. Every bag will be soft, roughly the same size and, above all, squishy. Squishiness is key. It'll make it easier to pack and unpack the boot of the car. And since every bag will be malleable and similarly proportioned, they'll also be *interchangeable*. It also, of course, means Dinah will no longer be able say this: 'Ben, all those suitcases are way too heavy for me, so I'll just marshal the kids into the hotel holding this virtually weightless Tesco carrier bag containing four felt-tips, leaving you stumbling towards the lobby with everything else, looking like Magnus ver Magnusson in the World's Strongest Man Lorry Pull. Don't forget my sponge bag. Let me tie its strap round your neck.'

'Well?'

'Good,' she nods.

'Good? It's a quantum leap. If this was chemistry, it would be the invention of the periodic table.'

'Love, you've bought some holdalls from Millets. Can we get on? Have you seen Charlie? Charlie!' she shouts.

There have been setbacks already. Not everything has gone to plan. For instance, none of us is wearing pants today. We're pantless. Our pants are unavailable, as Dinah's already packed them but doesn't know where. The oven's also picked this moment to stop working. The fan broke yesterday, after Dinah, contrary to our Baumatic Multi-Function Twin Cavity Cooking Theatre manual's instructions, used an 'abrasive cleaner'. And on top of this, we're currently in the midst of the annual summer ant invasion of the food cupboards. Every year in June, like it's the Isle of Wight Festival, every with-it young ant within a hundred miles of Brighton descends on our food cupboards to large it up in the dollops of spilt honey, jam and Bonne Maman Wild Blueberry Conserve.

'*Charlie!*' shouts Dinah again. 'Where is that boy?'

Phoebe enters the room. Dinah swivels her round by her shoulders and pushes her out of the door. 'Upstairs, get dressed, don't make any more mess with your Hello Kitty Beds, and not in here while Daddy's packing.'

'Why?'

'It's dangerous, sweetheart. Have you seen Charlie?'

'No. Why is it dangerous?'

'Because, a bit like a demented *The Cat in the Hat*, Daddy's made some very high piles of unstable cardboard boxes containing extremely heavy things like food mixers that might fall on our heads. CHARLIE!'

'I'm here,' we hear a voice say.

Dinah spins round. The walls of boxes have altered the room's acoustics, so it's hard to tell where sounds are coming from.

'Charlie?' She bends down. 'What are you doing in there?'

'Helping Daddy.'

'Get out this minute!'

He crawls out of the food cupboard. 'They don't make the squashy noise,' he says to me sadly.

'What?' asks Dinah.

'Charlie, go and get dressed with Phoebe,' I tell him.

'On Daddy's phone game,' he says. 'The ants don't make the noise like on Ant Smasher when you squash them.'

He shows us his hands. Studded with dead ants, they look like dimpled Garibaldi biscuits.

'He's killing ants for you!' Dinah looks at me despairingly.

'There's no ant spray and I've got loads to do . . .'

'That's not very Brighton and Hove, my love,' she says, and ushers Charlie towards the stairs.

Before he goes he asks, 'Daddy, if I get dressed quickly can we follow them back to their nest and kill them with the kettle, like what you said?'

'No, that's incredibly dangerous, Charlie. That would be very irresponsible parenting.' Then, as Dinah leaves the room, 'OK, if you're really, really quick.'

Following on from our last guidebook on Britain, we're researching a follow-up about France. Not only does it mean we're packing for a three-month road trip, but because we're renting our house out while we're away, there's the added pressure of having to leave the place in what the holiday letting agency call 'a hotel-standard state'. Which, because of its current messiness, puts this clean-up operation pretty much up there with what was required in Prince William Sound, Alaska, after the *Exxon Valdez* ran aground – if, of course, the *Exxon Valdez* had been carrying millions of tons of Lego bricks, Moshi Monster cards, Ravensburger jigsaw pieces, Squinkies, Hot Wheels cars, Thomas and Friends train tracks, half-eaten rice cakes, dried blobs of Play-Doh and thousands of tiny, loose Hello Kitty bracelet beads.

The kids are dressed and I'm ferrying a banana box of shoes downstairs and walking past the bathroom when I notice Dinah working a tiny pink hairbrush through her blonde hair. I do a double take in the doorway and moon-walk back a step.

'That's a doll's hairbrush.'

'I packed mine,' she says, not looking at me.

'With the pants?'

She nods.

'How many bristles?'

Dinah holds up four fingers.

'So you might as well be using a fork.'

The brush starts to play a tune. I pause to listen. 'Moptop Tweenybop?' I ask.

'Can you just get on with your jobs?' she says.

The doorbell rings. Dinah sighs and goes downstairs to answer it.

'Remember!'

'I know,' she shouts back at me. 'Be evasive about the Mr Muscle.'

And, as she leads the Baumatic repairman towards the kitchen ('And I can't understand it, because even though I only used soapy water, it just suddenly stopped working'), I pass her in the hallway as I head to Halfords to buy the obscure and frankly ridiculously random items the pernickety, clearly gay French police require you to possess to travel on their roads, which include, I kid you not:

- a pretty red triangle
- spare bulbs for your pretty red triangle
- a camp yellow vest
- a GB sticker
- headlight dimmers
- a 'slim' fire extinguisher
- a first-aid kit
- a breathalyser kit to blow into
- a Judy Garland CD
- a well-groomed poodle with a dog jumper
- and a pair of leather trousers with the bum cut out (probably, if they had their way)

The kids' voices echo in their empty bedrooms. Our first guests arrive in a couple of hours and the cleaning company will be here any minute with their mops and antibacterial guns. The car and its roof-box are packed and I'm doing a last check round when I see Dinah outside on the decking. She's sat on a wooden chair, looking down the garden, with one hand held up to her head. It takes me a moment to realise she's crying.

'Love?' I put a hand on her shoulder. 'You alright?'

'I'm being silly,' she says.

Minus a few patches, the lawn's grown back. For six months, during the building work, it was carved up and used as a storage area for slabs of insulation, timber and bags of cement.

'We're packed.'

'Give me a moment,' she says.

Charlie appears at the kitchen back door.

'Daddy?'

'What?'

He sees Dinah. 'Why is Mummy crying?'

I look at Dinah.

'Is it because of the ants?' he asks.

'No.'

'Is it because of the oven?'

'I don't think so.'

'Is it because she has no pants?'

'No.'

'Is it the nasty builders, Daddy?'

'And also because we'll be away a long time and Mummy will miss her home.'

'Daddy?'

'What?'

'Can we kill the ants now, with the kettle?'

Dinah waves me back inside.

'Course we can.'

'To the door, guys.'

The kids have their mini-rucksacks on – Hello Kitty (her), Lightning McQueen (him). Sunlight filters through the front door's stained glass. I can hear a seagull squawking and I can smell the sea on the wind.

'Goodbye, house,' says Dinah. 'See you in September.'

She kisses her fingertips and presses them to the hall wall. The kids copy her.

'Goodbye, house,' they say. 'See you in a million years.'

In the car, Dinah reads from my checklist.

'Tent?' she asks.

'In.'

'Passports?'

'In.'

'Wedding outfits?'

Dinah's cousin Zoe's getting married halfway through our trip, near Bordeaux. We have smart clothes for this.

'In.'

'Golf putters and balls?'

'In.'

'Are we really taking our own putters so we can sneak on to crazy-golf courses without paying?' she asks.

'Yes.'

'Isn't that a bit Alan Partridge, even for you?'

'Not at all. It'll save us a fortune.'

'Disney uniforms?'

'In.'

'Uniforms?' says Phoebe.

'Don't ask, Pops,' I say. I look at Dinah. Our trip ends in Disneyland, where my wife's been advised to take uniforms to prevent the children getting lost.

'What *are* the uniforms?' asks Phoebe.

'They're adapted Postman Pat outfits,' says Dinah. 'Tea flask?'

'In.'

'But Postman Pat's for toddlers!' says Phoebe.

'Do you want to get lost? My foldaway chair?'

'In.'

'No,' says Phoebe.

'Then you're wearing it. Master Document?'

'In.'

'No one will know it's Postman Pat, Phoebe. I've modified them. They look like boiler suits.'

'Are you and Daddy wearing one?' Phoebe asks.

I look at Dinah. 'Don't give her ideas, Pops,' I say.

'OK, that's it. Kids, are you all in?' Dinah asks.

From the front seats, we can't see the children. They're completely obscured by a wall of squishy bags.

'Yes, but I'm really, really squashed,' complains Charlie, who's having to sit cross-legged in his bucket seat because of the bags in the footwell.

'And I can't see, Mummy,' moans Phoebe.

'I've got three bags on my lap too,' says Dinah. 'It's Daddy's squishy bag system.'

'Teething problems. We'll tweak it on the ferry. Now, are we ready to start our AMAZING SUMMER?'

'Aww, my legs are so squashed,' says Charlie.

'It's like being in a dark, nasty cupboard,' says Phoebe.

'Guys, it's only a few miles. Wave goodbye to the house. Are you waving?'

'Yes,' come two disembodied voices.

'Mummy, Volume One, please, of Daddy's Ooh La La Mega French Holiday Compilation, please.'

And as I pull away and head towards the Newhaven ferry, Buster Poindexter is the first track on the CD.

'People in de party – hat, hat, hat,' he sings.

'People in de Passat,' I shout back to the kids. 'Guys?'

'Hat, hat, hat,' I hear their muffled voices reply.

CHAPTER 2

Underneath her suit jacket and tight pale-blue shirt, her breasts seemed to jut out horizontally for almost half a foot. It made me want to put my arms round her waist and pick her up, like an Oscar statue. She'd daintily brush her hair back over her ears and she walked with her hands tucked into her jacket pockets in a way that seemed charming, cute and unassuming. She was 22, with a round, smiley face, and she laughed silently, like Muttley, especially when she was pleased over a joke she'd made, often about her height. My wife-to-be was five foot exactly when I first met her, and liked to brag that she'd 'never ever' bumped her head. She had green eyes, dimples when she smiled, and claimed she was unbeatable at Buckaroo.

Dinah had started at the *Bucks Herald* as a trainee reporter shortly after me, but had a boyfriend, Serious Pete, who liked to listen to Billy Bragg in a Che Guevara T-shirt. He'd recently suffered a mini nervous breakdown that had resulted in him bashing a full can of Heinz baked beans against his forehead. It had been triggered partly by

Dinah's decision to move out of the flat they shared in Wigan to take up her *Herald* traineeship, and also because Labour had narrowly failed to win a by-election in Bury North.

The day I realised I had a chance with Dinah, I was introducing her to staff at St Tiggywinkles wildlife hospital in Haddenham, an invaluable source of space-filling picture stories featuring cute hedgehogs with legs in splints, bottle-fed otters and swans with bandaged wings. One moment, we were chatting about a rabbit with a severed ear she was writing a feature on; the next, she was hyperventilating into a paper bag.

At the Bricklayers Arms that lunchtime, over a pint and a chicken pitta pocket, she explained it was the red-legged tortoise with the cracked shell being carried into the hospital in a straw-lined box that had done it. She was chelonaphobic – frightened of tortoises and turtles. It was the result of being startled by a giant one, 'the size of a Fiat Uno', on a tortoise savannah when she'd lived in South Africa, aged seven.

On the way back to the office, she said, 'Ben, at some point you're going to think it's funny to buy me a plastic tortoise, or think it's hilarious to creep up on me with a picture of a tortoise. People have been doing this all my life. It's going to be tempting.'

I nodded. She was right. In fact, I'd already decided to raid the cuttings library for just such a picture to Post-it-note to her screen.

'Please, I like you.' She smiled. Her dimples appeared. 'Promise you won't do this. I'm absolutely serious. I really fucking *hate* tortoises.'

I promised, and that evening we went out for the first of

what would be many drinks in The Bell Inn in the Market Square. Afterwards she came back to the house I shared with my brother Buster to eat her chips and curry sauce and to beat us both hollow at Buckaroo. And when she drove back to her flat she swooped the wrong way round the mini-roundabout between our two houses in celebration because she knew then we'd end up together. It's something she didn't tell me for years, and which always makes me feel sad now when we fight because that night I had no inkling, unlike her, that twenty years later here we'd be married with two children.

We're in our cabin on the Newhaven to Dieppe crossing. There are lamps at the end of our flip-down beds. We have a small en suite shower and toilet and a little wooden table and chair beneath a round mirror. The kids are getting ready for bed.

'Is it true there are such things as witches?' I ask.

'No!' they shout.

'Is it true there are such things as ogres?'

'No!' they shout.

'Is it true there are such things as elves?'

'No!'

'Is it true there are such things as unicorns?'

'No!'

'Is it true there are such things as goblins?'

'No!'

'Is it true there are such things as Irish people?'

'No!'

'Wrong, wombats. There are millions of Irish people. Right, it's bedtime now!'

Charlie's still looking out of the rain-lashed porthole

for sharks with the binoculars that came free with his ham and chips at the Bon Voyage café.

'What are Irish people?' asks Phoebe.

'Posh lady,' commands Dinah.

Phoebe raises her chin haughtily as Dinah applies eczema cream to her neck.

'They're green, furry monsters with enormous red faces that—'

'They're people from Ireland, sweetheart,' says Dinah. 'Ireland's a country. Daddy's being silly. Charlie, put those down now.'

He lowers his binoculars and pulls on his pyjama bottoms.

'Daddy?' asks Phoebe. 'Can you do the "Eeny-meeny" song and chase us into our bumper beds?'

'Bunk beds, Pops.'

'Eeny-meeny' is the nonsense song my dad sang to me, my brother and my sister when we were kids. He always began slowly, then quickened up, and we had to be in bed and under the covers before he reached 'om-pom push' or else he'd tickle us half to death.

'Eeny-meeny. Macker-racker,' I say, and Phoebe, as usual, acts nonchalant, while Charlie puts his hands on his hips. It's exactly what we used to do. But now, as I speed up, their cockiness vanishes.

'Rare-eye-chicker-packer-lolly-popper.' I stare menacingly at them and they bump comically into each other, squealing with terror, as they scamper up the clip-on ladders to their bunks to be under the covers and avoid the tickling penalty.

'Well, I couldn't be happier,' says Dinah.

We're sat either side of the porthole, sipping red wine

out of plastic toothbrush mugs. The curtains are open and the room's partially lit by the luminous white surf arcing out of the side of the ferry. We touch mugs.

'Not all cabins have a porthole, you know,' Dinah says. 'Didn't I do well?'

'You did very well. I love being at sea.'

She laughs and leans forward. 'Do you, love?'

'I do. I should learn to sail.'

'But you hate getting water in your ears.'

'Because I have odd-shaped ears.'

She looks at each of my ears. 'That retain water, my love?'

'Yes.'

'What a remarkable man I married.'

'And I wouldn't go in the water,' I tell her. 'I'd have a massive yacht.'

'With a crew?'

'Yes.'

'Is this after your deal?'

The possibility of a new publishing deal for my novel has been the subject of some daydreaming.

'Exactly.'

'How much wine have you had?'

'Not enough,' I say, and I pour myself another, just as Charlie climbs down the ladder. I made him Head of the Bedchamber earlier and, taking the role very seriously, he keeps getting up to do things – to fetch Dinah and I glasses of water we haven't asked for, or to solemnly present us each with a spare teddy of his to use 'for the whole night, if you want'.

'Here are your glasses, Mummy,' he says now, having picked them up from the table where they were only an arm's length away from her.

'I don't need them, Charlie.'

'But I'm Head of the Bedchamber.'

'I know, but it's bedtime now.'

'Daddy, there's your book,' he says, pointing at *The Rough Guide to France* in front of me.

'Thank you, Charlie – I'll just leave it there for now.'

'Mummy, do you want your book?'

'Bedtime now, bubs,' says Dinah.

'Okaay,' he says sadly, climbing back up to his bunk.

'I fancy a stroll round the boat. And I might try to get hold of Buster before we lose the signal,' I say. 'Do you mind?'

'Is it a captain's stroll?' says Dinah. 'No, I don't mind. I'm sure the Head of the Bedchamber will look after me.'

'Mummy,' Charlie's head pops up in bed, 'do you want something?'

'No. Go to sleep now, Charlie.'

'What does retaining water mean, Mummy?'

'And you, Phoebe.'

'But I want to know why Daddy's ears are weird.'

'They aren't, sweetheart. It's Daddy who's weird. No more earwigging now. It's late guys.'

Apart from tattooed bikers drinking in the Agatha Christie bar, the ferry's quiet. People are reading or curled up sleeping, coats pulled up over their bodies.

I was 13 when my parents started taking my brother, sister and I to France. We'd catch the ferry from Weymouth after a week with my gran and aunty Romey in Sidmouth. We loved it in Devon, but France always disappointed. Gran and Aunty Romey's was all about us – beaches, the Radway cinema, donkey sanctuaries and outings to Exmouth. France was more for Mum and Dad. We'd visit cathedrals and châteaux or 'go for a mooch', as Mum would say, around French markets, where Dad would buy lamps shaped like Breton lighthouses and Mum would salivate over tubs of pork and apricot pâté.

I always loved the ferry crossing though. Dad was at his most relaxed then. It was before the stressful long drive to the campsite and the nightmare of erecting the family tent. He used to spend entire ferry crossings on the top deck, scanning the sea. Often I stood with him.

I'd decided to become a writer after finding, aged 14, in the creaky, round top room, amongst the cogs of the Buckinghamshire windmill we lived in, a brown leather briefcase containing the comedy sketches my dad wrote during his Cambridge Footlights days. The show had also starred John Cleese, Graham Chapman and the Goodies (Tim Brooke-Taylor, Bill Oddie and Graeme Garden), and had gone on to tour the West End and off-Broadway. It had launched my dad's comedy career that had ultimately propelled him towards his then job as head of BBC Radio's light entertainment. Finding those sketches had altered my relationship with my dad which had been an up and down one.

When I was growing up, my dad left the house before 6 a.m., never returning before I was in bed. At weekends, after a bottle of Woodpecker cider, he'd fall asleep in front of *Grandstand* in his armchair, saving his energy because 'next week's going to be a toughie'. We didn't see much of Dad and because of this, when we did, all of us were desperate to impress him.

My brother inherited my dad's athletic prowess. He represented the school at virtually every sport and the county for several. My sister was passed down Dad's artistic ability. She could play the piano and paint like an angel. However, I was so ungainly, I couldn't (and still can't) do a forward roll, and my solitary attempt to wow Dad with my drawing talent led to my Lifecycle of the Butterfly picture being gloriously magneted to the fridge door for a whole week until I was caught tracing a hippopotamus through greaseproof paper and it was silently removed. Without any discernible abilities, at some point I must have decided that if I couldn't be like my dad, I'd be the opposite of him instead. He was hard-working, so I chose laziness. He was extrovert; I became shy. Whatever he said, I doubted. Whatever he did, I questioned.

It was through Dad's sketches that we properly connected. They were written on very thin blue tissue paper and they made me laugh out loud. As well as presenting a new window through which I could try to impress him, they gave us something in common. He started bringing scripts home for me. We'd listen to radio comedies together and he'd tell me funny stories about writers and performers he worked with. On the ferry, I'd often show him my latest sketches. He'd read them, offer encouragement and write tips in the margin. 'Too obvious.' 'Remember the rhythm.' 'Move this line here.' Normally, at the end of one of these exchanges, my dad would hold his chin up and stare into my eyes, the surest sign of his love, and say something like, 'I hope you'll be a funny boy, my son. I should like that.'

While I followed my dad into writing, my brother Buster ended up in broadcasting. He works for BFBS, a British forces radio station, and is about to fly to Afghanistan to present a show there.

Standing at the back of the ferry watching the Seven

Sisters cliffs fade, I try to call him. The wind's picked up. White plastic chairs hover across the deck. But the reception's already gone, and I'm about to return to our cabin when I feel a hand on my shoulder.

'Ben?'

I turn round.

'It *is* you.'

'Richard!' I say, making out the tall guy in a hooded jacket. 'What are you doing here?'

'Same as you probably,' he says. 'Escaping the bloody kids.'

My friend Richard's family have based themselves next to the café on Deck 7. His kids, George and Gracie, are asleep in round-backed chairs and Sally, his wife, is holding a tray of food and drink.

'Mr Hatch!' she says. She looks at Richard. 'Told you.' Then at me. 'I knew we'd meet someone. We always meet someone on this crossing.'

Half an hour later, I'm telling them the builder story. 'You gave them £16,000 upfront! Shit!' Richard's saying.

The builder story's basically this: when my dad died a few years ago and left me some money, Dinah and I decided to spend it on the house – a loft conversion and kitchen extension. We got our three quotes, including one from a company a friend had recommended. This one came in the lowest by a long way, which, looking back, was the first danger sign. They were a small team – a father and son outfit – and they said they needed cash upfront to buy materials.

'So what happened?' Sally's saying now.

'They did work that *looked* expensive. They took a section of the roof off, built a breeze-block wall in the side-return – stuff that actually costs nothing. Then, one day, I was sat on the toilet upstairs. There's a strange acoustic in there that means you can hear as clear as a bell what's happening on the roof. Earlier, I'd been talking to Nick, the son half of the duo, the boss really. We'd been talking about putting a skylight in the dormer. I wanted one with self-cleaning glass because of the seagull shit.'

'Good idea,' says Richard.

'Yeah. Anyway, he explained they didn't work very well. So I'm on the bog afterwards, with the window open, and I can't believe what I'm hearing. Nick's talking to his crew on the roof saying, "So I told the fuckin' cunt, if you want to clean the fuckin' window, you can fuckin' get up there and clean it your fuckin' self."'

Sally's eyes boggle. 'Woah!'

'I know.'

'The other side of him,' she says.

'Exactly.'

'So what did you do?'

'I told our friend, the one who'd recommended them. She said it was just site banter. All builders put on a hard face for the lads.'

'That's probably true,' says Richard.

'That's what I thought, so I gave him the second lot of cash. Another £16,000.'

Richard closes his eyes. Sally winces.

'That weekend, Nick went to Brussels. He had the cash on him. We didn't know he was a reformed gambler. Our friend forgot to mention that.'

'He gambled it?'

'In a casino. And when he stopped paying his crew, they walked off-site. He followed them a few days later.

We got in a quantity surveyor. He estimated their work was worth £9,000. In the end, a friend of my brother's, a builder from Bradford, came down and lived with us. He slept on the sofa and did it on a day rate.'

'But it's finished now.'

'Yeah. We re-mortgaged. Took in students to pay the bills.'

'And how's Dinah been?' says Sally.

'Angry.'

'I bet.'

'But amazingly not with me.'

'What about the police?' asks Richard.

'They didn't want to know. It's a civil matter. There was no point taking him to small claims. He had no money. We'd just lose even more. So that's partly why we're here. We're like bank robbers coming out of retirement to do one more big job.'

'Another guidebook?' laughs Richard.

'Yeah. France.'

'I thought you were never doing one again,' Sally says. 'Didn't you almost get divorced last time?'

'The kids are older now.'

'Not much older,' says Sally, laughing.

'Plus, Dinah wants to become a French teacher.'

'Wow! Your lives,' says Richard.

'I know.'

'You should have rung,' says Sally.

'We've been like hermits.'

'You still should've rung.'

'So anyway . . . what about you guys?'

Sally smiles. 'Well . . .' and she looks at Richard, 'we do have some news actually.'

'It's probably going to lead to just as much chaos as your builders,' says Richard. 'And be as expensive. Sally's pregnant.'

'Three months,' says Sally. She rubs her belly in a circular motion, like someone cleaning a bowling ball.

'That's great news!'

'Bit of a shock actually,' he says, laughing.

'But a nice one,' says Sally, looking at Richard.

He nods. 'Definitely.'

I close the cabin door. Dinah's reading in her bunk. The kids are asleep. 'I just bumped into Sally and Rich.'

'Sally and Rich!'

'They're driving to the Auvergne. And guess what?'

'What?'

'Sally's pregnant.'

There's a slight pause. 'I can't believe you told me that second,' she says.

I change for bed and climb into the bottom bunk opposite Dinah. The boat pitches gently, there's a knocking sound – a loose screw vibrating somewhere in the metal roof.

I switch my light off and Dinah says, 'This isn't a criticism, but while we're in France, do you think we can not mention the builders?'

'OK.'

'I'm not having a go. I just want this to feel like a holiday.'

'Of course.'

There's a short silence.

'Hey, I've been reading about all the AOC registered cheese in Normandy,' Dinah says. 'AOC is a sort of quality rating. Do you know there are six altogether? We should make that a thing – try all the local produce. Good for info boxes. What do you think? I quite fancy that.'

'Give me an example.'

'In the Loire Valley they have tartes Tatin – apple tarts created by the Tatin sisters. And,' she says, picking up the book and reading, 'rillettes – chunky pork slivers from Le Mans. And there's praline from Montargis. Weirdly, it's made me quite excited.'

I draw the curtain across the porthole. Before I lie back down, I say, 'Can I say just one more thing about the builders?'

'What?'

'I don't really think I've ever fully acknowledged how great you were over it all. You could've blamed me – it was my fault – but you didn't. I forget that about you. On the surface, you're a bit of a panicker . . .'

'Thank you.'

'. . . you're a terrible panicker. But when it comes down to the really big stuff, you rise to the occasion.'

'I know you're buttering me up because you want to ask about having more children,' she says. 'But I'm too tired.'

'Did I say that?'

'I know you,' she says. 'You're working on me.'

'Well you're wrong because I meant that!'

'Good then can you try and remember this conversation tomorrow, when you're shouting at me for my map-reading?' she says.

CHAPTER 3

Draft guidebook copy:
Normandy is famously associated with the Second World War, impressionist painting and Camembert cheese. On D-Day (June 6, 1944) more than 160,000 British and American troops were put ashore here which ultimately led to the liberation of Europe, the defeat of Nazism and the war-film The Longest Day *starring Robert Mitchum. So grateful are the Norman people for this sacrifice that to this day it's not uncommon for those in cars bearing British number-plates to be beeped and wildly waved at by French motorists. The same result can also be achieved if you fail to give priority to the right on the Honfleur roundabout or, as we discovered, if you momentarily forget which side of the road you're driving on while exiting auto-route A29 because you're looking for a Squinkie in your daughter's footwell behind your seat. If you like to combine needlework with your warfare – and who*

doesn't? – at the Bayeux Tapestry you'll learn about the deft moral reasoning that meant French clerics weren't allowed to draw blood on the battlefield of Hastings in 1066 but were permitted to beat Englishmen senseless with maces. Mont Saint-Michel, meanwhile, is a beautiful island that resembles a Disney castle from a distance and on a summer's day enables you to imagine how earth would look like if mankind had the breeding capacity of rats. Other Normandy highlights include calvados, an apple brandy, Rouen, where Joan of Arc was burned at the stake for wearing men's clothes, and Camembert cheese. Invented in 1791, Napoleon III's favourite cheese on a cracker was issued as rations to French soldiers in World War I, was what Salvador Dali based his melting watch paintings on and is the only soft cheese we know of to feature as a murder weapon in a detective series (Avery Aames' Clobbered by Camembert). We liked Normandy. You will too. But be very careful in Rouen. Finding your way to a city centre hotel within the one-way system is like trying to destroy Voldemort's seventh Horcrux.

'Please calm down,' Dinah's saying. 'And stop doing that to the wheel. Do you want me to concentrate or not?'

'Just ring the hotel and get them to talk us in.'

'I don't know where we *are*, my love, so I can't.'

'We've been around this ring road four times. I am losing the will to live here.'

'It's very hard using this tiny map.'

Dinah's staring at a Google map on her phone.

'Where are the proper maps? We've brought about five.'

'I don't know. In the boot probably.'

'What are they doing there?'

'You packed the car. Look, can I just show you something? It says here rue Saint-Nicaise turns into—'

'I can't look at that. I'm driving.'

The sat nav interjects: 'Turn around where possible.'

'Can you turn that thing off before I chuck it out of the window?'

Dinah leans forward, but the TomTom's too far away. She starts to rock to generate sufficient momentum to lean forward enough, audibly straining as she stretches, but still fails to reach it. She unclips her seatbelt, but before she can detach the sucker, she's thrown back in her seat as I turn another sharp corner.

'I wish you'd drive less jerkily.'

'I'm following the road.'

'I might have gone through the windscreen then.'

'I could always have carried on straight into that building.'

Our new TomTom, that was fine on the two-hour drive from Dieppe, is having a meltdown in Rouen. Still refusing to acknowledge the existence of one-way streets, it recalculates the route again. The thick blue arrow now indicates we should cross a thronged pavement into a shopping centre, but it quickly thinks better of mass murder and has another idea.

'One hundred and sixty quid to have a psychopath in the car. You did check the maps were up to date?'

'Yes. They're the latest ones. Can you stop blaming me?'

'Please ring the hotel, love. I know you don't want to speak French because you're rusty, but help me out here. It's very hard driving on the wrong side of the road through a foreign city with this shitty thing telling me to mow people down in one ear, and you in the other giving me half-baked instructions from that postage-stamp map.'

'Riiiight!' says Dinah, theatrically. 'I'll make myself car-sick then.'

She turns round in her seat and rummages about in the wall of luggage, ignoring the kids' shouts as bags tumble on to their laps and heads.

'What are you doing?'

'I'm doing what you want, my love. I'm looking for the laptop to get the phone number of the hotel.'

'The laptop? Why do you need the laptop? Use your phone.'

'My contacts list isn't working.'

Dinah's iPhone is always either out of juice because she never remembers to recharge it, or is playing up because it lives in her filthy handbag, where liquids, dust and rotting children's snacks assault and corrupt its vulnerable orifices.

'You did back it up to iTunes before we left?'

'No, I'm sorry, I was busy packing your clothes and lying to the Baumatic man. Nope, it's not there,' says Dinah, harrumphing back into her seat and reattaching her seatbelt. 'It'll be in the boot with the maps.'

She starts burping now. 'I know you're punishing me, but can you please try not to drive so jerkily. I feel sick.'

We reach another crucial intersection. Charlie declares he's desperate for the toilet. I look at Dinah for direction.

'One second,' she says, holding up a hand and, after a pause so long I'm forced to make a decision at the crossroads, she does another tiny, dry burp. And that's when I see the sign for the multistorey.

'What are you doing?' says Dinah, as I turn off the main road and head towards it.

'He needs the loo. You're burping. I'm parking.'

'But we don't know where we are.'

'I don't care.'

'Go round one more time,' says Dinah. 'I think it is Rue Leanne. We should have gone left at that junction.'

'Nope.'

'But we know what to do now.'

'No, we don't.'

'But the hotel could be miles away.'

'We'll sleep in the car then.'

'Don't be silly.'

'No, I'm not driving any more. That's it for today.'

'That was *not* my fault,' Dinah's saying. We're parked on something like level minus 13 of the car park, probably not that far from the earth's crust. The atmosphere is pungent with exhaust fumes. It's hot and fetid, like a coal mine.

'I never said it was. Though it would've helped if the map-reader had had, I don't know, *a map*.'

'So it *is* my fault.'

'I never said that, but *yes*!'

'You've got to remain calm,' she says.

'I'm very calm.'

'You were shouting.'

'I didn't shout. I never shout.'

'You bashed the wheel. That's the same as shouting.'

'But it's not shouting, and we did almost mow down a party of schoolchildren.'

'Three children, my love!'

'Well, that's OK then. Just three children.'

'Look at me,' she says now. 'We knew this was going to happen. There are lots of major cities we'll have to drive into. Look at me.'

'I don't want to look at you.'

'Look at me.'

I look at her.

'I'm fine,' I say. 'Just don't ask me to drive anywhere else today.'

'Alright, you stay here. I'll go up top and try to find out where the hotel is.'

'Do you promise to ask people for directions and not just wander around?'

'Is that what you really think of me?'

'I know you hate asking for help. It's so hot in here. Are you hot? I can feel my eyes melting.'

'Do you want to go? I don't mind staying.'

'No, you go. You alright, guys?'

'I really, really need a wee,' says Charlie.

Dinah raises her eyebrows, meaning 'This is your problem now', and gets out of the car. As she heads up the ramp towards the exit, I wind the window down and shout to her in a way that makes me sound a bit like the ghost of Obi-Wan from *Star Wars*, urging young Luke to use his latent Jedi powers to fight the dark side, although in this case it's about directions to the Rouen Mercure in rue de la Croix de Fer, 'Use your French, Dinah. *Use your French!*'

I take Charlie for a 'nature wee' between two parked Renaults. I must be muttering to myself as I lift him up.

'Trust Mummy,' says Phoebe, still strapped into her

seat. She looks across at me. 'She'll be back soon. Trust her, Daddy.'

'I do trust her, sweetheart.'

'You have to calm down,' she says.

'I am calm, Pops. It's difficult, that's all.'

'And no bashing the wheel,' she says. 'That's like shouting.'

'It isn't shouting, Pops. Men bash the wheel to *stop* themselves shouting.'

'Actually,' her eyes go glassy, 'I need a wee too.'

What I don't realise is that we're parked on a slope, so, a few moments later, just as the last of the squishy bags are out on the tarmac, the two yellow rivers of Phoebe and Charlie's wees, despite my desperate attempt to dam them with the only thing to hand – the scrunched-up pages from a LD Lines ferry brochure – run straight into all the luggage behind the car. Naturally the kids think it's hilarious.

'Look at the wee, Charlie!' shouts Phoebe.

'Oh my goodness, the wee IS COMING!' says Charlie.

'Watch out, Daddy! The wee is coming!'

'Guys, can you just stand back so I can move the bags, please?'

'My wee is winning! My wee is so fast.'

'That's *my* wee. My wee is winning.'

'Charlie! That's my wee. That one's your wee.'

'Daddy, Phoebe's lying.'

'I'm not lying.'

'She is. She's saying that's her wee!'

'Charlie, *that's* your wee. Don't you even recognise your own wee? My wee is that one. *That* one's your wee. Daddy, isn't that Charlie's wee?'

'It's *not*! *That's* my wee!'

'*Guys!* For God's sake! Never mind whose wee is whose, can you help me move these bags? Please!'

To add to the madness, Charlie manages to drop the dinosaur jigsaw book he's holding into the puddle, forcing me to scrabble about on my hands and knees in the piss for drenched fragments of a triceratops' head.

'Everything alright?' says Dinah, when she returns.

'Daddy shouted again,' says Phoebe.

Dinah raises her eyebrows.

'You don't want to know,' I tell her.

'It's 300 metres away. That way,' she points, picking up a squishy bag. 'What's that horrible smell?'

'That's what you don't want to know.'

We're in a family room in the Rouen Mercure that has a small separate lounge. After checking in we spent the afternoon visiting the city's Musée des Beaux-Arts, where Charlie sent an earpiece-wearing security guard scampering after him when he punched a painting by Sisley. Before that, he and Phoebe had disrupted a service in Rouen Cathedral by playing 'Excusez Moi', a game they've invented that involves them backing deliberately into other visitors then flopping into each other in hysterics when they're told off.

We had the sandwiches we bought on the ferry for lunch, but couldn't find a single restaurant open before 7 p.m. for dinner, so ended up in the place du Vieux-Marché, where Joan of Arc was burned at the stake, using my AA membership card to spread Vieux Pané cheese on stale baguette, something the kids refused to eat because 'it's not normal cheese'. Back in the room, Charlie and Phoebe then managed to soak their only clothes not already drenched in piss earlier, by washing their bums, fully clothed, in the bidet.

'Let me feel it,' says Dinah. I pass her Charlie's milk. 'It's fine.'

I take it in to him. 'Warm it up,' he says, passing it back.

'Charlie, it *is* warm.'

'No, warm it UP!' he orders me, kicking the bedclothes with anger.

'Charlie, there's no microwave here. We're not at home. Be a bit adaptable, please!'

'WARM IT UP!' he shouts.

'Right, I'm shutting the door.'

'NOOOOOO!'

He sits up and takes the milk.

'Daddy?' says Phoebe, sitting up in bed. 'Is this a good Stanley impression?' Over the last few days, while we've packed the house up, the kids have gorged themselves on a Laurel and Hardy box set. Phoebe plucks and releases a few tufts of hair on the top of her head, while pulling a tearful face.

'It's very good,' I tell her.

'Laurel and Hardy are very careful with their hats, aren't they, Daddy?'

'They are, Pops.'

'And they always get into a fight with a small, shouty man with a moustache who has a pretty wife with wavy hair, don't they?'

'They do.'

'Can we watch Laurel and Hardy tomorrow on YouTube?'

'Yes.'

She lies back down.

'Phoebe, your teeth will stick out and you'll look like a rabbit if you carry on sucking your thumb.'

'Good,' she says, plugging it back in. 'I want to look like a rabbit.'

'You'll have to wear a brace and it hurts at the dentist.'

Her thumb comes out.

'Good girl.'

I flop down beside Dinah. She hands me a glass of wine.

'Did you hear that in there?' I take a large swig. 'It was like a Beckett play.'

'The UHT milk probably tastes different,' says Dinah. 'You told me to remind you to ring your brother.'

A few minutes later, I'm speaking face-to-face with Buster, using FaceTime on my phone.

'Want to see my armour?'

'Anything that makes your life seem worse than mine. You wouldn't believe the day we've had.'

Buster laughs. He's flying from Brize Norton to Camp Bastion tomorrow and is showing me his military clothing, holding up a blue flak jacket.

'Kevlar,' he says.

'That's what Kevlar looks like, is it?'

He picks up his helmet now. It's like a German's in the Second World War.

'Yeah, and it took me ages to get the right hat today.'

'Hat! It's a helmet, I think you'll find.'

He laughs.

'Is it heavy?'

'Very. And I've got to learn to do up the strap really fast. If there's a mortar attack on the base.'

'Please don't tell me things like that.'

'It almost never happens.'

'I still can't believe you're going.'

'Me neither,' he says. 'I wake up every morning and think, "Oh, yeah, I'm off to Afghan."'

'Be careful.'

'You know I will be.'

'Be extra careful.'

'You know what a coward I am,' he says.

'I do. And that comforts me. Now put on the . . . what do you call it, the *blouse*?'

He puts the flak jacket on, does up the straps. 'It's like having a bread board strapped to you,' he says, withdrawing a lump of black Kevlar from a pocket at the front. He knocks his fist against it, then reads me the instructions on the back: 'Wash with a soft cloth!'

I laugh.

'That's really important,' says Buster.

'Wash it with a rough cloth and . . .'

'. . . it doesn't fucking work,' says Buster.

He tells me about category 3 areas, category 4 areas. Hostile environment training. Chinooks, razor wire. He holds up a photo of his room.

'Basically it's a fruit container,' he says.

The room consists of a single metal bed. Beside it is a swivel chair and desk, his home for three months. Next door is the tiny radio studio.

'And that's it,' says Buster, laughing. 'And the toilet block hasn't been built yet. I have to take a bottle with me to work. The nearest bog is 300 metres away. The medical facility is close by, and Chinooks will be coming in overhead the whole time.'

We joke about how 'inconvenient' that is.

'Will you keep it down a bit!' I shout.

'I'm *trying* to get to bloody sleep!' shouts Buster.

'I've got a show in the morning!' I shout.

Buster goes through the landing procedure.

'Military plane from Brize Norton into Kandahar, where the Taliban first started. They turn the lights off when we land. We sit there in the Kevlar. Then Chinook to Helmand. Although we might get bumped in an emergency.'

'What happens then?'

'Land convoy. That's what you don't want. You get all the IEDs then, the improvised explosives, by the roadside. That's what gets everyone killed.'

'Right, and how would you get bumped?'

'I'm low down the priority list. Any troop movements and they need a helicopter. A casualty. Vital supplies.'

'Like what?'

'Anything. Not even that vital. A shipment of food arrives. Some fucking extra nibbles getting flown into the base, a sack of cashews, anything, and I'll be bumped.'

'The nibble flight.'

'The nibble flight and I'm off.'

'And on the base. You never leave it?'

'No.'

'Good.'

There's a pause.

'Any news on the book?'

'Nah.'

'So how's France?'

'OK.'

'And what about your driving?' he asks.

'Really jerky,' shouts Dinah, who's been listening in.

He laughs. 'What was that?'

Dinah jostles to get in front of the screen. 'He's already bashed the wheel twice, Buster.'

Buster laughs again. I shuffle Dinah away.

'My worry is you'll be a massive hit out there,' I tell him. 'They'll love you so much they'll want you to go to far-flung bases. You'll get into it. You'll start off saying no, but after a while, you'll think you know the risks better than you actually do.'

'People do get like that, I know,' he says.

'One day, towards the end, you'll think, fuck it, then you'll go. And that's when you'll be in real danger.'

'I would never do that. I've got too much to lose.'

'Promise me.'

'I promise you.'

'Good. And remember this moment. Look at me.'

Buster widens his eyes and stares at me.

'Look into my eyes and remember this moment.'

'I will, but I won't have to remember it.'

'You're off to Afghan in the morning!' I shout at the screen. 'To raise the morale of the British Army.'

'And you're in France, using a squishy-bag packing system,' shouts Buster.

There's a pause. He laughs.

'Dinah told Holly,' he says. Holly is Buster's wife.

I look at Dinah. 'Slagging off my squishy bags were you?'

I turn back to the screen.

'Actually she compared it to the invention of the periodic table,' says Buster.

'You're a part of me, you little twat. I'm only the way I am with you. If you weren't here, I would lose a piece of myself. Of the person I am when I am with you. You're like a limb.'

'I feel the same,' he says.

'It's a shit limb. An appendix or something. But be careful.'

'And you use your putters,' he says.

I look at Dinah again. Buster laughs.

'Why do I have to keep defending the putters?'

'And stop bashing the wheel. It's the same as shouting,' he says.

'It's not the same as shouting. I *never* shout.'

'Now he's shouting at *me*,' calls Buster.

'Stop shouting at your brother,' says Dinah, jostling to get back in front of the screen. 'I've already warned him about his shouting.'

Buster laughs and we hang up.

As part of a summer festival in the city, they're illuminating Rouen Cathedral with different pastel lights to mimic Monet's famous series of paintings. As I lie in bed, watching the curtains glow from green to blue through to pink, I find I'm thinking about Tring Road in Aylesbury, remembering when Buster, Dinah and I lived there.

CHAPTER 4

The house on Tring Road that Buster and I shared was owned by Mr Jefferies, a pensioner who ran an old-fashioned sweetshop next door. He'd crammed every flat surface of the place with hideous knick-knacks that were all carefully listed on the inventory ('China Owl in Flight, Wooden Hedgehogs Kissing, Mickey Mouse Teapot with Lid') almost as if he hoped we'd break them to compromise our deposit.

We didn't have a sofa, just these strange spongy seats that were more like footrests. They had no backs to them, which meant that, even after a hard day's work, we had to sit bolt upright at all times. This was hard because of the energy-sapping gas heater. We didn't know about carbon monoxide poisoning in those days, which is probably just as well for Mr Jefferies. But we knew what the heater did to us. Within ten minutes of entering that living room, when the heater was on, you were wiped out. It sucked all life from you. If you were off work and had things to do that day, you knew you had to do them before you put the heater on.

To make it even more unwelcoming, the room was dominated by a huge long-stemmed vase we used as an ashtray. It fell over once, containing six months' worth of Marlboro Light butts, spreading more ash round the house than the meteorite that wiped out the dinosaurs.

The kitchen wasn't much better. We ate kebabs off paper plates, the fridge never contained anything but lager and I Can't Believe It's Not Butter, while the oven was merely the world's least portable cigarette lighter.

Before he started at BFBS, Buster worked for BBC News and Current Affairs at Broadcasting House in London, where he didn't enjoy their snobbish attitude. He'd cycle to Aylesbury station on his bike with no brakes and spend all day cutting out news stories, sticking them to pieces of cardboard and getting patronised for not knowing who Lionel Jospin was, then he'd cycle home to sit in an ash-ridden, energy-sapping living room, on a sofa seat with no back, eating a takeaway on a paper plate.

Our one luxury was movies. Each night Buster cycled past Blockbuster to get out the latest action-adventure. *Die Hard, Die Harder, Die Hard with a Vengeance, Die Harder with a Vengeance, Die Harder with Harder Vengeance.*

The moment we both realised a woman was needed round the place came after we were almost reported to Social Services for child cruelty. This had happened because a busybody had mistaken the cardboard cut-outs Blockbuster had given us of Bruce Willis and Whoopi Goldberg that we kept by the dining room window for home-alone children. The figures were three-quarter-size replicas of the movie stars and, seen through net curtains, did look slightly like kids. The nosey woman who reported us was concerned that the youngsters seemed so forlorn with neglect that they just stared out of the window all day long. And she was particularly upset that one of them, despite it being winter, appeared to be wearing nothing but a blood-stained vest.

Dinah, now my best mate on the paper, moved into the boxroom where we'd locked away the knick-knacks. After a week, she'd introduced a washing-up rota, a no-smoking-inside policy and had showed us what a scatter cushion was. Within three, I was Ajaxing the bath in an apron with 'Mummy Likes to Keep Things Clean' written on the front and complaining when Buster came home so late he ruined the Nigella cottage pie with thyme and rosemary that Dinah had taught me how to prepare. We kissed for the first time in the Bricklayer's Arms two months later.

'What are we going to do?' she asked afterwards. She moved into my room, but she didn't mean that. She meant, what are we going to *do*?

Obviously get married, I said, and move into a thatched cottage with low ceilings, so she didn't feel so tiny, and live there with a three-legged cat called Mopsy. I'd grow shoulder-length hair and write dense prose, reserving my place at the top table of the British literary establishment, while she became a wizened old hack with a hatchet face, hypocritically moralising on the lives of the unwashed.

'Deal,' she said, 'but no cats. I *hate* cats.'

'Were you once surprised by a giant one the size of a Citroën Xantia?' I asked.

'Never reference tortoises, even in jokes,' she shivered.

The next morning, over breakfast, she called Serious Pete to break it off. 'I hope there are no baked beans in his cupboard,' I said.

'He'll be fine,' she said. 'It's *World in Action* tonight.'

* * *

It's been quite challenging to put an itinerary together for France, what with their 35-hour working week, the long lunches and extensive public holidays – not to mention the fact that, here, delegation seems all but illegal ('No, I cannot take a massage. You haf only to speak to Melanie. Goodbye').

It's sometimes taken weeks to reach a PR in the relevant tourist office with enough authority to issue us with a journalist pass for something sometimes as low-key as, say, visiting a prune museum. Often, having finally reached this person, we've found them too busy writing press releases designed to generate press interest in their region to actually speak to a member of the press who already *has* an interest in their region. To sanction our visit, the PR has then invariably needed the approval of their boss, who, in turn, has required the signature of a regional director, themselves beholden to the mayor, and so on up the hierarchy, until the final say on whether we get a family pass to see a short film about dried fruit in Languedoc-Roussillon has ultimately to come from the Elysée Palace, with President Hollande probably breaking off a conference call on the collapse of European banking with Angela Merkel and David Cameron to make the final judgement call. 'Yes, zey can see the prunes. No audio guide. They pay for parkink.'

To bypass this rigmarole, we requested a letter of accreditation from the Normandy Tourist Board, written in French. It verifies who we are, what we're doing and politely requests that attractions within this region assist us. The idea is that we hand it over, are allowed in free of charge and everyone's happy.

'He's not happy,' says Dinah. 'He wants an official press card.'

We're at the 360-degree cinema in Arromanches-les-Bains, and the man behind the screen has short, curly black hair, little round glasses and a mauve jumper draped jauntily round his shoulders. It's what Rolf Harris would look like if he was less avuncular, 30 years younger and French.

'But we haven't got one.'

'I know that, love,' she says. 'But he doesn't understand. He's French, remember.'

It's already been a fraught morning. Dinah's shampoo has joined the catalogue of items which we've left behind in hotel rooms. The squishy packing system's close to breaking down because we can never find anything, as all the bags look exactly the same. And, wired on their chocolate-based cereals, which is all the French seem to eat at breakfast (even All Bran has chocolate in it here), the kids have been out of control.

At the Bayeux Tapestry building we saw the 70-foot-long cloth depicting William the Conqueror's victory over King Harold in 1066, but there was a kids' audio-guide device that Charlie tied round his neck and insisted we lead him along by, like a dog. Meanwhile, earlier, at the Musée Eugène-Boudin in Honfleur, Phoebe had been rebuked by a security guard for shouting, 'And nobody will be any the wiser' in a hushed room full of household items from the nineteenth century.

I hand Rolf de Harris a Frommer's business card. He passes it like it's a specimen slide of botulism to the pipe-cleaner-thin woman beside him. She glances at it. They have a brief conversation, then Rolf returns it and says something.

'It's not a press card,' Dinah says, translating.

'In England,' I speak slowly to Rolf, 'to get an official press card . . . you must be a member of . . . the National Union of Journalists. But most journalists in England . . . aren't members of the National Union of Journalists. It's different in England. We're not . . . as unionised.'

Rolf turns back to the woman. They have a brief confab.

'Giving him a lesson in 80s British Labour relations, love? Why don't you tell him about Arthur Scargill, the Miners' Strike and that Chumbawamba record while you're at it?'

'It helps when you spell it out for them. I think he got my drift. But thanks for your input.'

And now the woman leans across Rolf, almost pushing him out of the way.

'Journaliste card!' she barks in my face. 'Journaliste card!'

After the director's been called, several phone calls have been made to the relevant authorities, a couple of forms have been filled out and our collective will to live has been sapped almost to extinction, Dinah's French secures our free tickets and we're led into a circular bunker that tells the story of the D-Day landings through a 20-minute film called *The Price of Freedom*. It's black and white, featuring occasional colour images of Normandy before, during and after the Second World War. The images are projected on to the concave walls. One minute it's sleepy farmyards and the kids are pointing at sheep and cows, the next it's footage of bodies lying tangled in barbed wire on Omaha Beach, or a bloodied soldier having an ear sewn back on by a field surgeon.

Charlie tucks his head into Dinah's shoulder, hiding from the rat-a-tat sound of heavy machine-gun fire that's also causing Phoebe to whimper in my arms. What's weird is that the clearly much tougher French kids are all calmly watching it like it's Roly Mo in *The Fimbles* discussing how a tambourine works in the underground library. When our children's cries of distress begin to outdo those of a dive-bombing Stuka strafing the French countryside, Dinah nudges me. 'Come on. Let's bin this', and we file out past Rolf into the sunshine.

On the grassy cliffs above us, there's a small memorial garden and below us, on the beach, lies the rusting hulk of the Mulberry Harbour.

'Too scary, Phoebe?' I ask.

She nods.

'Charlie, that's what real war's like.'

'Too loud!' he says.

'War is quite loud, guys. I'm sorry we frightened you.'

'Don't like war any more,' says Charlie.

It's a beautiful drive along the E5 through the Pays d'Auge, heading for Lisieux. We pass thatched cottages, fields of the cattle that produce Camembert and Pont l'Evêque cheese. There are orchards where the apples that Calvados is made from grow in green valleys. I'm still, however, trying to explain 'why they were fighting' to Phoebe.

'So, you know Germany?'

'Yes.'

'Well, a long time ago, it was taken over by a nasty man who wanted to steal everyone's countries with his soldiers. One of the countries he stole was France. America and Britain didn't like this, so we tried to take the country back for the French. Our soldiers landed on that beach we saw the film about and they fought with the nasty man's soldiers.'

'Why did they have guns if they were the good ones?'

'Well, the bad ones had guns, so to beat them, the good ones needed guns as well.'

'What was happening to that man's ear?'

'He was injured. When skin's torn, surgeons – they're like doctors – stitch the skin back together.'

'Does it hurt?'

'Not in a hospital, because they have anaesthetic. That makes it very cold so you can't feel it. But during a battle, there isn't time, so they stitch it up there and then.'

'Why wasn't the man crying?'

'Because he was very brave.'

'But why did everyone from Germany follow the nasty man?'

'Because he shouted a lot and made dramatic gestures with his arms and—'

'Like Mummy when Charlie knocks over his apple juice?'

I look at Dinah. 'Sort of, although I don't think Mummy wants to invade the Low Countries with Panzer tanks, do you, Mummy?'

'No,' she says.

'Mummy,' says Charlie very seriously, 'would never steal anyone's country because she's a *nice* mummy.'

'Thank you, Charlie. Now, guys,' says Dinah, 'we have a surprise. Daddy, do you want to tell them?'

'Guys, guess what?' I look at them in the rear-view mirror. 'Tonight, because you've been very good – well, quite good – we're sleeping *inside* a safari park!'

* * *

Our stilted lodge overlooks the muddy hippo enclosure and Gibbon Island, where a troupe of monkeys noisily swings about amongst the bark-less trees and dangling rubber tyres. There's a guest food hamper containing local cheeses, wine and pear cider.

The kids have had fun chasing the wallabies ('wobblies' Charlie called them) around the site and are now bathed and in bed. Sitting outside in the gathering darkness, the animal sounds carry through the air – the ping-pong noise of an exotic bird, the shriek of a chimpanzee and a distant roar of a lion.

'Some locally produced cheese, monsieur?'

Dinah passes a triangle of Camembert.

'Thank you. Pear cider, madame?'

'Thank you,' she says.

'So how's it going? Pleased we're doing another guidebook?' Dinah looks at me sarcastically. I laugh.

'It's like having babies,' she says. 'You forget the hardships.'

'Shall we have another baby?' I ask.

Dinah widens her eyes and looks across. She laughs. 'Are you serious? After the last couple of days.'

'What do you think?'

'I don't know. What do *you* think?' she says.

'I don't know, that's why I'm asking you.'

'I think I'm done,' she says. 'My love, I'm 40.'

The irony is we only had kids at all because of Dinah's ultimatum a few weeks before our wedding. 'I want to marry you but I can't lie – I want children. I know you don't but if you love me you'll trust me and go along with it. And if you don't . . . well . . ." And she'd handed back her engagement ring and gave me a week to make up my mind.

Several years later after Charlie was born, I thought that was it. We now had a boy and a girl. The set. I'd been a reluctant father for many reasons, chief of which was I thought they'd end up being as much as a pain in the arse to me as I'd been to my dad. And also because I selfishly thought they'd thwart my writing, which of course they had. Six months after Phoebe's birth Dinah, the higher earner of us, returned to work while I'd become a stay-at-home dad. While I'd never envisaged this happening, I'd loved every minute of it. I'd pushed first Phoebe then both of them around in their buggies. I'd changed their nappies, taken them to Little Dippers. I'd seen their first smiles, been bitten by their first teeth. Yet although they'd been the most rewarding years of my life, I'd also dreamed of having more time to write, which is why it's so strange that with this now on the horizon as Charlie's due to start school in September, I've found myself feeling so broody. 'What about your writing?' asks Dinah. 'I thought you wanted to get properly stuck in again.'

'I miss having a baby. You don't think there's another one of ours out there?'

I mime casting a fishing line and reeling it in.

'What's brought this on? Sally and Rich?'

'You know I've been thinking it for a while.'

'Oh, hello!' A wallaby's jumped right up to us. Dinah holds out her hand.

'They move so mechanically,' she says.

'Imagine moving like that.'

'I think it would be fun,' she says.

'It would get tiring. Imagine the day-to-day. Three jumps to get from the oven to the fridge. Two to the bin.'

'You're right, the little jumps would be tiring.'

The wallaby twitches its nose, before bounding away.

'And it would be two years of one of us not working,' says Dinah. 'And things have just stabilised.'

'But what if the book did well?' I say. 'You could take some time out. Go part-time.'

'But what about the teaching?' she says.

'I know. I know. But by not making a decision, we're effectively making a decision.'

'Because of this?' she says, tapping the contraceptive chip in her arm.

'Yeah. Did you know the honeybee has brain cells similar to ours? When they gather pollen, they lose hair and age faster than if they look after their grubs. Also, when they go from foraging for pollen back to caring for grubs, they're rejuvenated mentally and their hair grows back.'

Dinah glances at my receding line. 'I think it's too late for that, my love. What's up?'

I'm looking down at my own phone, which has just bleeped.

'An email from Henry.' Henry is my literary agent.

'How very apt,' says Dinah. 'What's he saying?'

'It's still downloading.'

Later, we're in bed, and Dinah's reading to me about Joan of Arc, as she tries to work out some copy for the guidebook.

'Basically, she was a farmer's daughter, a peasant, from Rouen. She had a vision that France would be rescued from misrule by the English and that the French king would be crowned in Reims Cathedral.' Dinah's trying to gee me along. The message from Henry wasn't good. A rejection from Penguin.

'Out of desperation, more than anything, when the French nobles heard about her visions, they popped her into some white armour and gave her 5,000 men to spearhead an attack on the English at Orléans. What's that like? Me going up to the Ministry of Defence to tell them I've had a dream about how to defeat the Taliban . . . What are you smiling at?'

'The thought of you burping at the controls of a white Chinook flying out of Helmand.'

'This sat nav,' she pretends to bash a joystick. 'Are you sure you downloaded the latest maps?' I laugh and she continues her story. 'So anyway, Joan wins all these battles against massive odds, recaptures fort after fort, reversing the entire tide of the war. She's shot in the head with a cannonball. She takes an arrow in the leg and another in the neck, then, just like she foretold, Charles VII is crowned in Reims Cathedral. That's definitely worth putting in.'

'Definitely.'

'And she was only 18. At 18, I was a busty wench in Camelot Theme Park near Chester and living at home. That reminds me.'

She picks up her phone and calls her mum and dad and I think back to when I was 18.

At 18 I decided to become a professional snooker player. The basis for this was I had my own snooker cue autographed by Tony Meo and on a small quarter-sized snooker table that I shared with my brother I'd recently achieved a break of 27. It would've been 35 if I hadn't had to use a 2b pencil instead of a cue to pot the black in the tight corner of my bedroom where the table didn't quite fit. It seems absurd, but I genuinely thought if I practised enough I *could* become as good as Steve Davis.

This snooker obsession helped explain my A-Level grades, which just scraped me into Bristol poly studying for a degree in social science. In fact with six hours of lectures a week the course was ideal as it gave me plenty of time to build up my safety game. My snooker dream was shattered the day I came home for Christmas. Having not attended even my six hours of lectures to practise in the Riley Sports Bar and Bingo Club, I told my dad I'd something important to tell him. As was customary we went upstairs to play a frame and discuss matters. I was hoping to demonstrate how good I'd become and use this to soften the blow that I'd soon be abandoning my studies to turn pro. As it transpired, my dad – not a very good snooker player – beat me by 100 points. What clinched it, and forced me to abandon the game, was not just the fact my dad was playing without his glasses on – they were at Dollond and Aitchison having the lenses altered – but that he also, at the time, had quite bad conjunctivitis. Barely able to see, with his eyes bloodshot and watering, my dad, who'd not hit a snooker ball since I last saw him three months earlier, had comprehensively beaten me at a game I was hoping to make my living at.

Other careers came and went after my mediocre degree in Business Studies at Sheffield University. I worked in a lawnmower showroom in Leyhill Buckinghamshire but was sacked for failing to attend a product awareness course in Stow-on-the-Wold, where the new Mountfield 345, excellent in wet grass, was being demonstrated. I sold photocopiers, then insurance. I worked in a pub, then a video shop. I was a postman before I was fired for losing a whole road's-worth of letters. I worked in the dole office. One time I even tried to set myself up as a private detective.

I put an advert in my local paper, the *Bucks Examiner*. Under the image of a large magnifying glass my ad ran: 'Marital surveillance?' Much to my parents' despair (I'd used our home number) I had plenty of enquiries, but for some reason hearing my mum shouting upstairs 'Benjy, there's a man on the phone who wants you to follow his wife, can you get out of the bath please?' tended to put off prospective clients. Once I managed to get myself sacked from selling advertising space at the *Independent* newspaper for writing a letter of acceptance for my job *un*acceptably. I was dismissed from Chesham McDonald's for wearing a dirty apron and from the Royal Bank of Scotland on Baker Street in London after accidentally mailing Michael Crawford's cheque book to the wrong address. Claiming it's what Frank Spencer would have done cut very little ice.

Around when I worked in McDonald's my dad gave me some advice. He said the secret of happiness was to do every job you were given to the best of your ability no matter what it was. At the time he was the controller of Radio 4. He was ensuring the Today programme ran smoothly and buttering up the Prime Minister, John Major, as the BBC's charter was up for renewal. What he wasn't doing was making sure the correct amount of lettuce was added to a McChicken sandwich. Mark Twain summed it up best: 'When I was a boy of fourteen, my father was so ignorant I could hardly stand to have the old man around. But when I got to be twenty-one, I was astonished at how much he'd learned in seven years.'

Except I was 25 when this turning point came for me. It was when my mum was diagnosed with cancer. My mum was the greatest mother any son could wish for. She took in ironing, used to do it in a blue boiler suit in the kitchen. She ironed so much her right forearm was the size of Popeye's. But more than that, she always took my side when I argued with my dad. That's why I decided to become a journalist. I wanted to make her proud. Plus I'd naively imagined the profession was a recognised nursery slope towards making it as an author.

CHAPTER 5

*D*raft copy for Guidebook:
The Loire Valley is famously associated with one towering woman of French history, Catherine de Medici. She was small, with sticky out eyes and aged 14 she married Henry, second son of Francis I, who became Henry II in 1547. Desperate to bear a child to secure the Valois line, Catherine resorted to daubing her lady bits with cow dung and drinking mule urine, presumably after rather than prior to sex. It worked and she went on to bear 10 children. When Henry II died in 1559 she became regent firstly to Francis II (aged 15) and then on his death to Charles IX (aged 10). Catherine, described as the most powerful woman in 16th century Europe, is condemned for the 1572 St Bartholomew's Day Massacre in which thousands of Huguenots were killed. Though on the upside she introduced the fork to France. Catherine's also credited with the invention of women's knickers. The story goes she was

desperate for something that would stop her showing off her foo-foo when she was riding side saddle (presumably because it was covered in cow dung). As a great patron of the arts she lavished fortunes on renovations at the Loire's Chateau Chenonceau where she spent the last 25 years of her life hosting cross-dressing balls featuring naked women aimed at inspiring her son Henry III to take an interest in his wife and produce an heir.

The soft climate of the Loire Valley also makes it the ideal environment to grow vegetables. Tours is famous for its French beans, Samur for potatoes, Anjou is a pear Mecca and Berry is of lentil-producing renown. We weren't as interested in the vegetables. Can you tell?

'Guys, I'm sorry – we thought that would be better,' Dinah's saying.

'It was rubbish,' says Phoebe. 'France is rubbish.'

'It wasn't rubbish, Phoebe, and France isn't rubbish.'

'Yes, it is. It's all about vegetables. You said it was a theme park. I was looking forward to the rides. It was *rubbish*.'

'It *was* a theme park,' says Dinah.

'Yeah, a theme park about *vegetables*! Who would have a theme park about vegetables?'

'Charlie, did you enjoy it?'

'It was rubbish.'

'Well, I'm sorry there wasn't a white-knuckle spring onion ride, guys. We did our best.'

'Everything is rubbish in France,' says Phoebe. 'The bread is sharp. They don't sell Moshi Monsters. The burgers don't have buns; they're just *burgers*. The beans aren't orange. And all the cheese stinks.'

'Phoebe, baked beans aren't the only beans in the world, and if you say the cheese is rubbish, I'm sure Daddy will have something to say.'

We're in the car outside Terra Botanica, Europe's first horticultural theme park, in Angers in the Loire Valley. Only the French would spend ten years and £70 million on a theme park dedicated to ingredients.

Spoiled by Pixar movies featuring imaginatively animated talking creatures going on epic adventures across time and space, a film about what happens to a drop of water when it gets sucked up by a magnolia tree didn't quite hit the spot. And as for the story of the hydrangea in the Plant Theatre, let's just say it was minus the plot twists our kids have come to expect in a narrative.

They weren't that interested in the display about the correct way to cook haricot beans either. In fact, the only ride even approximating our build-up was one where we sat in a hollowed-out, pedal-operated giant walnut shell that travelled slowly on rails not quite above the treetops, where we got to stare below at lettuce. Or, as Phoebe put it, 'I don't want to look at salad. I want to have fun.'

This is pretty much how it's been in the Loire Valley these last two weeks. We've been staying in a gîte near Loches, foraging further and further afield for more and more meagre attractions, and have come to the conclusion that basically all you can do here is drink wine (good) and visit châteaux (bad). We've been to Amboise, Azay-le-

Rideau, Château de Brissac, Blois Chambord, Cheverny and Chenonceau.

In British castles you expect a National Trust-style activity pack, peacocks to chase, maybe the odd colouring-in station for kids, or at the very least a grey-lady ghost haunting a draughty chapel to liven things up. In France, kids, it seems, are treated as though they're slightly shorter adults, so that even on a dedicated children's audio guide, there's little allowance made for their attention spans.

'Today, children, we are going to tell you all about our wonderful castle. But first some 'istory. When Philip IV died in 1314, Louis X, 'is eldest son, in'erited the throne. However, Louis X then died in 1316, leaving a daughter, Joan II of Navarre, and also 'is pregnant wife. The wife's son, John I, died in infancy. That meant Philip IV's second-eldest son, Philip Count of Poitiers, sought the throne to the exclusion of his niece, Louis X's daughter. This was opposed by nobles such as Odo IV, Duke of Burgundy, Joan II of Navarre's maternal uncle, and Charles Valois, Philip's uncle. Now let us move to the Long Room. There is a painting of a cat.'

Condemned to these meagre entertainment pickings, the children at least get to run around the wonderful open spaces, right? Wrong. How about this sign outside Château Chenonceau?

'Note to visitors: it is forbidden to move around noisily, to run, push one another, climb or shout. It is forbidden to sit or lean against furniture, touch objects, touch flowers, make things dirty, spit and draw graffiti. It is forbidden to relieve oneself. Or to change young children anywhere other than the toilets. It is forbidden to climb up trees, bring balls on to the site and walk on the lawns. It is forbidden to upset the circulation of visitors. Mobile phones must be switched off. Failure to adhere to the rules will lead to expulsion from the domain. Thank you for your cooperation. This place is under surveillance. Decree Jan 22, 2009.'

Short of releasing bull mastiffs into the grounds, filling the moat with piranha and rolling razor wire over the lawns, there isn't a lot more you could do to make the place any more child-unfriendly.

There are other gripes too. Things that you'd normally enjoy about France have become problems because of the tight schedule we're on. During our first week in France, for example, we enjoyed our special trips to the *boulangerie* to buy baguettes. How rustic and charming it seemed, buying fresh bread each morning, tucking that warm baguette, waistcoated in white paper, under your arm, after a cheery word with a local baker. Now we feel enslaved by this tyranny.

In England you're never more than 100 metres from a Londis, Happy Shopper or Tesco Metro that sell bread that's edible for days, weeks. In France, where you can only buy it from *boulangeries* that close for two hours in the middle of the day, occasionally don't open at all on random weekdays and *never* open on Sundays, the baguettes, which you'd think by necessity must last at least a week, are as hard as rounders bats after 12 hours. We've lost whole mornings scouring the French countryside, like Cro-Magnon hunter-gatherers, searching for bread. Like Dinah said one forlorn afternoon near Chateaubriand, when our starving kids had been reduced to sucking pickled onions like gobstoppers for sustenance, 'It's no wonder Marie Antoinette said, "Let them eat cake." She wasn't patronising peasants, it was practical advice. The lazy-arse *boulangeries* were probably all shut.'

But now, outside Terra Botanica, there are worse problems.

'Love, it's not working!'

'*And* the sausages are weird,' says Phoebe. 'They don't taste of sausages. Sausages should taste of sausages. Their sausages are *not* sausages.'

'Phoebe, I'm really not happy with this attitude,' says Dinah. 'If you want your choccy squares, you'd better buck your ideas up.'

Each day, like galley slaves motivated by rum, we apportion rations. Three squares of Milka chocolate per child per day, taken after fruit at lunchtime.

'It's not working,' I say again.

'What isn't?'

'The sat nav.'

I've been trying not to panic. But I can feel it rising in me. Not having a sat nav when you have my wife map-reading is a bit like being a sailor in the fourteenth century and attempting to round the Cape of Good Hope without a nautical chart. Put it this way, if I had a choice – lose the car's brakes or the sat nav – I'd gladly drill a hole in the driver's footwell and use my feet to slow down. Also, having a sat nav means vital brain cells required to remember to turn right or left at particular junctions are more usefully redirected towards establishing just who in the back was first to slap the other one round the face with the Villandry Gardens activity sheet.

'Give it here,' says Dinah.

She tries to switch it on. It doesn't work.

'And they trick you with their crisps,' says Phoebe. 'Their crisps taste of peanut butter. I hate the French.'

'Phoebe, shush! Was there water in your handbag?' I ask Dinah.

The glove-box catch broke a couple of days ago and now won't shut, so when we leave the car, Dinah carries the sat nav in her handbag. She opens her bag to show me it's dry.

'Could that mouldy apple core have soaked into it?'

'It needs charging, love,' says Dinah.

'It doesn't. It's broken. It's two and a half hours to Dol-de-Bretagne. We'll never make it. You said yourself you can't work out the maps. Actually, didn't you drop your handbag in the Artichoke Maze?'

'The blame game has started. Why is it my fault?'

'It *was* in your handbag. It's our longest drive. You don't understand how much I rely on it. You don't know what this means. It's a calamity.'

'I'll direct us,' says Dinah. 'Where's the map?'

'You want to map-read? But . . . but Dinah . . .'

And I feel giddy now. Terrible images return of researching our British guidebook. Getting cheered ironically outside Trenchers chippie in Whitby after 14 circumnavigations of the mini-roundabout; Scotland, when I finally had enough of her taking me through major cities because 'Inverness looked small on the map' and snapped off the rear-view mirror and threw it into the River Ness; the time she took us all the way to Cromarty because she mistook a lighthouse symbol on the map for one meaning Wi-Fi was available. And we can't even change places. Dinah won't drive in France.

'OK, so, we go back to Angers and then . . . where are we staying again?'

'Dol-de-Bretagne, but you need to look at the more

detailed map, love. The Michelin one. The one you're looking at has half the places missing.'

'That one gives me a headache. It has too many roads. So we head back to—'

'Too many roads?!'

'It's fiddly.'

'But they *are* the roads, love! They're the *actual* roads.'

'Do you want me to help or not? Just head for Angers,' she says. 'And stop getting your knickers in a twist. After that, it's the 963 to Rennes. It's simple.'

I pull away and, sure enough, five minutes later, Dinah says, 'Hang on, that's not right!'

'What isn't?'

'That sign for Le Mans. How did that happen?'

And now we're coming up to a toll. We'll have to pay a toll to go somewhere we don't want to be. Then we'll have to pay another toll to come back. And we probably still won't know where we're going.

The road widens. Cars spray in different directions heading for ten various toll lanes. The signs are in French and some have big letter Ts over them, others have Cs and Ms. I've no idea what the Ts, Cs or Ms mean. There are pictures of what look like credit cards, but are they season tickets? And there are images of coins or tokens. Should we have bought tokens?

'Which one?' I ask. Cars whoosh past us.

'I don't know,' says Dinah. She points. 'That one!'

It turns out to be an automated lane with no man to pay in person and, as we have no change or tokens, we reverse out and try another, causing three other cars behind us to back out as well.

'It's not my fault,' says Dinah. 'I can't read the signs.'

'But love, you're training to be a French teacher when we get back!'

'Go for that one – I think that means cards accepted,' she says, and we do, but then, because she's worried she won't be able to understand the instructions fully on the machine and doesn't want to put our credit card in without knowing what to do afterwards, I have to back out again. One man in a Renault Clio has now followed us into both lanes and is so furious he reverses wildly into a bollard.

Dinah says, 'These things happen when you go abroad. And you panicked me by shouting.'

Eventually a man in a high-vis jacket appears and points to the original lane we were in. He explains that we just pick up a ticket and pay when we exit the road. But now, at the barrier, Dinah can't reach the ticket through the passenger window. She removes her seatbelt and climbs so far out of the window it looks like she's trying to escape a kidnap attempt or flee a gearbox fire.

'Get closer.'

'It's your short arms.'

'You're miles from the kerb, Ben.'

'Stretch! It's not my fault your ancestors were iguanodons.'

A volley of beeps muffles her swearing as Dinah stomps out of the car. When she pulls the ticket out, the barrier rises.

'Quick,' I say. 'Before it comes down.'

When she climbs back in, Dinah throws the ticket at me.

'Belt on,' I say.

'Will. You. Give. Me. A. Second?'

I wait, my hand poised over the gearstick.

'Ben, you are *such* a shit driver. I'm sorry for that, kids, but he is.'

She clicks her seatbelt into the return. I glance at her arms.

'Shut up,' she says, 'I'm short so I have short arms. They're perfectly in proportion.'

A few miles outside Dol-de-Bretagne we stop at an Intermarché to buy tonight's dinner. It's taken an hour longer than it should have, mainly because for 15 miles we followed signs to a Carrefour supermarket until they petered out at a crossroads, where Dinah remembered that actually the word '*carrefour*' *means* crossroads.

The kids run up and down the aisles, throwing treats into their miniature trolleys – Menthe Cornettos, Milky Bars, honey-flavoured Cheerios, Chupa Chups lollies. Dinah pushes the main basket, while I go on solo forays for orange-rinded smelly cheeses and every mosquito repellent I can lay my hands on: Raid spray, Raid Night and Day plug-ins, Baygon, Pyrel Ecosphere and an insecticide in a giant red can called Special Volantes, which you could probably squirt an eagle out of the sky with.

I love French supermarkets because you never know what you'll find in them. We've seen live lobsters in tanks, profiterole-flavoured yoghurt, canned croissants, rabbit feet, and once I'm pretty sure we saw a skinned badger. We've come across fruit and veg that would be worthy of a picture caption in most regional British newspapers: tomatoes the size of footballs, aubergines a small child could hide behind and peaches so soft you can suck them down to the stone liked boiled sweets.

And, of course, there's the wondrous Brit aisle. Acknow-ledging the 12 million visitors a year from across the

Channel, the French reserve special shelves for us. It's instructional to see how we're viewed through the products we're deemed unable to live without: Marmite, Jacob's Crackers, McVitie's biscuits, Heinz tomato soup, Branston Pickle, Rose's marmalade and, unfathomably, Dr Pepper. Occasionally I've seen Pot Noodle, though I'm assuming that's a joke – something for the French to scoff at as they walk past it to buy their veal cutlets.

At the till, Dinah blames me for the huge bill.

'Two hundred and sixty-three euros!'

'That must be wrong.'

'How much is that spray?' She holds up the Special Volantes.

'It's not that.'

'Look at the size of it, Ben.'

'I'm telling you, the bill's wrong.'

She goes through the receipt, making shock discoveries.

'Jesus! Five euros for ground pepper! Deodorant: seven euros! I'd rather smell! Hang on, what's this?' she says.

There's one amount alone that's 89.60 euros. Next to the amount, it says: T. Plantin.

'T. Plantin. What the hell have you bought, Ben?' She rifles through the bags, looking for something exotic named T. Plantin, expecting it to be some monks' cheese I've spent a night's worth of accommodation on, or a mossie repellent so large you could attach it to the bottom of a helicopter.

'*Truffles*,' she says, eventually, pulling out a small jar. 'You've bought bloody truffles.' She shows me the receipt and the jar of Truffes Plantin.

'No way. They've added a nought. Ninety euros for *that*?'

'They haven't, you idiot. These are black truffles.' She shakes the jar in my face. 'They're more valuable than gold and you bought a whole jar to flavour a piece of cheap chicken. How can you not know that?'

CHAPTER 6

*D*raft Copy for Guidebook:
    There's a good reason why British people love Brittany. It's not the galettes, the moule mariniere or the 1,700 miles of sandy beaches, as enticing as they are. It's that Bretons hate the French almost as much as we do. The last region to come under the French crown in the 16th century, Brittany still considers itself a separate province, as witnessed by the 800,000 who still talk in the local dialect. There are also numerous evenings on campsites here that seem to end in late night Breton folk singing and flag-waving which aren't odd until you try to imagine staying in a Yorkshire Dales youth hostel and listening to locals carrying flaming torches and very loudly and quite aggressively belting out 'On Ilkley Moor Bar T'at' after midnight. There probably isn't a day in Brittany when there aren't women parading about in enormous coiffe lace headdresses while their menfolk blow into bagpipes and sing 'An Alar'h', a

patriotic song about cutting Frenchmen in two whilst still remembering to get the crops in on time. It's no surprise that the Asterix comics illustrated by Albert Uderzo were inspired by the Brittany's Côtes-D'Armor. In fact the Gaul's heroic resistance to the Roman invasion can itself be seen as a parable for Brittany's struggle to maintain its independence from the rest of France. Bretons have much to be proud of, of course. The 5,000-year-old megalithic stones of Carnac are some of the oldest man-made structures in Europe and extremely hard to push over as our children discovered, while its cider and crepes are deservedly world famous.

Frenchmen from Brittany who sound like wines include Chateaubriand, the writer and statesman. Dishes from Brittany that sound like Frenchmen include Andouille de Guéméné, *a type of sausage made from pig intestines, while drinks that sound like a Danish actor who might have starred in* Borgen *include Kir Breton, a cider-based aperitif.*

One of the liberating, though occasionally unsettling, aspects of France is its almost total disregard for health and safety. Almost 30 per cent of 18- to 75-year-olds here smoke because the ban on lighting up in public is largely unenforced. Motorway tailgating is not considered a traffic offence in France. And whereas in most developed countries the responsibility for not injuring yourself lies with the place you're visiting, in France it's down to you.

We realised this the first time the kids ran ahead at a château and almost toppled 60 feet into a moat through a gap in the battlements. French restaurants serve nut dishes without warnings, supermarkets sell unpasteurised cheese that would be burned in great pyres in Britain, and once we watched in astonishment as a fully grown circus lion was towed through Carnac town centre in the sort of trailer you'd normally expect to see wood chippings being transported in.

In Nantes they have a 45-foot-high, 25-foot-wide mechanical wood and metal elephant. Like some clockwork creation from a nineteenth-century Jules Verne novel, this beast resides on the outskirts of the city, like some caged King Kong, in a giant hangar. It takes 50 passengers a time on a 45-minute clomp around the Ile de Nantes. In Britain its route would be stewarded with the intensity of a royal walkabout. Yet in France, when we visited, small kids risked being stomped into pâté as they darted in and out of its tree-trunk-sized legs, with just a solitary, whistle-blowing security guard there to stop them.

However, there's one area of French life where this laissez-faire attitude doesn't apply. In fact it seems to absorb France's entire safety angst. Swimming pools. It's become a hobby of ours, finding ever more extreme French swimming pool safety signs. We've seen notices outlawing alcohol, topless sunbathing, jumping in, running, consuming and preparing food, bringing in glass, using mobile phones, shampoo, reading . . . even chatting has been banned. Once we saw a picture of a skeletal man in trunks with grotesque raised pustules all over his body with a red line through it. You might be vomiting and haemorrhaging blood, with ulcerated skin, but it's clearly still felt necessary to warn smallpox sufferers away from the water.

The campsite in Dol-de-Bretagne is like a proper resort, with mini-golf, takeaway pizza stands, restaurants, kids' clubs, a huge entertainment programme and lots of short-haired, sunburnt men standing around in Man Utd football shirts holding barbecue tongs. We're staying in a villa grand deluxe (as it's called), and have been at the indoor swimming pool a few minutes when the female lifeguard sinks to her haunches and points to a sign by the footbath. It's of a man in long shorts with a red line through it.

For every absurd sign we've seen, it's been just possible on each occasion to come up with a scintilla of logic for banning the particular activity or item referred to. Until now.

'Really, swimming shorts aren't allowed?' I ask the guard. 'Why?'

'They collect dirt,' she says.

'Dirt?'

'Because they are worn also in the day,' she says.

'But these are brand new. I cut the label off just now. It's the first time I've worn them. What am I supposed to wear?'

She points at the male swimmers around me. Everyone else is in 70s-style Speedos.

'I have to wear Speedos?'

'Yes.'

'Do I need a chest wig as well?'

She doesn't understand. 'No permis,' she says.

The pool's about to close. We only made it here by the skin of our teeth.

'We'll only be here 15 minutes. Please. I'll be so grateful.'

'You can buy a pair in the shop.'

I turn to Dinah. 'That's handy, isn't it? They sell them in the shop,' I say sarcastically.

Dinah turns away, not wanting to get involved.

'Please. We leave first thing in the morning. Do I really have to buy Speedos I'll never wear again?'

'Daddy,' Charlie shouts. 'You said you'd play with us.'

Charlie's in his stripy blue and white float-suit, with polystyrene buoyancy aides strapped in pouches round his waist which make him look like a jaunty suicide bomber, and Phoebe's in her Union Jack costume.

'Hang on, guys.'

'They are rules,' she says. 'For everyone it is the same.'

The French love of rules again.

'Daddeeee!' says Phoebe now. 'Come on.'

'One minute, Pops.'

'And what would you do if someone was drowning?' I ask the woman. 'Would you jump in?'

'Yes.'

'Ah, but you have denim shorts on. Are they new?'

She puts her whistle in her mouth.

'I'm sorry. Please, I want to play with my kids! They've been very disappointed by extremely poor vegetable rides today and . . .'

And now she blows it. When I still don't get out, she strides round the pool and enters the storeroom. Dinah looks across.

'You know everyone's staring at you.'

'It's *such* a racket. It's like trying to enforce a retro Leo Sayer perm, acting surprised when no one has the right haircut, then selling curlers in the camp shop.'

'Is it really like that?'

'It's exactly like that.'

A few minutes later, the lifeguard still hasn't re-emerged and I'm trying to coax Charlie into some breaststroke when a golf buggy pulls up outside the pool. The campsite manager is at the wheel. He carries a walkie-talkie and looks a bit like Alan Mills, the former Wimbledon tournament referee.

Dinah gives me an I-told-you-so look when the lifeguard points in my direction.

'Love, the high point of their day's been learning how to brown haricot beans in a skillet. I'm going to play with them. I am *not* getting out.'

Dinah laughs very, very hard when she sees me emerge through the foot trough.

'You lost that one then,' she says, when she's recovered.

The 15-euro trunks are black and shiny. They're tight, bulgy, uncomfortable and are basically like wearing dark cling film.

'On the contrary. I'm going to wear them all day and all night. I'm going to sleep in these Speedos, eat in them. I'll run in them, roll around in the dirt in them and then get in the next French pool we come across when they're absolutely filthy.'

'To expose the system?'

'To highlight the rubbish system.'

'I'm so proud of you.'

There's a pale moon over the campsite. Dinah and I are sat on the decking outside the villa, drinking wine and shelling pistachio nuts with our thumbnails. Karaoke's wafting up from the entertainment tent and the air smells of barbecuing meat.

'I wish you could've seen your face on the back of that golf buggy,' Dinah says, lowering her head abjectly, imitating me earlier.

In the end, I'd told the manager I was writing about the campsite for a guidebook about France. I don't think he believed me, but as a compromise, he'd given me a lift in my still-wet swimming shorts to the camp shop to buy some Speedos, the cost of which he said he'd add to our bill.

'I didn't bow my head meekly. I raised it *defiantly*.'

'You looked sad and defeated, like some French aristocrat in the tumbrel on his way to the guillotine.'

'I looked victorious and splendid, like Caesar in a chariot entering the Colosseum.'

She passes me a pistachio nut she can't open. I place my thumbnails inside the crack, prise it open and pass it back.

'Do you think the French love of rules and administration has something to do with the shame of occupation?'

Dinah laughs and shakes her head despairingly.

'Are you trying to turn what happened to you into a national failing of the French?'

'I'm thinking of the Vichy government. Is that why they obsess about procedure? Is it as a way of saying, "Look, this is why we collaborated, we obey the rules. We're not cowards, we're bureaucrats." Or is that why they acquiesced so easily in the first place, because they're people who do what they're told? "Marshal Petain is in charge and he says we round up the Jews in our village and hand them over to the SS, so let's blow whistles and do what he says."'

'It starts with Speedos in the pool . . .'

'Yes, and ends in a Holocaust.'

I close my eyes and Dinah smiles.

'I think you should learn some French,' she says. 'You're writing a guidebook about France, but you're missing the whole context because you don't speak the language. It's like doing a restaurant review without tasting the food. You're basing it on the decor and how clean the cutlery is. And how *have* you got to your age without knowing *any* French?'

At Chesham High School our French teacher was called Mr Gerard. Mr Gerard always wore the same, very tight, grey pinstripe suit. He wore half-moon glasses and desperately wanted to be seen as stern, but that was made slightly ridiculous because of the fact he had to sit on a cushion to see above the steering wheel of his Renault 5. He was about 60 years old, with white hair, and limped around the language lab in such an exaggerated fashion it looked like he was trying to free his right leg from a mantrap.

The lab was made up of a series of booths arranged around a command module at the front of the room, and we studied Longman's audiovisual French (*'Ecoutez et repetez!'*). We'd wear giant DJ headphones and listen to a series of unfathomable sentences about Monsieur Lafayette, the *bibliothèque*, Jean-Paul, Marie-Claire and the *jardin public*, then be asked to repeat them back by a man who sounded like Lloyd Grossman waking up in a stroke ward with a mouthful of gobstoppers. Mr Gerard could barely see above the rack of numbered buttons that fanned around him. These buttons allowed him access to our conversations, but meant that he was effectively only ever monitoring one child in 30. With these odds on our side, and his view limited, it presented a tremendous opportunity to crawl along the floor, commando-style, into someone else's booth.

'Bannister?'

'No, it's Hatch.'

'I thought it was Bannister.'

'No, it's Hatch.'

'Where is Bannister?'

'I don't know, Mr Gerard. This is Hatch.'

''Atch, you dopey boy, are you playing me for a fool?'

In the upper GCSE years it was rumoured that Mr Gerard had a wooden leg. As we were 13 years old and had read *Treasure Island*, we accepted this without question, so if Mr Gerard came anywhere near us, we'd slouch in our seats and try to kick him through his slacks, hoping to hear a clunk.

'Ouch! 'Atch, what are you doink?'

'Sorry, Mr Gerard.' Then, as he walked away, 'Must be the other one.'

The French language seemed utterly ridiculous to me. It seemed so implausible that a whole country communicated in this incomprehensible way. The verbs were impossible and the idea that every object had to be male or female made no sense. How could a vase be male? How could a spanner be female? And on what basis were these things decided? I dropped the language as soon as I was able and have progressed no further since.

After this start, it was a surprise in later life to discover there are British people who love the French and France. My dad was one. He loved the idea of what France represented – in particular, its aloofness and unbowed determination not to succumb and instead be a bulwark against the dumb, mostly American, ravages of our age, be they connected to film, literature, language, television, political debate or the clarified-butter-to-egg-yolk proportions of the ideal Béarnaise sauce. And while I admire this pig-headedness myself, there's no escaping the fact that no Frenchman has ever made me laugh. In fact, in the history of Europe, it's doubtful a Frenchman's ever made anyone other than another Frenchman laugh, through any medium other than mime.

At university I shared a house with my friend Sally, who read French. She had French friends, and they sat in our living room tossing their bouffant hair around, debating liberty and the nature of art when I was trying to watch *Going for Gold*. Decent-minded British students show off about musical tastes, their detached sense of irony and how many Jägermeisters they can drink before vomiting on the night bus. In France an alpha male has a coherent theory about the best way to create the illusion of light and movement in watercolours.

And as for French films. What, another quirky, pneumatic femme fatale with short, straggly black hair getting it on with a bearded, brooding, frustrated writer/intellectual in a polo neck? I tried to read *Remembrance of Things Past, Volume II* by Proust once, but gave up after I turned the first page and realised we were still on the *same sentence*! And as for Jean-Paul Sartre's existentialism – guess what? I already know it's an unforgiving, godless world where inanimate objects like toasters don't give a shit about me.

'I can see,' says Dinah, at the end of this rant, 'that you

have been badly bruised tonight. Go and have another
£10-truffle shaving to cheer yourself up. And, by the way,
if you understood French, you'd have been able to read the
label,' she shouts after me. 'You'd have known you don't
stack the world's most expensive delicacy, used sparingly
by the world's top chefs, on a two-euro chicken fillet with
bootlace oven chips.'

As we munch through the most expensive wine nibbles
in the world, I go through what's going wrong with the
trip. For a kick-off, France is too big. I'd assumed it was
the size of England. In fact it's four times larger. It means
we're driving too far. Too much time's being wasted
buying bread, and the tollbooths are bankrupting us.
We're not getting nearly enough sleep and I'm a little sick
of relying on Dinah talking for me. It feels like I've become
a selective mute. I can't even order my own dinner. '*Et
pour mon mari, le steak avec frites.*'

'Plus, we've been to far too many châteaux.'

'I've been saying that to you,' says Dinah.

'I know, and you were right.'

'Hallelujah!'

'We don't have to do things simply because they're in
the itinerary. We need to be more selective. Sod the Master
Document. Let's treat it as a menu.'

'I like that idea,' she says.

'We choose what we want to do. It's up to us. The
temptation is to try and do everything.'

'Your temptation,' she says.

'Mine, yes. We need to see the *real* France.'

'*La France profonde?*' she says.

'Exactly. We're doing obvious things. We need to do
quirky stuff that throws a light on the French character.

That's what will make a good guidebook. That's what'll be fun. There's a museum about onions in Roscoff.'

'An onion museum. Is that wise after today's vegetable events?'

'Adventurous stuff as well.'

Dinah gives me a concerned look now.

'What sort of adventurous things?'

'I don't know, I saw an advert for donkey trekking.'

Dinah pulls a face.

'Why are you looking like that? Why can't we donkey trek?'

'Because we couldn't llama trek.'

Going round Britain for our last guidebook, a supposedly restful afternoon's llama trekking ended disastrously, with Dinah being dragged around a field in rural Northamptonshire by an Andean llama named Paddywhack.

'They were llamas, and anyway, that was your fault, love. You were warned not to tickle his chin.'

'Love, we haven't got a good record with wildlife,' she says. 'We like it, but it scares us.'

'We're fine with wildlife.'

'The Kington small breeds farm?'

'What about it?'

'The goats that chased us on their hind legs.'

'What? Was this a dream of yours?'

'They attacked us, Ben.'

'Goats?'

'We had bags of feed and they were jumping up and drumming our bellies with their hooves.'

'Were there centaurs too?'

'The kids were crying. We had to leave.'

'Did a griffin take a swipe at us as well? I'm talking

about a donkey trek. It's not *Jason and the Argonauts*. We could time it to coincide with Phoebe's birthday. They'd love it. Look, I'll show you.'

'OK,' she says, as I walk down the decking steps towards the car to find the donkey brochure. 'But there'll be trouble.'

I'm ferreting in the kids' filthy footwells, amongst the mounting pile of attraction leaflets, lightly dusted with croutons of dropped baguette and apple cores, when I come across the DVD player lead. As I do so, it comes to me in a flash of inspiration. Suddenly I know why the sat nav wouldn't work. I open the glove box and compare the ends of these two sockets. Sure enough, I'm right.

'Where's your handbag?'

Dinah finds it and I empty its contents on to the picnic table.

'Wow!'

'It becomes a dumping ground,' Dinah protests. 'Please don't say anything.'

Along with things you'd expect, in my wife's handbag there is also: three tennis balls, a bank statement, a council tax bill, a clothes peg, nail scissors, two dice, ten jigsaw pieces, a broken pair of sunglasses, a single child's glove, a pair of Charlie's pants, a pair of Phoebe's pants, a pair of *my* pants, two Moshi Monsters, a light bulb, a Christmas bauble, a stick of rock, a tape measure, a pair of Charlie's socks, a pair of Phoebe's socks, a pair of *my* socks, superglue, a lump of Cheddar wrapped in cellophane from when she was on the Atkins diet, a WeightWatchers Lasagne from when she was on the WeightWatchers diet, Nurofen, a roll of Sellotape, a Lego car, an envelope addressed to Brighton University, a packet of chocolate buttons, a Club biscuit, two hair clips, her watch she thought she'd lost, my iPhone charger I thought *I'd* lost, three sets of unknown keys, nine Biros, four peanuts, a Crunchie wrapper, a table knife, a teaspoon, Calpol, a cup for Charlie's milk, four loose Fisherman's Friends that for a moment I think might well be mouse droppings and, right at the bottom, lying on a bed of sand, a tiny cap, a plastic screw and the spring from the sat nav.

I screw it all back together, plug it in and turn on the car's ignition. Three seconds later, the TomTom drum has never sounded more welcoming.

They say the state of a woman's handbag mirrors her life, and perhaps it's true, because Dinah's having an existential crisis in bed.

'Do you think I ricochet from one disaster to the next?' she asks me.

'What do you mean?'

'I'm thinking about teaching. That letter I haven't sent in: my acceptance form for next year.'

'Just send it in then.'

'But what if it's the next balls-up? The builders, this trip, your book. And today's a microcosm of it. Those truffles, the tollbooth, the sat nav. Why does it always happen to us?'

'This trip isn't a disaster, and nor will teaching be. And we don't know about my book yet. Just tidy your bag up, you dirty cow.'

She laughs. There's a blast of 'Agadoo' from the entertainment tent.

'You know what I mean though. We haven't officially been commissioned for the guidebook yet. What if that doesn't happen?'

'It will. Jake said it was 99 per cent certain.' Jake's my guidebook editor. 'You know how slowly their wheels turn. Stop worrying.'

'I know. It's not really that.'

She tells me there doesn't seem to be any straight line through our lives, like there is for everyone else we know.

'Like who?'

'Everyone. Everyone we know. It worries me sometimes.'

'You don't know what goes on under the surface. I'm sure it's not a straight line for anyone.'

'Everyone we know has stable jobs. They leave the house every day, get promoted, buy bigger houses. That's what happened to my mum and dad and yours. I'm worried it's because I'm a gadfly. I never stuck at newspapers. Just as I was getting somewhere, I moved into travel. Now I'm a freelancer. That's why I want to become a teacher, if I'm honest. I'm tired of the insecurity. All the pitching. It's exhausting. And I don't love French. Teachers are meant to love their subjects. That's what everyone says.'

'So? You'll love the kids.'

'I can't understand what French people tell me. I couldn't read that tollbooth sign. Plus I can't make my own children do what I tell them. How am I going to persuade kids I don't even know to learn French?'

'You know what you want to do, that's the hard thing. I'm the problem.'

She looks at me. 'Any news from Henry?'

'Not since yesterday.'

Yesterday I had another two rejections for my novel.

Dinah sighs. 'How have we ended up like this?' she asks.

'What do you mean?'

'In our 40s, tossing it off on some campsite in Brittany, eating truffles in our pyjamas.'

'You're happy, aren't you?'

'I do think about what other people have sometimes. Is that bad?'

'But do you want their lives?'

She doesn't say anything.

'OK, if you could metaphorically crawl into anyone else's booth right now and live their life, whose would it be?'

Buster calls before she can answer.

'Sandy and noisy,' he says, when I ask what it's like in Afghanistan. 'Helmand's busier than Gatwick. I haven't slept at all and every five minutes I have to dust everything. The sand gets everywhere, into everything. And I mean everything. Even your arse crack. You're actually told to wet-wipe your bum crack four or five times a day.'

I leave the bedroom and sit outside on the decking. 'Are you sure that's not just you?'

He laughs. 'They officially tell you that. There are memos about it. Bum rash is massive here. It's al-Qaeda's secret weapon. Everyone's either got bum rash, is recovering from bum rash or is about to get bum rash.'

'Are you saying you have bum rash?'

'Yes, I have fucking bum rash. But guess what? I've got some big news.'

'You're treating it with Sudocrem.'

'No,' he laughs. 'Although I am. David Beckham's coming out to Afghan. I've got to do an Access All Areas Q&A with him in the back of a flatbed truck in front of 2,000 squaddies, so I need you to come up with some material.'

'You're interviewing Becks?'

'Yeah, live, but that's embargoed. It's so fucking hush-hush, I'd probably lose my job if it got out.'

'Wow!'

'So I've got this opening gag. I introduce him, ambassador to Britain, former England skipper, Premier League title-winner, blah, blah, married to Victoria, former Spice Girl. Then I say: "I said to the men they could ask you any question, David, anything at all, provided it wasn't about your sex life." That'll get my first laugh. Then I pick a question from a box. They'll be on folded-up bits of paper. I unfold it, read it silently and chuck it away. Then I do the same again. I do it four times before I ask a question.'

I laugh. 'Nice. But you do realise he's going to be so charismatic, he'll just take over? That's what happened when – and I realise this is not in the same league – I interviewed Tony Slattery on stage at the Leicester Comedy Festival.'

'I can't believe you're comparing Tony Slattery to David Beckham.'

'Although Tony Slattery was more famous then.'

Buster laughs. 'And I haven't told you yet; I'm going to be live on Radio 1 for three 20-minute segments. They're flying a producer out here to sit with me.'

'Wow! That's amazing. That could be a massive break for you.'

'Nah, but it's a good distraction. There's nothing else to do here but eat spotted dick in the cookhouse and do press-ups.'

'And wet-wipe your bum.'

'Yeah, and clean my bum. Oh, I know what I was going to say,' he adds. 'There's a guy here – a bloke in signals – his sister works for *Tonight with Trevor McDonald*.'

'The ITV show?'

'Yeah.'

'I told her your story about the builders and he reckons she might be able to help. They investigate that sort of thing. Do you want her email?'

I'm taking this down when we hear the siren.

'A Chinook. That means a casualty's landing. Happens all the time. This line will go dead in a minute.' And, as he says this, it does.

CHAPTER 7

Dinah now worked at the *Northampton Chronicle and Echo*, while I was at the *Leicester Mercury*. We lived midway between our jobs in a cottage in Churchwalk, behind the Cherry Tree pub, which we nicknamed the Ooh Arr pub because there were always hay-dusted Land Rovers in the car park. The cottage had a hammock in the garden, wooden beams throughout and felt like the sort of place Hansel and Gretel might have discovered in the woods. We joked that it was made of marzipan.

It's the little things that make you love someone. Slightly deaf in one ear, Dinah was incapable of whispering. There was her jumpiness too. If I entered a room and Dinah had her back to me, I knew I'd have to announce my presence by making a non-inflammatory noise (a cough, a sniff, a scuffle of feet), otherwise she'd jump or lunge at me with whatever was in her hand. She had lots of OCD urges that I started off laughing at, but quickly learnt to obey without a word.

'It's an urge. Look at me three times, and on the third one, stick your tongue out.'

'It's an urge. It's about a staple-gun accident. Touch your toes twice then blink and smile.'

'It's an urge. Tap the coffee table and say the word saucepan in a drawn-out voice.'

'Your wonderful dwarf,' my dad called Dinah. My mates had become her mates, and she and Buster always took the piss out of me. ('Has he told you he looked like the brigadier from *Dr Who* growing up?' 'He didn't wear those green M&S army jumpers, did he?' 'With the darker green patches on the shoulders and elbows? Oh yes, he did.')

We didn't worry about the future. We didn't buy flat-packed furniture or talk about tracker mortgages and house prices. We raised our eyebrows at each other when our friends discussed their salaries. Our low income was compensated by great holidays blagged from the features desk. We wine-tasted in Italy, rode camels at the pyramids, cruised to Alaska. We were always broke, but were almost proud of this. We felt eccentric and worthy, driving around in my ex-police-dog-handling van that Dinah maintained still smelled a little of 'excited Alsatian sweat'. The hand-me-down clothes I received from my dad and my brother amused her. ('Buster's lost weight. I wonder what he's going to do with those black Levis. Shall I ask Holly?') And we laughed every day. There was nobody I wanted to be with more. We were never bored, never ran out of things to say.

It's hard, even now, to piece together why it changed. Firstly, there was what happened with my mum, I suppose, her cancer returning. But more importantly, and something I could never have guessed then was the effect her sister having a baby had on Dinah.

* * *

Our latest attraction visit is the Onion Johnny museum in Roscoff.

'Weeeell, I now know quite a lot about onions,' says Dinah in the car afterwards.

'Me too. I enjoyed that,' I say, looking in the rear-view mirror. 'Didn't you think that was fascinating, guys?'

In the museum, we discovered, amongst other things, that the stereotypical image most British people have of what French people look like is based solely on how onion farmers from Brittany used to dress (beret, stripy shirt, bike with a string of onions hanging from it) when they crossed the Channel to sell us onions in the nineteenth century. Our collective national perception of Frenchmen is coloured by the 100-year-old appearance of around 1,400 Roscoff Onion Johnnies too lazy to take the rough and more dangerous road to Paris, instead preferring to hop on a boat to England to sell their wares.

'Can we not talk about onions any more?' asks Phoebe.

'Putting those berets on, that was fun, wasn't it?'

'A bit fun,' says Charlie.

'Phoebe?'

She pulls a face.

'Really? What about carrying around that string of onions?'

'Daddy, there weren't many children's things,' says Phoebe.

'There were farm implements.'

She pulls the same face, and I look at Dinah.

'Let's see those posters you were given again.'

Phoebe's already discarded hers in the footwell. With deadened eyes, Charlie holds up his poster. It features a large, blown-up photo of a pink Roscoff onion. Underneath are the words: Fête de l'Oignon. It's a week-long onion festival we narrowly missed.

'Not keen, guys?'

'How is that interesting?' says Phoebe. 'It's not a toy. You can't play with it. It's not even an onion. It's a *picture* of an onion. We're children, Daddy! And children like toys. *Not* onions.'

'But you have had quite a few nice toys today, Pops.'

Phoebe opened her birthday presents in our Rennes hotel bedroom this morning. She got a Moshi Monster backpack, a Moshi Monster quiz book and a Moshi Monster teddy. We also bought her *Harry Potter and the Goblet of Fire*, three summer dresses, a pair of jelly shoes to wear when river swimming, four highlighter pens, 37 doodle mats, *Dr Strangeglove's Monstrous Biography* and a 'Beauty Collection' set – a packet of jewellery from the Carrefour called 'Ace all styles wonderful', featuring a plastic heart (silver), a plastic necklace (silver) and a plastic signet ring with a purple heart.

'Yes, but that was this morning,' says Phoebe. 'And it's still my birthday, and onions are not a good treat for a child.'

She kicks the poster in the footwell.

'How about we have a competition when we get in to see who can draw the best onion? I bet I can draw a *brilliant* onion.'

I look in the rear-view mirror and have to stop myself laughing.

'*Not* drawing an onion,' says Charlie, folding his arms.

'Phoebe?'

'Have you not been listening? Onions are boring for children.'

'Really?'

'*Yes.*' She nods. 'Of *course* they are. They're vegetables. Why is this whole holiday about vegetables? I'm sick of vegetables.'

'Really? A vegetable that can be used as a side dish, as a condiment *and* as a vegetable in its own right, *and* as the basis for soup, that's boring for children?'

'*Yes!*' they both shout.

'A vegetable whose seeds are planted between mid-February and mid-April and harvested in August, that carries an AOC-approved label to signify it's been washed by hand. That is not interesting?'

'Dad, can you stop now?' Phoebe says. 'It's getting annoying.'

'OK, let's have a quiz.'

'Yay!' says Charlie. 'A quiz!'

'Is it going to be about onions?' asks Phoebe

Since we stopped following the itinerary religiously, it's been better. Pin-balling around Brittany, we've been breaking up beach days with eccentric attractions like the bat museum near Pontivy and the seaweed museum in Plouguerneau. And, the other day, the kids had great, if highly illegal, fun trying to topple 5,000-year-old megalithic stones on a cycle ride around Ile-aux-Moines in the Gulf of Morbihan.

We've ruffled feathers at the Christian Dior museum in Granville, when Phoebe loudly referred to the rose bridal gown with a tulle yoke by Christian Dior for John Galliano as 'that red thing'; and in Concarneau we learnt Breton folk songs and also gave the kids a small budget to spend in a gift shop. Getting into the feisty spirit of the region, Charlie took a long time deciding which of several swords he wanted to buy. Like Hannibal at a blacksmith's, after sampling their blades with his fingertip and pretending to thrash his foes with each one, he opted for an orange one with a separate scabbard that I could use to swordfight him with. We never battle for long, though, as sooner or later Charlie will want his scabbard back, because the most fun he's having with his new sword (and it's something I remember well) is withdrawing it from its scabbard and, with a giant sweep of his arm, holding the orange plastic blade aloft and declaring, 'By the power of Grayskull!' or 'Behold the sword of glory!' and sometimes simply, 'CHARGE!'

Phoebe, by contrast, invested in a blue dolphin inside a snow globe that is itself encased within the serrated edges of a plaster clam shell. Her decision was based on pure beauty, with a pinch of price consideration, as she'd flip over the objects she liked and instantly go off any that were under the 4.50 euros Charlie's sword had cost. The snow globe, handed to her by the shopkeeper in a small bag of bubble-wrap, has not been opened since.

'Okaaaay,' says Phoebe, in a bored fashion. 'We'll have a quiz.'

'Phoebe, who was the boss of France in 1811 when it was discovered that iodine in kelp – remember, that's a type of seaweed, not an onion; this is not an onion question – was useful in treating injured soldiers' wounds?'

'I don't know. And I don't care.'

'Charlie? The boss of France. We've come across him a few times.'

'Actually, can we *not* have a quiz?' says Phoebe.

'The leader of France. Guess, Charlie, if you don't know.'

'William the Conker?'

'Conqueror, Charlie. William the Conqueror. Good guess, but it's Napoleon.'

'Daddy, I think it's time we said what we're doing next,' says Dinah, leaning round.

'What?' says Phoebe flatly.

'We're going to the museum of . . . the . . . endive . . . lettuce!' I say. Then quickly, 'Actually, guys, we have a surprise. Mummy?'

'We're going . . . ON A DONKEY RIDE!' says Dinah.

The donkey domain is deep in the countryside, near the bat museum, and we meet Maurice in a gravel car park next to his farm. Maurice, in his 50s, has sandy hair, a spherical head and round glasses. Looking a bit like a weather-beaten Benny Hill, he waves us through a gate into a field sprinkled with fresh aubergine-shiny balls of donkey shit, where three donkeys are grazing. Dinah speaks to Maurice in French, tells him it's Phoebe's birthday, and afterwards Maurice, who speaks no English, introduces Phoebe to one-year-old Bonhomme, who, as Maurice takes the reins of another donkey called Taquin, bites me on the bum, not hard but enough to make me shoot forward slightly. Maurice leads Taquin to a five-bar gate at the back of the farmhouse and says something to Dinah.

'You have to hit a donkey on the nose if he bites,' says Dinah, translating.

Maurice says something else.

'It's to train him,' says Dinah. 'Bonhomme is young. Older donkeys are the most gentle.'

Maurice says something else.

'We're going to have some cider now,' says Dinah, translating this.

Inside Maurice's kitchen, we meet Yvette, his wife, who pours the kids water and, from an old milk bottle, tops up our glasses with cloudy homemade cider. We're halfway through this bottle, having heard how Maurice bought his first donkey to keep the grass low in his fields, but bought more because Yvette liked them so much, when something surprises Dinah. 'Oh,' she says.

Dinah turns to me. 'Only the kids will ride a donkey. We're walking!'

We're both in sandals because we thought we'd all be on donkeys.

'Ask him how far it is,' I say. Dinah translates. I hear Mont St-Michel mentioned.

'Mont St-Michel! How far is that?' I ask.

Maurice says something. Then Dinah says to me, 'One hundred and thirty kilometres.'

We both look at Maurice, who laughs. He says something to Dinah.

'We won't be walking 130 kilometres,' she says.

Maurice fetches a map and shows us our 10km route. There are a series of staging points on it that he's named 'a1', 'a2' and so on, going up to 'a10'. Each corresponds to an intersection on the trek. On the reverse side of the map there are photos of these. Each intersection is overlaid with a blue arrow, indicating which way to go when we reach them. As Dinah explains this, I feel a growing sense of unease that increases as it dawns on me.

'He isn't coming with us, is he?'

Dinah says something to Maurice. He answers, then laughs.

'No,' Dinah says.

I look at her. 'He's leaving us in charge of a donkey?'

She says something to Maurice. He replies. She turns back to me. 'Yes.'

Maurice says something else. Dinah says, 'He now wants to show you how to stop the donkey running off when you lead him.'

'Running off! It could run off? And why am I leading him? Why has he chosen me to lead him?'

'I am just telling you what he's saying,' says Dinah.

Outside, Maurice hands the kids rusty wire brushes. He demonstrates how to comb a donkey's coat. Phoebe has a go and as Charlie walks behind the donkey to do the same on the other side, I tell him to be careful because Taquin might kick.

'Actually, do donkeys kick?' I ask.

Dinah translates. Maurice shakes his head very firmly.

Phoebe's already decided the French are cruel, having based this on three incidents: a) the child that picked up a starfish from a touch-pool in the Océanopolis aquarium in Brest and hurled it towards a rock; b) French schoolkids skimming stones off the back of a pygmy hippo in Branféré Zoo and Botanical Gardens; and c) seeing someone kicking a cocker spaniel across the Pont Neuf in Auray.

What happens next does nothing to counteract this. To further emphasise his point, Maurice goes behind Taquin, wraps his tail around his fist and yanks at it very hard. Taquin blows air out of his nostrils.

Maurice says something. 'Donkeys never kick,' says Dinah, translating. To further prove his point, Maurice grabs Taquin's right ear and tugs hard. Taquin blows more air out of his nostrils. Maurice now picks up a sharp-spiked tool.

'For goodness' sake, tell him I believe him,' I say. But Maurice is just checking Taquin's hooves with the spike, and says something else.

'Donkeys are calm,' says Dinah. Maurice spreads his hands out flatly to emphasise this. He says something else and Dinah translates. 'Now, because it is so hot, we will have more cider.'

Back outside after this, Maurice holds the blue rope around Taquin's head tightly in his bunched-up fist. He tells Dinah that you must never pull a donkey.

'Can you ask him why?'

'Otherwise the donkey will pull harder in the opposite direction,' Dinah translates.

Maurice then explains how '*marche*' means walk. And '*stop*' means stop.

He opens a gate. '*Marche*,' he says, and Taquin walks into the road. Maurice says something else. Dinah translates. 'Always walk beside the donkey. If you get ahead, he'll hang back. If you go behind, he'll drag you.'

'Drag me. He'll drag me? How fast do donkeys run?'

Dinah says something. Maurice laughs and says something else. 'What did he say?'

'He thought you were joking.'

Beyond the busy road, Maurice throws the saddle over Taquin's back. He lifts up Phoebe and puts Charlie on a blanket behind her. And now he says something, accompanied by fierce hand gestures.

'There is something that is more important than anything else,' says Dinah. Maurice speaks. 'There is one thing you must *never* ever do,' says Dinah. Maurice carries on talking. 'It is very, very important. Do not let him eat anything by the side of the path. Never let that happen.'

Maurice says something else. 'He is repeating himself. You must not, under any circumstances, let him eat anything by the side of the path.'

'Why, what would happen if he does?' I ask.

Dinah says something to Maurice. 'That won't happen,' says Dinah, translating.

'But what if it does?'

Maurice says something else.

'You will not let that happen,' says Dinah.

The first hour's great. I lead Taquin through the first two intersections and the kids have fun shouting, '*Marche*, Taquin! *Marche*!' every time he slows or lowers his head and tries to eat the long grass at the side of the bridleway. '*Bon âne*,' (good donkey) we declare whenever he speeds up or lifts his head after we've commanded him to do so.

'Enjoying it, kids?' I ask.

'This is fun,' says Phoebe. And it is. We're in the countryside, seeing the real France. Doing something new. And it starts to feel like we've cracked it. Not just this expedition, but France generally. It's all due to the routine we've created. Basically, the kids watch cartoons on the Gulli channel in the mornings, while Dinah dresses them, leaving me to pack the bags and load the car. At breakfast, Dinah finds a quiet corner of the hotel restaurant and here I steal food from the buffet. I wrap rolls in napkins and slip them across to Dinah at a signal from her that nobody wearing an apron is looking. She secretly loads these parcels into her carefully positioned handbag. It's a ritual Dinah hates and she'll be grumpy and resistant ('Too many staff today' 'Why do I have to do this bit?' 'I'm not doing it if you take Merzer cheese. They'll smell it on the way out'). However, once the food is safely stashed, we are elated with our small victory and this sets the jubilant tone for the day.

This solves the baguette-foraging issue and another problem too. Eating out in France is cheaper at lunchtime, so that's when we have our hot meal of the day, usually a cheaper plat du jour. We save our thieved picnic for the evening. This means we no longer have to wait until restaurants open at 7 p.m. to feed the kids, so they get to bed earlier, meaning they're less cranky and Dinah and I get a peaceful evening.

To cope with the long drives between attractions, we've effectively reordered time itself by drawing a distinction between English and French minutes. Without being precise, we've told the kids that French minutes are longer than English ones, which, because neither of them can multiply or tell the time, gives us an instant get-out if they feel a journey's taking ages.

'But you said ten minutes!'

'Ten *French* minutes, Phoebe.'

'Aww, I hate French minutes. They take ages! Why can't they be English minutes?'

'Because we're in France.'

By the time we reach the next intersection, I'm able to sense the right moment to drop behind Taquin to up his pace and when to move just in front to slow him down. I'm usually jumpy around animals. I've never been a dog owner and don't really trust anything with four legs that's larger than, say, a domestic cat, but today I feel myself bonding with Taquin. I pat his head, stroke his nose and keep up a running dialogue as we proceed between the hedgerows, receiving the occasional twitched ear for a reply.

But after the intersection, all the cider's caught up with me and I need a piss. Leaving Dinah with the reins, I nip through a gap in the hedgerow. When I emerge, I can't believe my eyes. Taquin's feasting on grass by the side of the path.

'Dinah!?'

'He's only having a bit.'

'But that's the *one* thing he said not to do.'

'Stop panicking. He'll be fine,' says Dinah. 'He's probably starving, poor thing.'

'He's hungry, Daddy,' says Phoebe. 'Aren't you, Taquin?'

Straightaway, it's more difficult persuading Taquin to move. I have to say '*Marche*' very firmly two or three times and before we reach the next intersection, Taquin stops again to eat more grass. Because it's the first time he's disobeyed me, rather than lose face, I decide it's best to pretend we stopped *deliberately*, to let him eat. 'Go on, Taquin, have a little bit more then. But that's your lot, OK?'

But he's detected our weakness because by the time we reach the next intersection, Taquin's spending longer in the bushes eating grass than he is walking. Close to the five-mile halfway point, Taquin's rogue behaviour goes up a notch. He veers right, despite us all shouting at him, and climbs a two-foot-high, precarious, narrow grassy bank to reach some elderflower. To get there, he has to stride through an overhanging bramble bush that rips Phoebe's T-shirt and scratches her chest. She starts to cry.

'Right! That's it,' says Dinah. 'He's out of control. He's hurting the children now. They're coming off.'

'Love, if they get down now, we'll never make it. It's miles.'

'What if he falls over with the kids on him?' she says.

'Falls over?!' exclaims Phoebe, looking round, alarmed.

'Dinah, he's not going to fall over. He's a donkey. Donkeys don't fall over. Come on, let's all calm down.'

Eventually, after he's had enough elderflower, Taquin climbs down. We now decide Dinah should go on the inside and act like blinkers. If he can't see the grass, he might behave better. We manage to cover 100 metres like this.

'I think he *was* just hungry. We're sorted now, aren't we, Taquin?' And I'm in the middle of adding 'Let's get a lick on while he's cooperating', when Taquin finishes chewing the grass he has in his mouth and immediately heads into the bushes for more. He drags me along as I desperately try to yank him back, shouting, '*Stop*, Taquin! Taquin! *Stop!*' Then there's a muffled cry from Dinah the other side of him.

'What's up?'

'What do you think? He's barged me into the hedge.'

I walk round the side of Taquin and peer into the bushes that Dinah's pressed into.

'If you push, love, he'll do the opposite.'

'Thanks, donkey-whisperer. But when he stops dragging you around, I might listen to you.'

'I want to get down,' whimpers Charlie.

'He's out of control,' says Phoebe.

'He's not out of control. We're not leading him right. He's just a donkey. It's our fault.'

'Love, my leg's bleeding, Phoebe's bleeding, Charlie's crying. It is a *little bit* out of control. Let's get them off,' says Dinah.

I take the kids down. For the next twenty minutes, we shout at Taquin, then we coax him. We do everything we can possibly think of to get him moving, but there's a fence with long grass that he's leant over and he's not budging.

'Look at him, stuffing his face,' says Dinah. 'He doesn't give a shit. I'm getting a stick.'

'No, let me have one more go. *Marche*, Taquin! Taquin,' I whisper in his ear. '*Marche*! It's me. *Marche*! Do it for me, Taquin. *Marche*. Taquin! Come on, Taquin. *Bon âne*. *Marche*, Taquin!' I move closer for a tighter grip of the reins. I stroke his nose and carry on whispering in his ear, and Taquin's just lifted his head from the grass when Dinah clouts him on the arse.

'Dinah, for God's—' And I feel such a sudden and incredible pain shoot up my leg from my toe, I drop the reins.

'OUCH! YOU TWAT!'

Dinah runs round the other side.

'What? What's the matter?'

'He's on my *fucking* toe. Get him off me.'

Dinah tries to push Taquin off me, but he doesn't budge.

'Give me that stick,' I shout. 'Quick! QUICK! He's breaking my toes.'

Dinah hands me the stick and I thrash Taquin four times on the arse, as hard as I can. 'Get off me, you fat shit! GET OFF!' Finally Taquin lifts his leg and I hop away.

'It's not Taquin's fault, Daddy,' I hear Phoebe say, as I try to bend my bloodied, probably broken middle toes. 'It's your fault. You don't know how to lead him.' And when I look up, Dinah is calling the emergency number on the map.

Maurice arrives in a Jeep, looking now like a very cross Benny Hill. He slews the Jeep up on to a grass verge and, without a word, strides straight past us and up to Taquin. Holding the reins in one hand, he punches Taquin hard in the middle of his face with the other. Taquin whinnies. Maurice then ties Taquin to a fence, returns to the Jeep and, again without a word, opens the passenger door. Scared and shocked, the kids climb into the tiny back seats with Dinah, while I take my place sheepishly beside Maurice.

Dinah tries to explain what happened in French. 'You have to lead a donkey,' she says, translating Maurice's response.

'Tell him it was you who let him eat.' Dinah tells him. 'Tell him he stood on my bare toe.' Dinah tells him. Maurice says something. 'What did he say?'

'He said that's why he wears boots.' I look at Maurice's boots. He says something else. 'You have a souvenir of your trip,' says Dinah.

'Ask him what the symptoms of a broken toe are.' When Dinah stops talking, Maurice laughs. Back to happy Maurice, he says something else.

Dinah translates. 'He says that if it goes black, your foot is broken.' Maurice laughs as he sees my face react to this.

'Ask him how soon it goes black.'

Dinah translates, 'A donkey weighs 250 kilograms. A quarter of a ton. It will go black very quickly.' Maurice laughs so hard, he takes his eyes off the road. He's still laughing as we pull into his drive. Here he parks and says something to Dinah. She starts to translate, but I already know what it means.

'Are we going to have more cider now?' I ask.

Dinah nods.

* * *

The Kerurus Campground is in Plounéour-Trez, on the north-west tip of Brittany. It sits on an estuary off La Côte de Granit Rose. Some of the mobile homes are privately owned, and Elsie, who manages ours for a friend, is waiting for us when we reach the security barrier. She opens the gate and we follow her up a gently rising gravel track. In contrast to Dol-de-Bretagne, every car here is French. We pass a table tennis table and football nets. The mobile home, painted in lighthouse-style horizontal red and white stripes, is on a small hill that overlooks the Bay of Goulven. There are two bedrooms, a kitchen-dining area, and, from the living room, a sea view.

Elsie shows Charlie and Phoebe a drawstring bag which contains rainy-day games and a book for each of them about shells. She tells us how to work the microwave and, as she walks outside to check the gas bottle, Dinah says to me, 'There's loads in the fridge. Look!' Inside there's Breton cider, crêpes, a jar of caramel sauce, butter, orange juice and two packets of butter biscuits. 'And look at that view.'

When Elsie returns, she writes down the name of the best nearby beach.

Keremma Beach is a short walk away, down a sandy path between two banks of mobile homes. It's still warm and sunny. We walk along the narrow grassy dune, passing a row of green bubble tents belonging to a French school party. They're in regimental rows, overlooking the sea. The kids – boys and girls aged about 11 or 12 – have bed sheets wrapped round their midriffs with 'Français' written on them in red and blue marker pen. The theme tune to *Chariots of Fire* is playing on a sound system as they take it in turns to wrestle in pairs on crash mats for cardboard Olympic medals.

On the beach, Dinah sits on her matriarchal picnic chair, in her huge brown sunglasses. Phoebe draws rabbits in the ribbed, still-wet sand that's a silty grey under its brown crust, while Charlie and I build a shark sand sculpture. I draw the shark's outline with Charlie's wooden spade and dig a trench around the circumference, turning the sand into the centre. When it's high and full, I mould the sand into shape with my hands, while Charlie pats it smooth. We make teeth with white cockle shells. Charlie scores the gills with a stick and I make eye sockets from inverted limpet shells ('Olympic shells', Phoebe calls them) that we fill with two small pebbles for pupils.

When a Frenchman walks past with his girlfriend and stops to admire what we've done, it reminds me of my dad, who used to make us the greatest sandcastles you've ever seen when we were on holiday. Unshackled from his swivel chair on the management floor of Broadcasting House, his whole energy would be directed at us for two weeks. He'd build magnificent walled medieval cities of sand that people would take pictures of as they passed.

It was the most terrible thing my dad ever said, when he admitted, a couple of years after Mum died, as we sat in the garden at my stepmum Mary's house, that actually he'd never enjoyed these summers, that the responsibility – for giving us a good time, making sure we were safe – weighed too heavily on him, so that he was always relieved when we were back at home. We'd loved those holidays and our time with him. Those holidays had been the essence of our childhood. And in saying that he'd never felt the same way, it was like my dad was rewriting family history, erasing himself from the rosy picture we'd all painted. It took me a long time to understand why it was he felt that way. It was part of his need to be in control, something that's impossible with three young kids. And also, I think now, it's a generational thing. He worked. Mum looked after us. So while it was a holiday for her, it was a culture shock for him. In a funny way I think it partly explains my love of these family road trips. They're exactly what my dad would have hated.

The tide comes in at walking pace, and half an hour later, the shark crumples into the water, pleasingly leaving just the dorsal fin visible for a while. Charlie waves his spade at the approaching sea and shouts, 'Germans!'

'Why Germans?' I ask.

'Don't know,' he laughs.

Phoebe finds a starfish, but has watched *Finding Nemo* so many times that she's disappointed that it has no human face when she turns it round. Families pad down the wooden steps for end-of-day swims. An exultant swallow rises above the water, its wings tipped back in an ecstasy of flight, and I'm overcome with a sudden desire to swim. I take my shirt off. 'I'm going in.'

Dinah's shocked. 'In your shorts and pants?'

I've never swum in Brighton in our seven years there. I haven't bathed in any sea since childhood. And even then, I never enjoyed it. I preferred to watch my dad in the water with my sister Penny and Buster, while I sat instead on the picnic rug with Mum, rolling my cricket die.

'Who's coming?' I ask.

'Me!' says Phoebe. Salt aggravates her eczema. Normally she sticks to the pool.

'And me,' says Charlie.

We wade in together and, past the rocks, the sand is smooth. At the point where our shark was, the water's over my shorts. Phoebe lowers her shoulders underwater first. She leaps up, panting, out of breath, laughing. 'Daddy, that is *so* cold! Charlie, I double-dare you to go in!' I crouch under next. Charlie, in his pants, is sucking in his concave white stomach, still walking out. He has a huge grin on his face and there's a squeal of delight in his throat every time the water laps to a new level. And he's so like me when I was his age, so, so like me, I feel for a moment I've become my dad, encouraging him, cajoling. 'Get your shoulders under, that's the key. Come on! It's lovely when you're in.' It's too shallow to swim, so we sit in a line, the sea up to their necks, excavating the seabed, running wet sand through our fingers, betting on which boats the incoming tide will refloat next.

'The blue one.'

'I think the blue one too.'

'Pick your own one, Charlie.'

'But I want the blue one.'

'It's no fun if we don't have our own ones.'

'OK. The white one.'

'The white one that's right at the back?'

'Actually, the yellow one.'

'I think there should be prizes,' I say. 'If yours is the next boat.'

'Prizes?'

'Butter biscuits.'

'How many?' asks Charlie.

'One.'

'Four?'

'OK, two.'

'Three?'

'Don't push it. Two.'

Charlie wins the first go, Phoebe the second. Out of the water, when I put my shirt on, I can remember that childhood sensation of material over a salty back – how it feels like a loose thread of cotton tickling. My toe's throbbing a little, but it's not broken, and I feel intensely happy. The kids are enjoying themselves. We still have weeks to go, and there's Phoebe's birthday dinner to come – sausages and mash, with crêpes for dessert.

The kids are drawing with their rainy-day pens, eating their butter biscuit prizes, and I'm playing patience. Dinah's chopping potatoes for dinner, intermittently reading out bits about the history of Brittany: how the Celts fled Cornwall and called the new country they'd landed in Bretagne, as it was so similar to the one they'd left behind; how it hadn't become part of France until 1514. 'And where we are now, Finisterre, literally means "end of the world". It was the last part of France to be annexed to the crown. Can you move those cards now? I need to lay the table.'

And when my mobile rings, I can somehow tell from the urgency of its vibration that it's Henry. Henry almost never rings me. I always ring Henry. Even when I ring Henry these days, I never speak to Henry. I speak to his assistant, Nicola.

'Be-ehhhh-n,' says Henry, dragging my name out.

'Heeeenrrrrry,' I reply.

'How's France?'

I tell him some mishaps and although I'm trying to make the stories funny, Henry doesn't laugh, but just keeps saying things like: 'Oh dear. A broken toe isn't funny. My father-in-law broke his toe' or 'That must be tough on the kids' or 'An onion museum on her seventh birthday! Oh dear!'

'Listen,' he says, eventually, ending the small talk. 'I wanted a quick chat before I disappear again.'

'You off again?'

'Uganda.'

'Wow!'

'With my daughter. We're going to see the silverback gorillas. She wants to teach them sign language in her gap year.'

'Lovely way to spend a gap year.'

'It is. Look, I'm sorry, I don't have a contract for you in front of me. It's not like the old days, when I think it took, what, 48 hours with your first book? Nowadays books have to go to marketing departments. There are acquisition meetings. Sales have a look at it.' He reads out the names of five more publishers that have said no to my novel. Not for us. Don't like the premise. Not sure if there's any audience for this kind of thing. We don't do this kind of thing very well here.

'Now, there are other options. Mills & Boon,' says Henry.

'Mills & Boon!'

'I know, I know. But they have radicalised their list.'

'Really? *Mills & Boon*?'

'They have a crime section now, and they're moving into other genres. I just want you to know that they're up my sleeve. Another option is Amazon.'

'I didn't know they published books.'

'Online. For the Kindle. They take 30 per cent. The author takes the rest.'

'And they market it?' I ask.

'Er . . . no.'

'Oh, so self-publishing, you mean. Vanity publishing.'

'Indie publishing.'

'But it's the same thing.'

'Yes.'

'I see.'

'Of course, I want us to go with a mainstream publisher, but this is just so you know there are other options. Or you could blog the book. We could set you up with a website.'

'Blog it?'

'I'm being realistic,' says Henry, more curtly.

'I appreciate your honesty, Henry. You've been a great help . . .'

And he has. It was Henry who discovered my first novel in the slush pile at the Brown Thorn agency 13 years ago.

'I'm sorry, Ben,' says Henry. 'The big authors are doing very well, but it's feast or famine. Middle- to lower-ranking authors have been squeezed. Anyway, take some time out, have a think about what I said about Mills & Boon, then get another proposal to me.'

'OK, thanks, Henry. And thanks again for—'

'Actually,' he says, 'send it to Nicola.'

There's a pause, while I digest this bump down another step in my importance to Henry.

'Ben?' he adds.

'Yes,' I say, hopefully.

'Can I ask a favour? Where have you been that you enjoyed? I have a week in August and I'm thinking about France.'

'Arzon was nice. Boaty and expensive. I know, it sounds like another planet, doesn't it? They came from Arzon. Nanoo-nanoo.' It goes quiet on the other end of the phone. 'It's near Carnac,' I say, snapping out of this.

'Thank you. Goodbye, Ben,' he says, and the phone goes dead so suddenly it feels like a physical slap in the face.

After her cake, Phoebe's final birthday treat is watching 20 minutes of the Laurel and Hardy movie *The Flying Deuces* on YouTube with Charlie. It doesn't matter that it's black and white, that we watch it on a tiny screen and that I have to explain what some words mean ('"Quite a dish" means someone who's good-looking' and '"Swell" is what they used to say when something was good'), they love the slapstick, the pokes in the eye, the custard pies and bangs on the head. Phoebe particularly enjoys Ollie falling in love and is so embarrassed for him, she sometimes has to hide her face ('Oh no, he's going to give her the ring'). She can copy the balletic, nervous movement of Ollie's fingers on his tie when he's feeling flirtatious in the presence of a pretty woman. Afterwards, Phoebe reads *Harry Potter* to me.

'Let me tell you what's happened so far,' she says. 'Harry's gone to stay at Ron Weasley's and Hermione is there too. And Dumbledore, he's the headmaster of Hogwarts – he's nice. And it's funny at the Weasleys' because the dad doesn't know about money. He thinks a five is a twenty, and things like that. And Harry keeps having to tell him, because he lives with Muggles, so he knows about Muggle money, and the Weasleys are all wizards, and Harry has this scar on his head. It was done by Voldemort.'

Throughout all this, she rolls her eyes and makes exaggerated gestures with her arms.

'And sometimes, Daddy, when Harry does something embarrassing, I have to . . .' she mimics putting the book over her eyes.

'That's because you're identifying with him. We'll have to think what you're going to read next. I doubt you'll be able to go back to fairy books after this. You want real characters now.'

'If it was a choice between telly and Harry Potter books, I'd choose my Harry Potter books.'

'That's great.'

'And when I grow up, I'm going to write books like you, Daddy.'

And as Phoebe tells me more about the convoluted plot, I'm picturing the black spined Penguin Classic edition of *War and Peace* that my dad gave me after my first book was published. He'd written inside the cover: 'One day I hope you'll write something as good as this. I am so proud of you, my son. And so would your mother have been.'

Back in the living room, Dinah has the Mills & Boon website up. They have about 13 imprints, called things like Medical, History, Blaze, Sexy and Modern. We look at Blaze. All the books have covers featuring dark-haired, shirtless men with six-packs. The first book blurb says: 'City-slicker Rafe Locke is no redneck and refuses to buy into the whole cowboy thing. That is, until he sees engineer Meg Seymour. It's not long before she's enticed Rafe into riding, roping, country dancing . . . and a whole lot more!'

Dinah skips to Desire. We read another. 'Sherri Dalton knows all about hot, stormy weather – the kind where all a girl wants to do is strip down to her lingerie. Despite being a successful, attractive weather girl, nothing can prepare Sherri for being stranded in a real-life hurricane with gorgeous, arrogant Terrence Hudson, the son of a billionaire financier. While the gathering clouds bring gales and pounding seas, Sherri and Terrence walk right into a storm of passion.'

After this I Google 'eBooks + Amazon' and learn that anybody can upload an eBook on to Amazon at no cost. Amazon simply takes 30 per cent of the profit.

'It will be alright, my love.' Dinah taps my leg under the covers.

'I know. I'm actually thinking about what you said before.'

'What was that?'

'About how I'm missing the context here.' I've started reading a book by the former *New York Times* reporter Adam Gopnik. It's about his family moving to France, and it's made my guidebook seem pale in comparison and made me want to improve it.

'You were right, what you said. My sole interactions are saying "*merci beaucoup*" when we're given free tickets and "*au revoir*" when we leave.'

'Do you want to say something insightful about the French, like Adam Gopnik?'

'I do. I want to relate their personality as a nation to a moment in history – the Franco-Prussian War of 1870 – or to the way their plugs are two-pronged not three. It's hard to do that when all you've got to go on is what inflection they say "*bonne journée*" to you in when you leave with a baguette.'

'Do you want me to teach you some French?'

'Will you? Words. Not grammar. It's too late for grammar. Words I can use.'

'OK. *Vache*?'

'What's that?'

'Cow.'

'Great. I'll use that tomorrow.'

'*Boeuf*.'

'I know that. That's beef. I'm good on beef.' A wave of tiredness floods over me.

'And—'

'Actually, I think that's enough.'

Dinah switches the light off. 'I do think you should try to think of proposals for Henry. And it's just his opinion, remember.'

'I'm fine,' I tell her.

'Good,' she says.

She rolls over and now, for some reason, I think about the famous Philip Dunn picture of the blown-out red and blue deckchairs on a windy Brighton day, against the backdrop of the Palace Pier. I imagine being back home in the study in September. The kids at school, Dinah starting teacher-training at university. Writing up this guidebook will take a couple of months, but what will I do after that?

Charlie shouts out, 'Daddeeee?' Dinah bangs her head down on the pillow.

'What?' I call back.

'I need a poo.'

'You do it,' I shout back.

'I want you to do it,' he calls.

In bed, Charlie's wearing his Ben 10 pyjamas. His dark eyes and white skin make him look as blank and innocent as a freshly made gingerbread man.

'Come on then.'

He throws his covers back, shuffles ahead of me and sits on the toilet. His bum sinks low into the bowl. He rests his elbows on his thighs, holding his head in his hands. 'I don't want to be silly tonight. I'm tired,' he says.

'Good.'

He jumps down from the toilet and, in the same movement, pulls his trousers up with both hands. He washes his hands. I steer him back to the bedroom. On a spare pillow on the floor beside their double bed, Phoebe's arranged her birthday jewellery. On the bedside table is the plaster dolphin on its raised plinth of Horrid Henry books. She has her left hand tucked awkwardly under her pillow, so she remembers not to suck it.

CHAPTER 8

Dinah called me from the kitchen and there was something in her voice that gave me a clue, because I braced myself before I sat down in the little rocking chair in the hall and picked up the phone. My mum, who had been a week away from her two-year all-clear, was whispering, and I remember her voice, the fear in it.

'Benjy,' what she always called me, 'I think it's back. The cancer.'

About three months before this, when Dinah's sister's son Hugh was born, we'd been at the hospital a few hours later. The following weekend, we then went to see Hugh 'in his home setting'.

'I'm Hugh's godmother!' was Dinah's startled response when I'd complained, a fortnight later, that another 130-mile round trip, this time to drop off a Humphrey's Corner mobile, was overkill. After this, photos of Hugh appeared on our fridge and on our mantelpiece. 'I can't help it,' Dinah would say, cooing over nappy adverts on telly. 'It's my biological clock – it's been turned on.'

I treated it as a joke, like one of her urges. I didn't take

Dinah seriously until the weekend her friend Kat came to stay with her boyfriend, John. Dinah and Kat's lives had always followed an uncanny parallel. They lived a street away growing up, went to Midlands universities and both ended up as journalists. We were in the Ooh Arr pub and I can't remember how the subject came up, but Kat, lording it over John, said, 'I've told him, if he doesn't give me a baby by the time I'm 30, I'm out of here. If he won't give me one, someone else will. I'm terrible to him, Dinah. Aren't I, John?'

John rolled his eyes at me and Dinah piped up, 'Me too.' And when I stared at her, she said, as if it was something we'd discussed many times and that I'd been unreasonable about for years, 'Well, you can't hang around at 30.'

I expected her to blame it on the wine the next morning. Instead, we had the first of what would be many rows on the subject. She told me we were on a treadmill, had thought so for a long time. I accused her of being unsupportive about my mum. The biopsy had revealed the cancer had reached my mum's liver and she'd been given six months to live. I was spending most weekends back at home. And now Dinah was putting this pressure on me. She said she couldn't help the timing. She had to be honest with me. Would I have preferred her to lie? We didn't own our own place, like our friends, we weren't married, like many of them. Her mum, her sister and everyone at her work, she said, wanted to know why – what was wrong, why hadn't I asked her to marry me? In truth, the reason I hadn't asked her wasn't that I didn't want to get married. It was because I was now worried we'd be one step nearer the next thing – children. The truth was, her broodiness had frightened me.

* * *

We're in a hotel in St. Nazaire, in Loire Atlantique. The kids are next door, watching *Voilà, Scooby-Doo!* while Dinah's lying on our bed, watching me pack up. She cricked her neck earlier sleeping on a bolster last night and walked to breakfast like a doll bent into a strange, unnatural shape.

'Tell me the nightmare again.'

'I was being attacked by a cat,' she says.

'A serval? Did it have pointed ears?'

'No.'

'A mountain lion?'

'I don't know.'

'A lynx?'

'I'm not sure.'

'You were moaning.'

'I was frozen with terror. I couldn't even shout out!'

I remember that we're going to an aquarium later.

'Is it turtle anxiety?'

'You know what it is.'

Dinah climbs off the bed. To do this and keep her neck rigid means she has to inch down the mattress, bending her knees and shuffling her bum along after her feet, like a jackknifing caterpillar. At the foot of the bed, she lowers her legs and rises to a vertical position, keeping her back so rigid, it's like watching someone erecting a totem pole.

'Ah, it's canoe anxiety,' I say. 'Can I say something about that?'

'What?' she says.

'Now, I know you're not doing it on purpose, but can you try not to communicate any fear to Charlie today?'

'Love, I'm very careful not to show my fear.'

I move into the bathroom to pack the things in there. Dinah rotates her whole body to face me. She takes a series of small steps, so she doesn't have to turn her head.

'Do that again,' I say.

'Why?'

'You look like Herman Munster.'

'What?'

'That's how Herman Munster turns round.'

'I *am* actually in pain here, you know!'

'Sorry. Anyway, all I'm saying is that Charlie takes his cues from you. Any look or nuance.'

'What have I done?'

'Drilling him earlier on what to do if the canoe capsizes!'

'He needs to know about safety.'

'By telling him how to swim for air pockets, and to float feet first in fast-flowing water, to avoid hitting his head on floating debris?'

'You know how many nightmares I've had about him drowning.'

'I'm just saying, from now, you know, let's be cool.'

'I think I'm being very cool.'

'And, if I were you, I'd stop assuming strange postures and act normally. Eventually your muscles will warm up. You'll damage them even more if you walk around like Barbie at the back of the closet with her head round the wrong way.'

'Any more sensitive advice?'

It's been a tough week. We thought we'd cracked it, but it turns out we haven't. What's changed is that tourist board reps in this region, and sometimes even museum staff, have started wanting to *accompany* us around attractions and sometimes to lunch. It means they've watched our kids misbehave at close quarters and have struggled to know what to say when, for example, Charlie has scooped up mashed potato with his hand shaped into a bear paw and fed himself, like Winnie the Pooh.

Each day's been an exhausting copycat of the last, where we race to a new town, meet some new tourist officer who hands us a goodie bag containing USBs, CDs and a telephone directory's worth of literature in French, most of which we then discard in our hotel-room bin after cherry-picking it for stickers, pads and free pens.

After this we spend the day with a rep – a Bernard, a Delphine, a Gerard, a Sandrine – during which time they provide regional delicacies for the kids to dry-wretch at, dispense local knowledge about their town's history in relation to the 100 Years War, the 30 Years War, the Wars of Religion, the First World War and the Second World War. They then show us fortifications built by Napoleon, boast about their journey time to Paris and their casino (all French tourist reps are, for some reason, hugely proud of the organised pontoons taking place in their towns), while also being evasive about the mosquito threat.

After that, they give us tickets to attractions, where the tours, conducted exclusively in French, are usually about a very specific element of the town's heritage – rope-making, salt-harvesting, oyster-farming – before they finally leave us their business cards, after being mildly affronted when we try, and fail, to persuade them not to come to lunch and dinner with us as 'it will be chaos with the children'. Then, the next morning, the roller coaster begins again. L'Orient, Pornichet, La Roche-sur-Yon, Guérand and today St Nazaire. The endless positivism about a town's mojette beans or a tapestry made on an unusual vertical loom can be wearing, but harder is having our parenting so closely watched.

There was a book out recently, I can't remember its name – *Why French Children Don't Throw Food*, *Why French Children Always Say Please and Thank You*, *Why French Children Are So Well Mannered They're Probably Getting Saturday Jobs as Equerries*. Something like that. French kids *are* generally better behaved, it's true, but there's a reason for this. It's because they get walloped all the time. *La fessée*. The smack. Kids are whacked left, right and centre in France. We've seen it countless times – at Suscinio Castle, the Carnac stones, Arzon harbour. Shushing is part of the same thing. In Britain you'd never shush someone else's kids, especially if their parents were within earshot, and doubly so if you didn't know them. In France old ladies have shushed our kids. Shopkeepers have shushed our kids. Bus drivers have shushed them. In Angers they were shushed by a beggar trying to sleep in a bus shelter. They were even shushed by a security guard in a room at the Castle of the Dukes of Brittany that was completely empty apart from us and the security guard.

This has all taken its toll on Dinah, even before the cricked neck. There are heavy bags under her eyes from the early starts. She's run out of contact lenses and there's been no time to get more, so she's in her glasses with the wonky frames that make her look like Eric Morecambe just after he's cracked a gag. With no spare time for washing, the roof-box is a giant laundry bin full of dirty clothes. And it's her third day in the same summer dress, which is so encrusted with kids' food, she doesn't so much lay it across a chair at night as *lean* it up against things.

Even the car's having a downer. The miasma around the cheese box is so strong that the other day I actually saw someone walk past the boot, stop, pull a face and look around, sniffing. The boot hinges have also somehow rusted away – or perhaps the smell's actually corrosive. Anyway, they no longer work, so we have to prop it open with a golf putter.

We arrive at the beach in St Nazaire and the canoe man, Didier, shows us various-sized orange life jackets.

'Are there dangerous fish?' asks Dinah.

'Danjerus fish!' says Didier, handing me a life jacket. He's about 35 and is wearing long shorts, a sleeveless fleece and shades.

'You know, poisonous ones,' says Dinah. 'Stonefish, that sort of thing?'

Didier smiles at his flip-flops. 'No, zare are no danjerus fish.'

'Dinah,' I say, because Charlie's looking on, 'remember what we said.'

It's fair to say my wife's an anxious person. She's scared of tortoises and turtles, as I've said. But you can add to that all insects and a large percentage of birds. She's scared of ghosts, fair rides. She's frightened of bees, wasps, earwigs, open fires, candles, trams, the dark, the semi-dark, guinea pigs, pigs, horror films, thrillers, serial killers, pictures of intestines, snails, slugs, mummies, newts, frogs and cats. Before we had kids, I saw it as a laughable quirk that I could never impersonate a zombie, pretend to be possessed by the devil or hum the theme tune to *Jaw*s. Now we have kids, it's made Dinah, if anything, worse, because she's transferred this fear on to them.

It started after Phoebe was born, when she confided to a midwife her fear that our baby would be smothered by a domestic cat. She was quickly assessed for post-natal depression. She wasn't depressed, but I can see why the midwife thought she might be. After all, we didn't have a cat.

After that, it was the washing machine. Dinah was convinced that Phoebe, who couldn't yet crawl or even recognise her own hand, was going to climb into it, somehow turn it on, close the heavy door and colour-wash herself to death. And do you know any other mothers who print off stories about the untimely deaths of young children and leave them on their partner's keyboard in the study, with 'FYI' written in red pen over the top? A child in Arbroath falls into a grain silo, a four-year-old in Sydney is stung by a stingray, and I'm informed – in order, presumably, that I can tweak my risk assessment of grain silos and Great Barrier Reef predators accordingly.

When ironing, Dinah practically seals off the area with Police Aware tape. We're not allowed to open the window upstairs, and Charlie and Phoebe are so terrified of being run over after my wife's horror stories ('THEN YOU WILL BE DEAD IN THE ROAD AND THAT WILL BE THAT') that they panic whenever they hear an engine start. They're not allowed unsupervised baths ('Enamel is hard, Ben!') and the stair gates would probably still be up now if the kids hadn't long ago learnt to climb over them.

So although canoeing doesn't sound much, in our world, this is the high-risk equivalent of another family ski-dooing to the North Pole to spend a fortnight working at an environmental observatory electronically tagging polar bears.

'And are there any strong currents?' Dinah asks now.

'Currents?' says Didier.

'Tides,' says Dinah. 'Are the tides dangerous?'

Didier points towards where the Atlantic meets the mouth of the Loire River. The cruise ships refitted in St Nazaire use that channel and, as he fetches life jackets for the kids, Dinah raises her eyebrows at me, as if to say, 'See, that was worth discovering.' When Charlie's jacket proves a little loose, Dinah puts her hand inside the front of it, to show me how much room there is between his chest and the straps.

'Love, this is not the Kon-Tiki raft. We'll be in a few feet of water. He'll be fine.'

'It doesn't fit him, Ben.'

I ask Didier for a smaller one.

'Smaller?'

'My wife thinks . . .'

'Ah, OK, your wife . . .' he says, and he trudges back up the beach to his Land Rover to find one in a different size.

Afterwards, Didier leads us to a small jetty. He unscrews the dry-bag lid. We place valuables and a towel inside it. Didier slides in four paddles, then helps Dinah into the boat. Phoebe climbs in next, but Charlie resists.

'Charlie, you're in charge of spotting herons and cormorants. In fact, if you see one, I think that might be worth a choccy square, don't you think, Mummy?'

'Definitely,' says Dinah. Then, as Charlie reluctantly takes the middle seat beside Phoebe (I'm in the stern, Dinah has the bow seat at the front), she says to Didier, 'And if there's an accident?'

'You shout 'elp,' he says.

'And you come running?'

'Wif an 'arpoon for ze shark.'

Charlie looks round. 'He's kidding, Charlie.'

Dinah says, 'Sorry, and the mouth of the Loire is . . .'

Didier points.

Dinah paddles on the left and I take the right side with Phoebe. To begin with, we keep rotating 360 degrees, or we veer towards the beach, where we're in danger of being capsized by a wave. There's some bickering.

'Lean forward slightly, love, keep the blade vertical and drag the water back in a long stroke.'

'It's you,' says Dinah. 'You're the helmsman. It's up to you to make it go straight.'

'Look at me,' says Phoebe, dabbing her paddle into the water. 'I'm doing well, aren't I?'

'Look at Phoebe, Mummy,' I say.

'Mummy, look!' she shouts.

But, because of her neck, Dinah can only turn a fraction. 'Wow! That's great, sweetheart.'

'But you didn't see, Mummy. Look!'

'I saw you, Pops. That's great.'

'Mummy, look properly!'

'Sweetie, I saw.'

'Charlie, are you sure you don't want a go?' I ask. Charlie, who's being tonked lightly on the head with the handle of Phoebe's paddle every few seconds, shakes his head and continues his wildlife vigil.

Slowly we learn to keep the boat travelling, if not totally straight, then at least generally forwards. To our left is the open sea; to the right, the shore. We pass the St Nazaire Statue of Liberty, presented to the city by the American government after the First World War. There are birds perched on it.

'Any cormorants, Charlie?'

He shakes his head.

The water glistens in the sunshine. We pass the headland. The beaches become resorty, with large white hotels. Further out, cruisers pass, with speedboats dragging inflatable bananas.

'Drag one hand in the water,' says Phoebe. 'It's really cool and nice.'

'Charlie?' I ask.

'Don't want to.'

'It's OK, bubs. Look, Mummy's putting her hand in. The man was joking about the sharks.' He shakes his head.

Even with Charlie's lack of co-operation it's a pleasant way to spend a morning. We're on our own. It's peaceful. We're not outdoorsy types, but I'm beginning to see the attraction. It makes me think about the dad in the Roald Dahl story *Danny the Champion of the World*. He was the best, most exciting dad in the world, Danny said about him. He taught Danny how to poach by leaving soaked raisins threaded with horse hairs, so that when they were swallowed by the pheasants in Hazell's Wood, they became lodged in their throats. For some reason, as they retched and attempted to dislodge the raisin, the pheasant would stand stock-still, enabling him to be captured. He taught Danny other poaching skills, and how to drive an Austin 7 and how to take apart and put back together its engine. In comparison, there's very little I can teach the kids. Charlie isn't that interested in football, and although I've taught Phoebe to play chess, she still cries every time I take one of her horsies, making it difficult to move her along.

But here we are canoeing.

After half an hour we turn round and we're not far from home when the wasp lands on Dinah's back. A butterfly flaps its wings in Asia and, according to chaos theory, it can cause a natural disaster in the Midwest. For us, a wasp works just as well.

'Daddy!' shouts Phoebe. 'Look! A wasp!'

'Oh yeah.'

'Mummy!' shouts Phoebe. 'You have a wasp on your back!'

Charlie looks round at me, scared.

'It's alright, Charlie. It just thinks Mummy's a flower because of her bright life jacket.'

'It'll fly away in a minute when it realises its mistake,' says Dinah.

The wasp does, but the trouble is, it lands on the front of Charlie's life jacket. He stands up, the boat rocks and he cries out.

'Sit down, Charlie,' I say. 'It'll go in a second.'

The wasp takes off and now lands back on Dinah's jacket.

'Mummy! It's on you again!' shouts Phoebe.

'Is it?' says Dinah, and when Charlie stands again, I lift my paddle past Phoebe's head, and I'm about to flick the wasp away with the blade when Dinah half-stands at the exact moment Charlie jumps into my lap. I fall back, my paddle lifts and it clonks Dinah on the head. Unbalanced and taken by surprise, she falls sideways and tries to hang on to the gunwale. For a moment it's as if she's wrestling with the front of the boat, which rocks dramatically from side to side. It reminds me a little of how Tarzan would tussle with a crocodile in the old black-and-white Johnny Weissmuller movies. But then Dinah rolls, almost deliberately it seems, into the water. The boat corrects itself. Time freezes. I see a graceful heron arrowing a few inches above the water in the opposite direction. I have time to wonder what we'll eat for dinner tonight and then the peace is broken by Dinah emerging breathless from the water, scrabbling for the side of the boat. She tries to haul herself back in, but hasn't the strength. 'Ggggget . . . mmmme . . . oooout!'

I move down the boat and I try to heave her in, as she attempts to lever herself up and over the side, but the boat tips violently again. Phoebe stands. I tell her to sit down. Charlie starts to cry. Dinah's now half in, half out of the boat, draped over the side. She looks like some wanted cattle rustler strapped across a bounty hunter's saddle in the Wild West.

I return to the stern, move Charlie to the middle seat and paddle forwards three strokes on the right. 'Tttthe Llllloire!' shouts Dinah. She can't see over the boat because her head's so low and she can't bend her neck.

'What?'

'Ttttthe . . . fffffucking . . . Llllloire. Ooooopen www-wwwater.'

'Love, I'm turning round.' And I raise my eyebrows towards the kids.

'I'm . . . sssssssorry, aaaaam Iiiii . . . sssssswearing in ffffffffront of the . . . chchchchildren?' she asks.

'I'm completing a ferry glide. Stop panicking.'

'Iiiii'm . . . fffffffreezing . . . fffffucking cccccold.'

I paddle three strokes on the other side. Dinah slips back into the water. She hangs on, her arm draped over the boat. Phoebe moves down the boat to stroke Dinah's hand. Charlie's in my lap, his head pressed into my shoulder.

'I'm sorry, love. I was trying to flick the wasp away. The kids moved.'

'Sorry, Mummy,' says Phoebe.

'Sorry, Mummy,' says Charlie.

'And you have to bend your knees when you stand up in a boat. You didn't bend your knees.'

Dinah tries to say something, but I can't make out what. She's shivering too much. All I can just hear is: 'Fffffffucking.'

Ten metres from the beach, it's shallow enough for Dinah to walk. Her skirt clings to her legs as she wades to shore. I jump in and steer the boat by the prow, following Dinah, with Charlie on my shoulders. Once I've pulled the boat up on to the sand, I go back for Phoebe. Dinah's now prostrate on the sand, lying face down in a star shape, resembling a shipwrecked Robinson Crusoe or, minus the axe in her back, an Agatha Christie murder victim.

'Towel,' she says. I open the dry-bag. She snatches it, sits up and whips it round herself, before hunching forward, shivering.

'Take your top off.'

She doesn't reply.

'You'll get hypothermia. Take your top off. I'll shield you!'

'You should've changed into your swimming costume before,' says Phoebe, helpfully. 'Like me. My bum's wet, but it's a swimming costume so,' she stretches her arms out, 'it's OK. Mummy, you've got seaweed in your hair.'

I unbuckle Dinah's life jacket and peel her wet shirt over her head. She shudders in just her knickers and skirt. I slip my shirt off and place it over her head.

'Give Mummy a hug, guys.'

Phoebe and Charlie cuddle Dinah, one either side. Dinah looks up. 'I was worried,' she shudders violently, 'about the Loire.'

'I know. But I was just turning round. We were miles from it. I'm still trying to work out what happened. I knocked you with the paddle. You fell sideways. Then it was like you rolled in deliberately. One moment, you were on the side, the next . . .'

'I thought the boat was capsizing.' She closes her eyes.

'So you jumped in to save the kids?'

She nods, looking tearful now.

'Did you, Mummy?' says Phoebe.

She holds Dinah's face. Dinah nods again and looks away.

'Give Mummy a hug, guys. She sacrificed herself for you.' We all put our faces together.

'Better?' Dinah nods.

'More cuddles, guys.' We cuddle again.

'The Hatch sitcom continues,' shivers Dinah.

I look at my watch. 'I hate to say this, but we'd better get going, love. If you want to change, I mean. We have the submarine tour and the aquarium shuts at four.' Dinah's head is wrapped in her arms. She doesn't reply. 'Love? Hello, can you give me a response?'

'Here's one,' she says. And she slowly raises her middle finger.

Later that evening, Dinah's sat at the table in our hotel as we wait for the restaurant to open, raking the mossie bites below her knee so rhythmically it looks like she's playing an invisible double bass.

'You need to put something on those or they'll get infected.'

Ignoring me, she picks up a piece of stale baguette, then tries to cut a section of sausage off with a plastic spoon from the hotel's tea and coffee tray. The spoon snaps, as does Dinah.

'This is shit,' she says. At the same moment, as if to reinforce this appraisal, Charlie knocks over Dinah's paper cup of wine.

The submarine tour didn't go well. 'I'm being Laurel and Hardy' has become the kids' excuse for random acts of comic violence. And in the torpedo room, Phoebe shoved Charlie through a hatch into a sonar machine. Dinah was so furious, she clouted Phoebe on the bum with a water bottle she had in her hand. It got worse at the Croisic aquarium when we walked past a tank of green turtles and the kids saw one that was upturned, wriggling on its back.

'Shall we tell them on the way out?' Phoebe asked.

'No!' said Dinah.

'Mummy!' said Phoebe. 'It'll die.'

'Good,' she said.

'But it'll die!' repeated Phoebe.

Dinah said nothing. I stared at her. '*OK*, tell them,' she said.

The keeper came. He righted the turtle.

'Well done, Phoebe. That was kind,' I said, and I looked at Dinah.

'You know how much I hate turtles, Ben,' she said.

'Love, for the kids' emotional health, and because we don't want them to grow up to be psychopaths and dismember local cats and dogs . . .'

'Well done, Phoebe,' she said, grudgingly. Then under her breath, 'Horrible little green shits.'

'You used the s-word *again*, Mummy,' Phoebe says now.

Dinah closes her eyes. Charlie fetches a towel from the bathroom to clear up the wine and Phoebe says, her eyes sparkling, 'Daddy, Mummy *keeps* using the s-word.'

'Sometimes adults do that,' I say, 'when they get really frustrated.'

'Is Mummy frustrated?' asks Phoebe.

'Yes,' says Dinah. 'Now go and do your teeth, Phoebe. It will be too late when we get in from the restaurant.'

Charlie spills his apple juice trying to mop up the wine, and also knocks a piece of Vieux Pané cheese off the table. Dinah tries to take the towel from him before he can cause more damage.

'I didn't mean to,' he says, pulling on the other end of it, refusing to let go. 'It was an accident. *I* want to do it.'

'Charlie!' I say.

Phoebe returns from the bathroom. 'I can't find my toothbrush,' she says, and Dinah holds her head.

'That's because you probably left it at the last place as you WANDER AROUND WITH IT THE WHOLE TIME!'

I take the towel from Charlie, who senses that Dinah's raised voice means hanging on to it is now not worth the struggle. I clear up the apple juice and the wine, then pick up the now hairy piece of cheese.

'Go on, go and have a shower,' I tell Dinah. 'Clean your bites.'

She stands up and I pull out Phoebe and Charlie's sofa bed. I experiment with the lighting, for when we're back. The only way for there to be enough light in our family room for the kids not to be scared at night, but for it not to be so glaring that it keeps Dinah and I up is to have the mini-fridge door open. The only trouble then is the smell of Vieux Pané that permeates the room.

When it's time to go, I find Dinah sitting on the bath rim. She has her head in her hands. The kids have used up her new shampoo making one of their 'magic potions'. This multicoloured potion's in the sink. They've also used half a tub of her Pond's hand cream and most of the toothpaste. I start to tell Dinah about the mini-fridge and she holds up a hand to stop me.

'This is *not* a holiday, Ben,' she says.

The argument happens in the restaurant. Arguing with my wife is a bit like a James Bond shootout in a fairground hall of mirrors. I can win what I think is the real argument and all that happens is another pops up behind me, this one being what I supposedly should have been aiming for. I shoot at that, think I've hit the target, but it's another illusion; the mirror shatters and two more pop out, about obscure, seemingly unrelated topics, so that eventually I'm out of bullets, defeated and still don't know what the hell I'm supposed to have done wrong.

In Le Skipper the decor is what the French consider chic – recessed spotlights, black leather chairs and wooden floors. The first sign of trouble comes after the waitress leaves the table, having taken our order.

'Can you not drone on when I'm speaking French? It's off-putting,' Dinah says.

'I wanted you to ask about the sauces. What sauces there are influence my choice of meat.'

'Trust me, I know how you feel about your sauces.'

'Really?'

'Really,' she says.

'OK, what sauce would I have with lamb then?'

'Mint,' she says.

'Wrong. Teriyaki. What sauce would I have with beef?'

'I don't know. But this is very boring,' she says.

Half an hour later, Dinah's eating oysters with shrimp and sea snails, and I'm having the steak with garlic butter, while the kids are playing their nightly game of Who Has the Longest Chip? There's also a fringe event – Who Has the Shortest Chip?

'But no breaking them in half,' Phoebe's saying.

'I *know*,' says Charlie.

'They have to be *naturally* small,' she says.

They're presenting chips to each other, talking in the New York accents they think make them sound cool. 'I'm like, this is *my* best chip. It's so *cool* and long,' Charlie says.

'And this is, like, *my* best chip. Check it out. It's called a *frite*, but I call it a chip, cos, like, I *want* to.'

'Are we allowed to talk about what happened on the submarine now?' I ask.

'That did *not* hurt her,' spits Dinah. 'That bottle was empty.'

'Kids,' I say, 'do you want to play round the corner?' There's a games area in the restaurant. The kids run off.

'I'm not saying it did. But the anger in your face, love.'

Dinah closes her eyes impatiently. 'If you must know, I was feeling very uncomfortable, or else I probably wouldn't have done it,' she says.

'What?'

'My tummy's been a bit funny. It's still a bit funny now, if you must know. I was struggling to suck a fart in. There. Satisfied?'

'Why were you holding it in?'

'Pressure.'

I stare at her. 'I don't understand.'

'The pressure in the submarine,' she says.

'You thought your fart might alter the pressure in the submarine?'

'I don't know,' she says. 'The gas.'

'It wasn't even underwater, love.'

'Well, anyway, it would have been selfish because of the smell.'

I start to laugh.

'And, yes, I have a temper. I admit that and I'm sorry. But thanks for highlighting that weakness.'

'OK, calm down.' And I should leave it, but I can't help myself. 'No, I've got to ask. What did you think would happen if you farted?'

Dinah won't look at me.

'Did you think you'd create a vacuum? That we'd all get sucked through the torpedo tubes because you ate your cheesy crêpe too fast at lunch and got a bit of wind?'

Dinah has her hand on her chin and looks at me. 'I'm always your fall guy, aren't I? Take the piss out of Dinah.'

'What?'

'Stupid Dinah who doesn't know how submarines work or how to ferry-glide a canoe.'

'What are you talking about?'

'I never do that with your weaknesses. How embarrassing you are about mosquitoes, for example.'

'I'm embarrassing?'

'Yes, you are. Do you know you stink of Raid all the time? It's like a permanent cloud around you. I can hardly breathe half the time. You're like that character who's friends with Charlie Brown.'

'That's because this place is reclaimed swamp.'

'You're ridiculous about them, Ben.'

'Swamps are where they breed.'

'It's practically the first thing you ask everyone. "Have you got mosquitoes?" You're obsessed. And do you know what time you stopped banging the walls last night, trying to kill mossies? 2 a.m. That's just selfish.'

'You have a few quirks too, you know.'

'I'm sure I do,' she says. 'But at least I'm not moody.'

'Moody? I'm never moody.'

'Your moods change all the time,' she says. 'Inconsolable when we get lost, then, when we find out where we are, it's like nothing's happened.'

'That's because the driving tires me. Every day I'm driving the same distance it is to Aunty Romey's.'

'Which is another one of your quirks,' she says. 'Any drive is always calculated in relation to driving to your aunty Romey's. That's two Aunty Romeys. One Aunty Romey. Your obsession with getting me to ask people for directions or for help. That's another. You're never happier than when I'm asking someone something.'

'That's because it's what I'd do. If I'm lost, I ask however many people it takes to find where it is I want to go. That's actually one of yours – your *reluctance* to ask people. And while I'm on yours. Tea. Your obsession with drinking tea each day, and your dissatisfaction if this is denied you.'

'I do like my tea,' she concedes.

'You're furious that flask is used to prop the glove box shut.'

'I am, yes.'

'And also your attempt to inveigle Phoebe into your tea-drinking ways.'

'She likes a nice cup of tea.'

'Only because you offer her one. She'd never ask for one herself. And I've got news for you – she's only in it for the biscuit!'

Dinah hits the table. 'Stop it. I'm angry with you and you're trying to make me laugh.'

'And the other one is your chair. You carry your chair everywhere. Correction. *I* carry your chair everywhere.'

'I like to sit down.'

'But on that *particular* chair.'

'It's comfy and I don't like sitting on the ground.'

'That's quite a quirk. And another one – how you hate eating picnics in front of people.'

'I don't like eating them in front of people sitting in restaurants, no.'

'Because you feel they'll look down on us?'

'Yes.'

'You're ashamed of our picnics?'

'I am ashamed of the big Marmite pot.'

'Because we look parochial?'

'Yes.'

'And what else?'

'I hate the smelly cheese box.'

'Is the cold sausage alright?'

'I don't like chopping it on the Tupperware lid of the box.'

'That's why we have to find secretive places to eat lunch?'

'I can see people looking at our kids and thinking,

"They don't even have plates." And I haven't even mentioned the gravel.'

'Gravel?'

'Every time the kids go anywhere near gravel, you panic.'

'They're not used to the surface.'

'They've never seen gravel before?'

'Not in such quantities.'

'What are you talking about?' she says. 'You ridiculous person.'

'They gravel everything in France. Haven't you noticed? Everyone knows that about the French. I wouldn't mind, but they don't even play boules any more. Have you seen one boules match since we got here? It's their national sport. They've gravelled everything to fit in with this. And if you're bringing up gravel, I'm bringing up your sandals.'

Yesterday at the pool someone walked off in Dinah's size 38 Birkenstocks and left a pair of 39s behind instead. Since then, like Cinderella's prince, Dinah's been checking everyone's feet.

When the kids return, we stop arguing and order dessert. We start to eat in silence. It's always up to me to begin a rapprochement. Dinah never admits she's wrong and therefore never has to apologise. She can quite happily go to bed angry, but that's something I'm incapable of.

'If you ever remarried, I expect you'd have learnt quite a bit from this experience,' I say. I'm joking, trying to lighten the atmosphere a little, but Dinah remains stony-faced.

'This is incendiary,' she says.

And now I'm angry. I only ever become angry with Dinah when she's angry with me first. I think to myself, 'How dare you be angry with me? I've done nothing wrong.' Now I want the row out. Because even worse than her being angry with me is her suppressing her anger with me.

'Come on, what would you look for?'

And Dinah appraises me. Her eyes are now cold, slanting, and they take me in with a withering disapproval.

'No,' she says, 'I won't say.' But I can't let that go. Phoebe shows me a picture she's drawn, of what she calls 'the crab hotel'. It's a purple hotel with a huge crab hanging over the entrance, with a sign reading 'Free hot chocolate and coffee in your room'. I show it to Dinah, but she doesn't acknowledge it. Instead she sits with her elbow on the table and a hand over her mouth, looking down at the tablecloth.

'It's lovely, Pops.' Phoebe starts to draw another picture. And something destructive in me makes me ask the question again.

'Come on, what would you change?'

Dinah looks up and says in a voice I hear as though I'm underwater, 'You'd be softer, kinder.'

It's like she's sucked the air from me. I feel numb because, knowing her so well, what she really means is: I wish I'd married someone better. We don't speak through dessert and, some time later, I hear Phoebe's voice drift across the table: 'Daddy?'

'What?'

'Are you tired?'

'No,' I tell her.

'Then why are you staring like that?' She does an impression of my face.

'You're right, I am tired.'

We walk back to the hotel in the dark. Dinah holds

Charlie's hand when we cross roads and Phoebe holds mine. I ensure I don't get too far ahead, so Dinah can't accuse me of storming off. In the room, she puts the kids to bed while I go to the bar to write up my notes. I drink a small Affligem beer in a scarlet leather chair at a soulless white table in front of a TV showing Euro pop.

Dinah's fed up with the trip and is taking it out on me. But we're not just here for my guidebook – she's also here to brush up her French. Kinder and softer – the words go round my head. In my mind, I have a clear idea of who Dinah's judging me against. When we fall out, I'm always compared to her father, who received several powerful electrical shocks during his 30 years as an emergency lighting engineer, to keep a roof over the heads of his family. Bert's stoic, gentle and kind. But at the same time, I know she also wants more than what her dad provided – a bigger house, holidays, Boden dresses. I think of some of her mini-infatuations with my friends over the years: her regard for Banny's dedication to the office and bringing in the lucre. It's because my book's flopped, I think. That's what it is.

I also know this bundle of fatigue and disappointment in me, most evidenced by her refusal to entertain the idea of a third child, is never going to be faced squarely. It's an ill-defined shadow tailing my wife, who only references it in the odd squiffy barb, such as tonight's. And if that tripped so easily off her wine-reddened tongue, what more lies beyond?

As I drink my beer, I imagine being single. I think about the pretty waitress with the grey-green eyes and the one wonky tooth, and her leather trousers and the green bra strap casually and erotically on display beneath the thin strap of her black top, who served us tonight. In this intense environment of travel, it's like some particle accelerator of marriage. Strange new elements of our relationship emerge under the bombardment of the mileage and rigour. It's speeded things up. It might have taken four years to reach this point in Brighton. We need to discuss things, but the schedule won't allow it, so they blow up in our faces.

But as I get further down my drink, I start to feel bad. I haven't said goodnight to the kids. They'll be calling for me. Tomorrow will be a nightmare if we don't make up. And I suppose Dinah didn't want to go canoeing and I did knock her into the water. And it's true, I did wake her on last night's mossie hunt. Then there was my inquisition about the bottle-whipping of Phoebe. That would have annoyed her. Have I been unkind? Not on purpose. Have I been thoughtless? The trouble with being thoughtless is that, by its very nature, you won't know you've been thoughtless because you won't be able to think it's thoughtlessness, as you're too thoughtless to have the thought.

I imagine going upstairs and using that circular argument to explain my behaviour. 'The problem with being thoughtless, Dinah, is that, by its very nature . . .' I smile to myself, imagining her withering response to this. Somehow it bridges a divide between the Dinah of earlier and this more friendly Dinah that I'm imagining. Sometimes, when we're going through a bad patch, Dinah reverts to before we were married, how she saw me when I was more selfish. In this mood, anything I do is scrutinised for self-interest. It's a downward spiral after this. She never listens to my side of an argument in this state and always assumes she's right and thinks worse of me for disagreeing. But then that's because she normally is right. She's not always right for the reasons she thinks she's right, but more often than not, she *is* right. Have I made a terrible mistake? On past experience, the likelihood is, yes. I finish my drink and return to the room.

I knock on the door. Dinah, in her nightie, opens it wide without a word and moves back into the room, signifying there's been no mollification in my absence. The kids cry out for a cuddle. I kiss them goodnight. Dinah's lying on the bed, turned away from me. To be kind, I fetch her a glass of water and put it by her bedside table.

'Goodnight,' I say, to be soft.

'Night,' she says, flatly.

'I'm sorry,' I say.

'What for?' she says.

'Because my book got rejected.'

'It's not about your stupid book.'

'Well I'm sorry anyway.'

'You can't be sorry if you don't know what you're sorry about, you idiot,' she says.

For a moment, I think about returning to the bar, behaving in the clichéd manner of the wronged man, but that would only make it worse, so instead I go straight to bed, without even applying mossie spray. The air-con comes on in fits and starts. The duvet's so thin I could probably fold it up and store it in my bumbag, and I'm so unwelcome beside my wife in this bed, I don't even feel I can root around for my pyjamas in the bag, so in the end, and to guard against mossie attack, I sleep in the clothes I wore in the restaurant and breathe through my mouth to block out the smell of Vieux Pané. But actually, I don't sleep. What I do is lie there thinking.

CHAPTER 9

The final time my mum was compos mentis, I cut her up a bowl of strawberries. Alone in her room in the Chiltern Hospital, I tried to feed her, but she fell asleep between mouthfuls because of the diamorphine she was on. 'Hello, darlingth,' she'd slur when she woke, forgetting where she was. When she slipped into a coma we sat round her bed, dabbed her lips with a lemon swab. We brushed her hair, watched her chest rise and fall until, finally, one time it didn't make it back up and she died, and even though I knew it was coming, it was still a terrible shock. Every morning for weeks I woke short of breath. It seemed impossible that my mum was dead when there were strands of her ginger hair still in the sink, perfumes of hers in the bathroom and her duffle coat was hanging in the porch.

When you no longer want the same thing as your partner, you stop talking about the future, and soon after you stop talking about the future, you stop talking altogether. Now every time Dinah made a beeline for a baby, it felt like she was nagging me. Each time I left the room when a nappy advert came on, it looked like I was making a point.

The funny thing was, I wasn't against kids per se, but more what they turned you into. Every friend who'd had a child (and there were many now) had suddenly, without exception, acted like they'd been body-snatched. They stopped coming to the pub, moved into the burbs for gardens or to be on waiting lists for schools with better than average SATs scores. Their lives became ruled by this foot-long Little Emperor in a rayon blanket. Then there were the endless dinner parties that deteriorated into discussions about what buggy to buy – the Maclaren stroller versus the Phil & Teds three-wheeler. How many cubes of butternut squash little Tommy consumed at lunchtime, cot rub, nappy rash, Aquatots.

'It will be different when they're your own,' Dinah said. But what if it wasn't? It was too late then. Surely I wanted kids one day, she said. 'Don't you want miniature versions of us running around saying the things we say?' Yes, I'd agree, *one* day. But I was stalling. It got so every time the phone rang after 8 p.m. I dreaded answering it, anticipating another mate with their big announcement – an engagement or a baby. There'd always be a terrible silence afterwards from Dinah, normally followed by another night on the sofa for me.

Then there was Smith. She was 21, on work experience at the paper, and while she laughed along with the other reporters, who all had a bit of a thing for her, she was always strangely serious with me. She'd make a big point of asking after my mum, her pinched face almost seeming close to tears as I passed on the latest bad news. I don't know why this felt so appealing. Maybe it was the contrast with Dinah's joie de vivre. Perhaps it was that Smith was younger and wasn't thinking about marriage and babies.

It also felt like I was changing. One lunchtime she told me Nelson Mandela was her hero. She said this with tears in her eyes and I felt incredibly drawn to this passion. On another occasion she told me about an ex-boyfriend who'd beaten her so badly she'd ended up in a hostel for battered wives. They were now friends. 'He got jealous and couldn't help himself,' she said soulfully. Before my mum died, I'd had a theory that everything was capable of being reduced to a joke. After my mum died, I realised how naïve and thoughtless that view was. I'd joined the Samaritans and stopped being able to do death-knocks at the paper. Of course, it didn't harm matters that Smith was very attractive.

On a curry work outing, just before her work experience placement ended, I engineered it so I'd be the last one in the taxi when she was dropped off. Outside her flat, I kissed her on her forehead and told her I thought she was very special.

Smith moved to London the following week to take up an internship on *The Times*, and I was in turmoil. I'd only spent half a cab ride alone with her and barely knew her, but in the absence of more information, I filled in the gaps myself. She became the most faithful, honest, honourable, tragic woman in the history of the world. We exchanged a few old-fashioned letters. I was being a fool and slowly I came to my senses. But it was already too late. I came home from work one evening and found Dinah in her coat, sat on the end of our bed, crying. She told me that the weekend before, when I'd been with my dad, she'd met someone, had slept with him and she was leaving me because I had made it clear I didn't love her.

We're in Fouras, near La Rochelle, on the Petit Train. They don't have open-top sightseeing buses in France, but tiny blue-and-white land trains, fronted by miniature mock steam locomotives. To maximise passenger embarrassment, this particular Petit Train also has a steam engine sound effect. The driver parps on this button whenever we're either a) paused at traffic lights or b) outside chic-looking restaurants with al fresco tables. It's a bit like sightseeing in a Noddy car. Dinah's nickname for it is the Wally Trolley.

The driver's enormous, and she keeps burping. Her commentary, through the fuzzy speaker, has the imperative and rapid cadence of a captain advising passengers of the mustering points for lifeboats following a catastrophic iceberg collision. She issues her volley of garbled French, then snaps her microphone off, quickly dries her armpits with a towel she keeps on the passenger seat, burps, then resumes driving.

On the way here this morning, Dinah played Billy Bragg and Sting on the stereo, bands she listened to before we met, bands she listens to when we fall out. She sang along, every word a reiteration of how life was better before I came along. I sat back and raced the sat nav's predicted arrival time and retaliated, letting my mind wander as I steamed along the autoroute, thinking about a drive I'd done from Byron Bay to Noosa down Australia's Sunshine Coast during our break year, when I travelled the world and, for a week, fell half in love with an organised Dutch girl called Anneke.

The kids are sat in the first seat of the Petit Train, in front of us, exaggerating how we're being thrown about by shunting from one end of their banquette seat to the other, giggling crazily and occasionally sliding to the floor. This is aided by the fact that normal traffic rules don't apply to the Petit Train. In possession of various swipe cards, drivers are allowed to magically lower the stone bollards that bar other motorists. They can mount pavements, jump red lights and happily scatter tourists by swinging into crowded pedestrianised streets. In fact, if she wanted to, this sweaty driver could probably drive into local celebrity designer Philippe Starck's house, ride around his kitchen island a couple of times, blather some rushed nonsense about his iconic plastic chair, wipe her sweaty armpits on his tea towel and smash back out into the street through his bay window, and I doubt there's anything Philippe Starck could do about it.

I look at Dinah. 'A sweaty girl,' I say.

'Who loves her work,' she says.

It's the longest conversation we've had today.

Ile-d'Aix is a 20-minute ferry ride from La Pointe de la Fumée in Fouras-les-Bains. On the island, cars are banned, so passengers pull belongings along on small metal trolleys. At the other end, we select bikes from a hire shop on the wharf. Phoebe chooses a pink bike, Charlie's on a child seat behind me and Dinah has metal panniers either side of her back wheel to hold her handbag and the packed lunch. The island's two kilometres long, 600 metres wide and its focus is a tiny village north of the wharf. Here, four streets (rue Gourgard, rue Napoléon, rue Coudein and rue Marengo) bisect. It's where most of the island's population of 200 live, without a resident doctor. The one-storey houses are shuttered, with faded, pastel-coloured walls, while purple hollyhock, a triffid-like weed, grows dramatically between every crack of pavement and masonry, sometimes climbing ten feet high. The village, full of rusty bikes, has a shabby-chic *Vogue* photoshoot quality to it, so that any minute we half expect to pedal into a stick-thin supermodel in a diaphanous dress with tiger stripes on her cheeks and heavy gold eye shadow, haughtily sniffing a solitary red rose. But at the same time, the place carries a strange air of impermanence, like it's just waiting for a wave to roll in and claim it.

Out of the main village, the land's flat and the coast muddy. We ride towards Fort Liédot, a sunken ex-prison, once a Napoleonic fort, where the former Algerian prime minister Ben Bella was interred in the 50s. Phoebe weaves in and out of puddles, so she doesn't splash her legs, forcing me to slam on my goose-honk-sounding brakes. The birds chirp loudly in the trees, and we see the occasional flash of sea, mudflat, sandy creek and oyster farm whizzing by through the branches of the coastal pine trees.

'This is lovely,' I say to Dinah, slowing down.

'Nice there are no cars,' she concedes.

Before we fork right to the bay of Anse du Saillant, the path rises and Phoebe's bike becomes stuck in fifth gear. She veers from side to side, straining to climb the hill, before giving up.

'I can't do it,' she says.

'Change gear, Pops. It's easier in a low one.'

'I can't,' she tells me. 'This bike is rubbish.'

'Phoebe!' says Dinah.

'But it won't change.'

'You have to get a bit of speed up,' I tell her.

Phoebe tries, but wobbles alarmingly as the only taxi operating on the island appears behind us. She dismounts to let it pass and we all stop. Dinah's bike, over-weighted, slides from under her on the gravel. The pedals rasp her shins as it crashes to the ground and the contents of her handbag spill into the road. When Phoebe repeats that her bike's rubbish, Dinah snaps.

'Right, let's go back,' she says. 'Back we go, Phoebe! Another thing we are incapable of doing.'

'Nooooo!' says Phoebe.

'Dinah!' I say.

'No, I'm tired of it! We're clearly not capable. In fact, let's pack this whole thing in. That's it for me. We cannot even go on a simple bike ride. It's beyond us.'

'I'll change her gears,' I say. 'Just hold my bike.'

I try to dismount, but it's hard with Charlie behind me.

'It's easier if I do it,' says Dinah. 'Get off, Phoebe!'

'That's not very nice,' says Phoebe.

'Love, it's her first time with gears,' I say.

Dinah sits on Phoebe's bike. She tries to ride it to change the gear. 'My legs are too long. I can't do it.'

'Here, give it to me.' Dinah climbs off the bike and holds my bike upright as I put Phoebe's on its rear wheel. I turn the pedals with my hand and change it into first. 'There. Come on, let's go.'

The rain increases in strength so gradually that we're not aware of it until we're soaked. My linen trousers become see-through, Phoebe's bum's wet and Charlie's shivering. We shelter in the Napoleon museum on rue Napoléon. It was the emperor's home for three days in 1815, following his defeat at Waterloo. He came here to plot an audacious escape to America before surrendering to the British. To make a museum about one of the most enigmatic figures of the nineteenth century boring is hard, but they achieve it. The most interesting thing is the pub-style sign outside, showing Napoleon standing, bizarrely, beside a zebra, as if this were what he rode into battle on. The museum has statues and quasi-religious paintings of Napoleon, but they're primly covered with cloth, protecting them from the sunlight, which you have to lift up to view. Our guide points at objects and says things in French that Dinah, straining to hear, translates half-heartedly for Phoebe.

'Following the battle of something or another, Napoleon imposed terms on Prussia which continued until the death of . . . I missed the next word . . . which brought on the war of something or another.'

I break away, find a bench downstairs and call Buster.

'Alcohol fuelled?' he asks about the row.

'We'd had a few drinks, yes.'

I go through it – the canoeing, the restaurant, my storming off to the bar.

'The stupid thing is that I thought I was perfectly in the right at the time.'

'I do that,' says Buster. 'I'm always going to bed thinking I've won arguments. There should be an umpire. Someone to test both parties for alcohol consumption.'

'Ben subsequently tested positive for banned red wine,' I say.

'And the result of the argument has been declared null and void,' says Buster. Then, 'You know what to do.'

After hanging up, I write Dinah a letter of apology in the note app of my phone. In Napoleon's bedroom, there's a painting of him sat at a small table in battle dress in front of his wife, Josephine. He's clenching his fist with one hand, signing a surrender with the other. Appropriately, this is where I hand Dinah my phone. She reads, scrolling down with a finger. Five minutes later, she passes me her reply.

It says: 'I could not have had any idea you were going to ask that question in the restaurant. I wasn't planning to say that to you. But I won't say you couldn't be kinder or softer. You are an unusual person and I fell in love with that odd, funny, uncompromising man. When you are single-minded, it often works to my advantage, although sometimes, when it works against me, the result is that I feel railroaded. I have not said anything about what Henry said, to give you time to digest it, but I have been surprised you've hardly mentioned it, when it has such repercussions for our lives. Remember how you were going to earn the money so I could do the teacher-training? I love you, and our marriage is not shaky. But we must be allowed to examine it periodically and shout if we spot a gremlin creeping in. You are the chairman of Hatch Plc and I was only being the MD, pointing out something that needs board-level attention. I love you, D.'

We hug in the middle of the now empty room. Dinah puts her head on my shoulder and weeps. Her stomach quivers against mine.

'OK, let's get out of here. We've got a packed itinerary and we need to do every single thing on it,' I say, and she chuckles despairingly at my railroading joke. 'We alright?' I ask.

'Yes,' she says. 'Did you like the way I said you were the chairman?'

'That was the best bit.'

'I thought you'd like that,' she says.

'I'll try and be kinder,' I whisper. 'I'll try not to railroad you.'

'I'm sorry I upset you,' she says.

The next high tide isn't until 3.30, so after lunch we visit the African museum, further down the street. We see the camel, now stuffed, that Napoleon rode during his Egyptian campaign in 1798. Along with the zebra picture earlier, it confuses Charlie, who starts to see Napoleon as some sort of Bernie Clifton figure, riding a menagerie of different animals into battle. There are stuffed leopards, badgers, cheetahs and a crocodile.

'This one?' he asks of each in turn. 'Did he ride this one?'

That evening we're in a chalet on a campsite on the outskirts of Angoulême. The kids are in bed. 'Is this a good time to talk?' Dinah says.

'I'm in a bit of a mess, aren't I? I don't know what I'm going to do,' I say.

'I can't lie to you,' she says. 'You *are* in a mess.'

How did I get in this situation?

After Dinah left me, I quit my job on the paper and moved to London. I bought a flat in Ealing using the money my mum had left me for a deposit and I lived there, like a wild animal, for six months. I went to bed at irregular hours, got up at stranger ones. I forgot to eat, bathe, shave and clear up. I chained-smoked, drank, swore at the telly and watched chip remains harden on the floor. I left the flat so infrequently that just buying a packet of Wotsits from the Happy Shopper over the road became an adventure, and I became so ill-used to company that my social skills evaporated almost entirely. I forgot how to speak to people, left long, uncomfortable silences in conversations because I couldn't remember how to respond to the day-to-day news of others, or else I became so excitable that I couldn't stop talking, at breakneck speed, about the inconsequentialities of my day. 'Slow down, slow down, you're saying you bought a packet of crisps at the Happy Shopper.'

But I wrote a lot too. I wore out two keyboards and three mouse mats. I sent my manuscript off in ten manila envelopes to literary agents the day before I let the flat and left the country to go travelling. I went travelling because I didn't want to be around when the rejections came in.

Halfway round the world, in Thailand, I got the email from Henry saying that he wanted to sign me up. Three weeks later, on the fifth floor of a shiny chrome and black glass building near the Eros statue off Piccadilly Circus, he was telling me I'd be marketed as an exciting, young new writing talent, that there was interest about a TV adaptation. They had a reciprocal arrangement with an office in Hollywood. My novel would be sent to Miramax, although Henry saw it more as a three-act comedy-drama on BBC Two.

I left that building so high on pure joy, my body didn't seem big enough to contain it all. It fizzed around my head like a swarm of bees, almost blinding me, so I was nearly run over crossing the roundabout at Piccadilly Circus. I wanted to jump, run as fast as I could, shout, scream, get drunk and cry, all at the same time. 'I'm not a waster' I wanted to tell everyone I knew and had ever met in my life. I'm an exciting, young writing talent. I had incredible daydreams. I was meeting Baby Spice and telling her she was my favourite. I was on the *Chris Evans Breakfast Show*, making jokes with his posse. It felt like I'd taken this risky shortcut across inhospitable terrain that everybody thought I would flounder in, and yet somehow I'd burst through a hedge, like the Anthill Mob on the *Wacky Races*, and come out ahead.

Not long after this, Henry landed me a two-book deal. That summer, there were tube posters about my novel up at Victoria Station, a stack of 50 copies on the three-for-two tables of my local Waterstones and I was a guest on the Mel and Sue radio show. The first novel did OK; so did the second. But I decided not to submit a proposal for book three. Instead, I'd write it out of contract. That was the idea. But without a deadline, time ran away from me. Before I knew it, weeks became months, and months turned to years. The longer I took, the more perfect the book felt like it needed to be, to justify the time I'd spent writing it. And as my life circumstances changed, the novel trailed in my wake, constantly evolving and needing to be rewritten to reflect how differently I saw the world. The resulting hotchpotch is the book Henry's just rejected.

Now I look at Dinah. I've been telling this story for a while. Her head's down. 'I know, my love,' she says, 'I know, but it might be you have to take a few years out. Do something else. Come back to it when you've got your mojo back.'

'I've always wanted to be a carpenter.'

'A carpenter!' says Dinah.

'When I was a kid, I made the aircraft carrier HMS *Invincible* out of balsawood. It had guns, two decks, a turret. I put Airfix planes on it.'

'But what's the reality of that?' Dinah says.

'I know. I'm not going to be carefully planing some baby's manger I've been specially commissioned to make out of walnut. I'll be hanging 14 doors on a shop-fitting job in London Wall, or reattaching an old lady's skirting board with a tube of No More Nails. It's not an option, is it?'

'When we get to Zoe and Alex's – before the wedding and after it – we'll have some spare time. Take the laptop with you, go off somewhere and think of some ideas for Henry. That's all you can do.'

'I do have one idea.'

Dinah looks at me.

'You remember Nick Hornby's *Fever Pitch*?'

She nods.

'Trailblazing book about men, football and relationships. Redefined the genre of male fiction.'

'Go on.'

'How about in a similar vein I write the definitive novel about hypochondria. Everyone would be able to relate to that. Deep down we're all hypochondriacs.'

'You are, you mean.'

'Trust me, all blokes are.'

'My dad isn't.'

'Alright, apart from your perfect dad who suffered for six months with his goitre before it burst and splattered your mum with pus and he *had* to go to the doctor, every guy deep down is a hypochondriac.'

She laughs at this and, encouraged, I go through a possible first chapter about nits. As an 11-year-old boy, opening the batting for Kelvin House during an intramural Chesham High School cricket match against Wren House, I became so convinced that the thunder flies attracted to the brightness of my whites were nits, I deliberately got myself bowled out by Andy Garstang in case the close-in silly-point fielder noticed the black bugs and I ended up with the nickname 'Fleabag'.

'Is that true?' says Dinah.

'Yeah. Although it wasn't Andy Garstang. It was Peter Galsworthy, but he actually died soon after school so that might muddy the hypochondria theme a bit.'

Dinah makes a winding-up, get-to-the-point motion.

'OK, so basically it's a love story, a romance, but it's interlaced with the major public-health scares of the last 30 years, starting with nits. The next chapter could be about, I don't know, when I was 12 I thought I was growing a third testicle.'

'You thought you were growing an extra testicle?'

'It was my epididymis. It's a tube on top of your balls.'

'OK. So what's the romantic story you're attaching to this phantom testicle?'

'I haven't thought of that yet.'

Dinah bites her lip.

'But do you like the structure? Hornby did Arsenal's league season in 1989. That was his framework. Mine could be major hypochondria episodes. I could make something out of love being like a virus. How the character thinks he's in love when he's not. You know, make it a metaphor.'

'Hmmm,' she says.

'I've got a title too. Not, *Fever Pitch* but *Fever, Itch*. You know itch, because of the fleas . . . I could even call it Nit-lit. That could be its genre.'

Dinah pulls a face.

'That's a joke by the way. But seriously, there'd be a

CJD chapter. Avian flu. Then I had that rectal probe for prostate cancer. Remember that? Actually there were two rectal probes. Although I might have to condense them into the same chapter. Two anal inspections might be too many. What do you think?'

Dinah doesn't say anything so I remind her I write books in a different way to lots of other authors. While they think of the plot then research, I collect experiences then make a story from them afterwards. For this book the research is done. That's the beauty of it.

'It's like Ainsley Harriott in *Ready Steady Cook*,' I say, putting it another way. 'Someone brings in a few ingredients. A potato, a tin of tuna, noodles and a lettuce and then I have to make a meal out of it all against the clock. The only difference is I'm not competing against Antony Worrall Thompson. What do you think?'

But when I look up, Dinah has her head in her hands and she just repeats that I should have a proper think at Zoe and Alex's.

CHAPTER 10

*D*raft Copy for Guidebook:
The Dordogne, within the region of Aquitaine, was one of the last areas England held on to during the 100 Years War. It's now one of the most popular areas of France for Brits to buy second homes. Hotter than Atlantic-facing areas and with less rainfall, it's nickname is the fruit bowl of France. Home to the Agen prune, the enormous Marmande tomato, there are also huge orchards of plums, peaches and nectarines along with melon fields and asparagus beds. It is also renowned for foie gras. In recognition of this there's a museum in Frespech, Souleilles, dedicated to the 2,000-year-old delicacy that involves farmers force-feeding male mallards with maize through a funnel until their livers bloat to 8 to 10 times their normal size at which point they're slaughtered and their livers are served with small crustless slices of toast, making you wonder

what future delicacies the French are working on. Are they somewhere persuading sheep to drown themselves in Dr Pepper to see what the resulting cutlets taste like? Or maybe there are female goats being force-fed biscuits until they burst and shower their pastures with a tangy new type of intestine-veined cheese.

Regional highlights here include the highest sand dune in Europe, the 108-metre-high Dune du Pyla, Château de la Rochefoucauld, where we sipped Parisian tea with the chatelaine who showed off about her family's 28 relatives guillotined during the French revolution while our son did likewise about his ability to burp-talk. While in Bergerac you'll find Europe's sole museum dedicated to tobacco. Famous people who have no association with the town of Bergerac include Jim Bergerac the Jersey-based detective with a nose for major clues, and Cyrano de Bergerac, who just had a major nose.

'Good heavens, Alex wouldn't tolerate having a car this dirty.'

Dinah's cousin Zoe and her fiancé Alex used to live in Brighton but moved to Duras in the Lot-et-Garonne two years ago, and now have an old farmhouse, two gîtes and six acres of land. Zoe's wearing a Roman-style white tunic. Her straight blonde hair's in a hippy style, with a flower in it, and she's holding a half-empty baby's bottle while leaning into the car through Dinah's window. 'Some of the bigger Carrefours have a valet service, you know.' She sniffs tentatively. 'What is it?'

Dinah looks at me. 'Cheese,' I tell her.

'He keeps buying monks' cheese,' says Dinah, climbing out of the car, and hugging Zoe. 'I can't stop him.' Zoe laughs.

Alex appears, shirtless and in flip-flops, and shows me the plot in front of the house where I'm to pitch our tent. I'm in the middle of laying out the groundsheet when some of his nieces and nephews wander over in swimming costumes. One of them, a girl of about 14, says to me, almost accusingly, 'You're a writer.'

'I am.'

'What's yer name?' Her accent is broad Lancastrian.

'Nick Hornby,' I say.

'Nick Hornby. Really?' Her eyes light up.

'No.'

They dim. 'Oh.'

'I'm Ben Hatch, but you won't have heard of me. I'm a middle-ranking author. We're getting squeezed.'

'Do you write about elves?' she asks.

'No.'

'My uncle writes about elves. Goodbye,' she says, wandering back to the pool.

'You'll see him tomorrow,' says Alex.

'Has he got pointed ears and a resistance to the extremes of nature?'

'Yeah, he's from Burnley,' says Alex. 'And of course you know who else is coming . . .' Standing in profile to me, he bends his forearms towards his chest, while holding an imaginary pistol. He then swings round to shoot at my head, all the while humming the James Bond theme tune. One of Alex's cousins works for MI5.

'She's coming?'

'She might already be here, Ben.'

'Undercover?'

He narrows his eyes. 'Or maybe you've already met her . . . in disguise.'

'Your elf-obsessed niece?'

Now we both hum the James Bond theme tune.

We eat at a long wooden table and benches that Alex has made himself from old beams which overlook a field owned by the French farmer next door, Marc.

'So delicious. I forgot that milky smell,' says Dinah, with their baby Harry on her lap. 'And look at those springy cheeks!'

The prawns are fresh. There are homemade sausages and terrines of vegetables Alex has grown himself. They have anchovies, olives, three local cheeses and a pork dish with a delicious olive tapenade. Charlie and Phoebe have folded smoothly into the gang of Alex's older nephews and nieces.

'This is lovely,' says Dinah.

'The good life,' says Alex, topping up our glasses.

'And is it?' I ask.

'It is,' he says.

'Really?'

'It takes two days a week to maintain this place.'

'The outside?'

'Cutting the grass mainly.'

'And the rest of the time?'

He reaches for a leg of pork. 'We eat and drink mostly. Nothing much else to do, Ben.' Alex is a former photographer and used to do shoots for *Wallpaper* magazine. One day he and Zoe just decided they needed a challenge.

'Amazing that you actually did it.'

'It was hard. In the winter, when it was freezing; when I had the builder coming at eight. But I've learnt so much. And it's great for Freddy and Harry.' Freddy's their two-year-old. 'They have all this.' Alex spreads his arms. 'Freddy steals pudding from the guests. We don't know where he is half the time. In fact . . . where is he, Zoe?'

We hear a tractor starting up. 'I think he's about to plough that turnip field for Marc,' I say.

Alex laughs. 'Peas actually. The year before, maize. Next year, turnips.'

And, as he talks, I imagine Dinah and I doing something similar, jacking in our English lives, buying a big, rundown French property with land. Dinah could freelance for travel mags and I'd look after the kids. We could have as many as we wanted then. A whole litter of kids. I picture them all crawling over me like kittens in a basket on a Saturday morning in bed.

Dinah asks how well they've integrated.

'We know Marc,' says Alex. 'Them across the road. We were at a party the other day. But it's hard when you don't speak the language.'

'And it's so expensive,' says Dinah.

There are bits of red flower in the salad. I pierce some with my fork. 'You can eat that,' says Alex.

'Really? And you grew them yourself? You planted them?'

'It was all here,' says Alex. 'Just unloved, like this whole place. It is expensive though,' he adds.

'Are French wages higher?' asks Dinah.

'They're lower,' says Alex. 'But they lead a simple life. They spend half their money on food and drink. They have two weeks off, stay in France and never go out. They're conservative.'

'That's it?' says Dinah.

'They're not interested in money,' says Alex. 'We have three bread shops. Not one of them opens on Monday. You'd think one of them would think, "Aye aye, I could make some money here."'

'But no . . .'

'No. It doesn't interest them. They buy local food, which is better quality. They buy French cars. And that's how they survive. I wanted to buy that field,' he says, nodding towards the one sloping away from us. 'The maize grows two metres high. We couldn't see anything and felt hemmed in. But I was at a local do and this farmer said that was a British attitude. Forget feeding people, I wanted to clear a field of food for my view. He had a point.'

Zoe lights a citronella candle. 'You get mossies here?' I ask.

'When it's really hot.'

'Show them,' says Dinah.

'I saw,' says Alex. 'You should be in a colony, Ben.'

Freddy comes up, dressed as Buzz Lightyear. He throws an arm out to one side and runs after it. 'I Buzz,' he shouts.

'You're not,' says Alex.

'I Buzz.'

'You're Freddy, my son.'

'I Buzz.'

'You're not Buzz.'

'You're in tuddle,' he says.

'I'm in trouble, am I?' says Alex.

'Big tuddle. Biscuits?' demands Freddy, holding out his hand.

'Biscuits later,' says Alex.

Freddy nods and walks off. 'Biscuits later,' he repeats.

Later, the kids are in their sleeping bags in the tent and we're outside on the decking beside their pool, on sun-loungers cranked back to horizontal. Earlier we'd played a few games of fancy-dress table tennis in the games room in pairs. Zoe and I against Alex and Dinah. Every time a player lost a point, they put on an item from Zoe's dressing-up rail. By the end, I was in a Saxon jerkin and Lincoln green trousers held up with a cowboy gun-belt, with a feather boa and papal cross round my neck. Now, under the cloudless sky, we're spotting shooting stars. The meteor shower happens annually. Small, icy rocks a few millimetres across are released from the comet Swift-Tuttle by the sun's heat. They travel at 7,000mph and burn up at an altitude of 30 miles. Alex's read up on them in the Duras ex-pat newsletter, which is full of the major concerns here – the best way to make nutty Camembert pâté, an animal husbandry page about alpacas and advice on the best time to dig up potatoes.

'Wow!' says Zoe. 'Did you see it, Dinah?'

'Where?' she says. Zoe points.

'That was amazing!' I say.

'Missed another one?' says Alex, laughing at Dinah. For some reason, she's always looking the wrong way.

'I was tracking the satellite,' says Dinah.

'You have to look generally upwards. Don't focus on one area. Shall I check the kids?' I ask.

'I'll go,' says Dinah.

And as she gets up I say, 'Wooooow!' Alex and Zoe say it too.

'I know you're joking,' says Dinah. I laugh. She walks behind the pool.

'How many millions of years have those rocks been circulating the earth?' I say. 'And we witness them burn up in our atmosphere lying here.'

'The greatest show on Earth,' says Alex.

I imagine I'm a Roman or a caveman or a medieval knight, who'd have seen exactly the same spectacle I'm looking at now.

'Will you ever come back to the UK?' I ask Alex.

'When the kids are older.'

'Why?'

'There're no jobs unless you want to be a farmer. The secondary school is miles away. The kids that go stay with other families during the week because it takes so long on the bus. I wouldn't want that,' says Alex.

'There!' I shout, as a white light tears a small diagonal rip in the firmament, disappearing almost instantly.

'And another one,' says Zoe, pointing. 'There!'

'Wow!' I say again.

Dinah returns from checking on the kids. 'I told them that if they didn't go to sleep, Alex would come over.'

'You used me?' says Alex.

'I see that becoming a theme,' says Zoe. 'Wherever you go, picking on some random bogeyman to shut them up.'

'No, it's always Alex,' I say.

'Even in England,' says Dinah.

I pretend to be quietening the kids. 'Listen, guys, if you're not quiet, Alex will catch the ferry from St Malo as a foot passenger, be picked up by his friend in Portsmouth at the other end, and he'll be furious when he gets here because it's a six-hour crossing, a three-hour drive and it costs £150, and Zoe probably won't remember to vacuum the pool when he's away. Now GO TO SLEEP!'

Zoe and Alex laugh.

'So what did I miss?' Dinah sits back down.

'Three meteors and some aliens in a UFO showed up,' I say.

'Ben beat them at table tennis,' says Alex.

'No backhands,' says Zoe.

'No hands at all,' I say. 'Just tentacles.'

'Zoe made them wear fancy dress,' says Alex.

'Come back with my feather boa,' Zoe shouts at the sky.

There's the whoosh of a car on the road behind us.

'The first car for an hour,' I say. 'Cars passing your house are rarer than shooting stars.'

'Put that on TripAdvisor,' says Alex, and he and Zoe get up and say goodnight, leaving Dinah and I alone.

'I think I've fallen in love with France,' I tell her.

'It is lovely here,' she says.

'It's like the whole country has been arranged for the benefit of the people who live here. Do you know what I mean? Not for big companies.'

'It's heartwarming.'

'It's annoying to start with, but not being able to buy bread between 12.30 and 2 is the equivalent of us getting put on hold by EDF or TalkTalk for an hour.'

'And there's no road congestion,' says Dinah.

'The food's better. You don't feel you're going to read about contaminated beef or how eating apples will give you cancer because of some shit they've sprayed on them.'

'They are cute, the French,' says Dinah.

'But what would it be like living here?' I ask.

'I'd miss our culture,' says Dinah.

'Would you?'

'You would too.'

'What is that though?'

'I don't know. Radio 4, the TV, our shared sense of humour,' she says.

'What else?'

'Stephen Fry. Yorkshire tea.'

'Is that it? *QI* and a brew?'

'What about family?' she says. 'My mum and dad. Buster, your sister and Mary. It's never going to happen.'

'I know.'

We stare at the sky.

'Wasn't Harry cute?' she says.

'He was gorgeous.'

'And Freddy's hilarious. What was it?'

'Biscuits later,' I say.

'Biscuits later,' she says, nodding like Freddy.

'How old's Zoe?' I ask.

'A year younger than me.' We watch the sky. Dinah misses another shooting star. 'I think that argument helped,' she says, still staring up.

'I was going to say that.' She looks at me.

'It cleared the air. You've been kinder since. I've noticed that,' she says.

We change for bed a little while later, and I'm fast asleep when I wake to find Dinah standing over me, shining a light in my face.

'I want us to have sex,' she whispers. She crouches down. 'But we've got to do it right now.'

'Now?'

She bends right down over the airbed and whispers in my ear, 'White stuff came out. In the bathroom just then. Some albumen. It means—'

'Some albumen?!'

'That means I'm ovulating. I know the signs.'

I sit up. 'But I thought . . . the implant . . .'

'They stop working after a few years.'

'How many years?'

'I don't know.'

'How long's it been in?'

'Since Charlie was born.' I try and do the maths, but I'm still half asleep.

'Come on,' she says and pulls me up.

'We're going for it then, just like that?'

'That's what you want, isn't it?'

I start taking my pyjama bottoms off, but she wants me to follow her.

'What?' I pull them back up. 'Where are we going?'

She leads me up the path. The front of the house is open. Inside, she directs me towards the downstairs bathroom. Inside it, the sink's full of soapy water. A sponge is floating in there. Dinah laughs nervously.

'Just come in here,' she says.

When she sees me take in the sink, she says, 'Your groin smelt a bit earlier. It's not your fault. It was quite a long drive.'

'You're rinsing me down like a dog?'

A few minutes later, back on the airbed, I'm struggling. For one thing, it's like trying to have sex on a bouncy castle. But also, just when I'm getting somewhere, my mind seems to mentally look around inside my skull and say things like this: 'Hang on, in a month's time neither of us will have a job!'

'It's not happening,' whispers Dinah.

I also find I'm getting slightly irritated with Dinah's insistence. I get a torch shone in my face, hear about some albumen and I'm supposed to leap into action after being hosed down.

Afterwards, we whisper in ever-decreasing circles of misunderstanding.

'I know you get a certain number of days a month. I know I said I wanted another one – I do want another one – but we haven't discussed the new information, the lack of a book deal. If you weren't retraining as a teacher . . .'

'I know it doesn't make sense,' she says. 'It didn't make sense when we had Phoebe or Charlie. You make sense of it afterwards.'

'But love, with everything else going on.'

'No, it's stupid. You're right,' she says.

'It might not be.'

'I'm agreeing with you,' she says. 'It's stupid.'

'But now you've almost persuaded me.'

There's a pause.

'You'd have done it if it'd been in the Master Document,' she says. She laughs and I laugh, but it's a mad laugh.

'Bloody hell,' she says. 'What's happening to us?'

'I don't know.'

'That was crazy.'

'You didn't wake up with a light shining in your face and a voice demanding sex after a basin wash.'

'Maybe I imagined the albumen.'

'There's that sexy word again.'

'Daddy!' says Phoebe. She's in a separate pod with Charlie, on the other side of the tent.

I look at Dinah. 'Phoebe, it's the middle of the night.'

'I don't like this sleeping bag.'

'What's wrong with it?'

'It's all slippy.'

'That's how sleeping bags are.'

'I'm cold.'

'Well, put a jumper on.'

Dinah says, in a flat voice, 'Your bag's outside the pod, Phoebe. DO NOT knock over the wee bucket.'

We hear Phoebe's zip then a telltale clatter.

'Mummy?'

'What?'

'I knocked over the wee bucket.'

CHAPTER 11

It's like *My Big Fat Gypsy Wedding* meets the car-cleaning scene from *Pulp Fiction* the next afternoon. I've spent the morning thinking of book proposals for Henry in Zoe and Alex's study and return to the tent to find Dinah in a frenzy. She's wearing a dust mask and an apron of Zoe's. The car stereo's on full blast. All the car doors are open, so's the roof-box and boot, while all the clothes Dinah's washed are hanging off it, drying. Boxer shorts dangle from the wing mirrors, my Lacoste shirt's hooked over the aerial. Kids' tops are spread over the bonnet. The groundsheet's flapping in a tree. The deflated airbeds are doing the same. And Dinah's scrubbing the car seats, on her hands and knees.

'I like what you've done to the place.'

She pulls back the mask. 'Do you know how many toenails I found under your seat?'

'Tell me.'

'Twenty-four!'

'That's more than I have toes.'

'I know, you freak. Right, you need to dress the kids and get ready yourself. All the clothes are in that bag. Had any ideas?'

'Yeah.'

'Good. Tell me them on the way to the church.'

Twenty minutes later, we're standing in Zoe's room.

'Charlie's pants?' I ask.

'In the bag,' she says.

'Looked. All I've found is this one wet pair drying on the bonnet.'

'Charlie!' shouts Dinah.

'What?' he says, appearing in the doorway.

'You'll have to wear your swimming trunks as pants.'

I've already had trouble convincing Charlie to wear a waistcoat and bow tie. He shakes his head at this latest indignity.

'What would happen if I microwaved them?' I ask Dinah.

'What?'

'Charlie's wet pants. It's metal that catches fire, isn't it? Can you microwave pants?'

'It doesn't sound a very good idea,' she says.

'Come with me, Charlie.'

We walk to the house.

'I don't know,' Dinah shouts after me, looking concerned. 'His little bum.'

I look back at her. 'His little bum?!'

'We're dabbling in things.' She frowns. 'I mean, what happens if there's, I don't know, some radiation lurking in them.'

I stare at my wife.

'It might affect his, I don't know . . . his, you know,' she lowers her voice, 'fertility.'

'Do you think there was radiation lurking in your baked potato last night?'

She thinks for a moment. 'OK, but do them on a low setting.'

'Do you want me to prick them with a fork as well?'

I microwave Charlie's pants for ten seconds at 350w and when I pull them out, they're dry. 'Charlie, your father's a genius. Go and show Mummy your microwaved pants.'

'Now, bear in mind this is rough, OK?'

I'm telling Dinah my book ideas on the way to the church, as she puts her make-up on in the vanity mirror. Basically my plan is to write a book about the meaning of life. But rather than being a worthy philosophical look at the subject, it'll be one of those male quest books – *Playing the Moldovans at Tennis*, meeting everyone else in the world with the same name as me, etc. Only instead of the joke being that I'm treating something trivial incredibly seriously, I'll write trivially about a serious subject. And what more serious a subject is there than the meaning of life?

'The meaning of life?' says Dinah. 'You think you can write a book solving the puzzle of the meaning of life?'

'I'm not going to solve it, obviously.'

'OK, shed some light on the meaning of life. A subject that's evaded philosophers, scientists and the greatest minds for more than 5,000 years.'

'Why not?'

She looks at me. 'You just microwaved pants.'

'The pants worked. How are the pants, Charlie?'

'Good,' he says.

'OK, so how are you going to tackle it?'

'I thought I might write it with someone else.'

'Love, I'll be teaching, bringing home marking . . .'

'I was thinking of Buster actually. I could co-write it with him.'

'With Buster?'

'Yeah.'

'A book about the meaning of life. With Buster! He's never written a book in his life. He doesn't even read books.'

Dinah's phone rings. It's her dad. Bert and Marian have landed at Bordeaux Airport, but are having problems finding the venue. Dinah directs them and although I wasn't going to say it, promised myself I wouldn't say it, I can't stop myself.

'And I had one other idea,' I say, after she hangs up. 'This isn't about writing. It's quite radical.'

'Go on.'

I look across at her. 'OK, we know letting the house works, right?'

'Yes.'

'So we extend the principle.'

'And?' she says.

'And we let the house out for a year.'

She looks at me, her mascara wand poised. 'A year?'

'And we take the kids out of school.'

'Sorry, is this the school we've just got them into?'

'Yes, but only for a year . . . and . . . we travel round the world. We use the income from the house to finance it.'

She looks at me, waiting for more.

'You can write articles on the places we visit. You're always saying you're a travel journalist that doesn't travel much. We tent it, which will be cheaper. Hot countries in the winter.'

'We tent it for a year?!' She screws her mascara lid shut. 'Have you completely forgotten last night?'

'Obviously we'd have a better tent, one with loads of compartments. And the other advantage is, it would give me something to write about. Graham Greene moved around as a diplomat. His novels are all based on his travels. It would give me material. Plus it gets us both out of the study. And the kids would learn more than they ever would in school.'

Dinah blinks slowly.

'We could camper-van around America, for instance. Imagine listening to Joan Armatrading in the Nevada desert. The Grand Canyon. Wyoming, Colorado. We'd home-school the kids. Get some Jolly Phonics-type workbooks. You could even be in charge of the Master Document this time.'

'Do you mean that?' she asks.

'Yeah, I actually don't like organising it. I'd love you to plan it. I was thinking about it last night – travel, it's in our genes. It's part of being human. I think it's why I like it so much. It's only in the last 3,000 years that humans have farmed. Did you know that? Before that, for thousands of years, we followed herds. We were nomads. What we're doing now, it's in our genes. We just happen to be in a Passat.'

And just as I start to think we're on the verge of something marvellous, Dinah turns to me. 'So, me retraining as a teacher means nothing to you then?'

'Er . . . no. I didn't say that. It's just . . .'

'Never mind that it's what I've been working towards for over a year.'

'Of course, it's important. It's massively important. It's just . . .'

'It doesn't mean a thing to you, does it?'

'Of course it does. Our lives are interconnected. Everything we do matters to the other person, but . . .'

'But what?'

'I don't know, you could delay it for a year. Or we could go to Quebec.'

'Quebec?!'

'They speak French in Quebec. Or Tunisia. That's French-speaking, I think. Or is that Morocco? One of them is. You could teach there. Google French-speaking nations – I bet there are dozens. You'd learn French quicker speaking it every day.'

Dinah turns away.

'I said it was radical. I'm just throwing things out. You wanted to go for another baby last night. This is no more radical. OK, maybe we could delay my plan for a year, or two years, or until you finish the teacher-training. I'm thinking aloud . . .'

CHAPTER 12

Zoe was given away by her father. Dinah cried during the vows, and now we're at the *vin d'honneur* (the reception), in a nearby country hotel, a few miles outside Duras. It's a former château, with creaky wooden floorboards, and Charlie and Phoebe have disappeared with their cousins, leaving Dinah and I dangerously unencumbered. Daiquiris in hand, we've just filed past Zoe and Alex into the dining room, where three large tables each have numbers on them. These numbers make up the date Zoe and Alex met – 10/12/2004. On one side of me, I have Dinah, who's next to Bert and Marian, and on the other side, it's Gus, the elf writer, who's in full tuxedo and is telling me about how putting an elf on the cover of his last book quadrupled sales. It's the same with an orc. But it's always a mistake to emboss a hobbit. I ask him why.

'They don't like hobbits in Germany.'

'Is that where you sell your books?'

'They sell millions in Germany. And they love elves.'

'I'd never have guessed it.'

'They're not gay elves,' he says.

'OK.'

'No. In the past, elves were sort of gay. In *Lord of the Rings*, they're effeminate.'

'Were they? I can't remember.'

'They minced.'

'Did they?'

'They were homosexual constructs. My elves are aggressive. They're like the SAS of the underworld.'

'Wow, I'm going to put an elf on my next book cover. And an orc.'

'You should do that.'

The first course is pigeon. It's served on a bed of . . . 'Glazed oats,' says Gus, leaning over. 'That's what they are.'

'I thought they were seeds. Stuff from a pigeon coop. Pigeon feed. I'm rambling. Listen to me. Wow! The daiquiris are strong! How do you feel?'

'No, they're glazed oats. I had a bramble.' Gus vibrates his head as if clearing it. 'So what do you write?' he asks.

'Comedy fiction, but also guidebooks.'

'I wrote a 20,000 word novella. That was comedy.'

'Was it funny?'

'No.'

'No?'

'No.'

I look at his wife, on the other side of him. She shakes her head and laughs.

'I did it for fun.'

'And was it fun?'

'Not really. But there's always comedy in the underworld. In the stories I write. I like to lighten it up.'

'How?'

'Situations.'

'That elves get into?'

'No, not elves. It's always serious with elves. Other creatures.'

'Do you have a set number of mythical creatures or can you invent them?'

He leans back in his chair and stares at me. He has grey edges to his hair and a dickie bow he's tied himself ('Because you must, post-40').

'You can never invent them. They're timeless physical constructs. Although you can play around with their characters.'

His wife says something to him, and Dinah's dad, Bert, now leans across to ask how the trip's going. Then immediately, once he has my attention, he starts telling me about Widnes rugby league. Bert, a former electrical engineer, has three main interests now he's retired: collecting small change in a pewter jug, telling stories about electrocutions and power surges in the workplace and Widnes rugby league. He was reading a book about the Super League on the plane. It was about the injustice done to his home-town team of Widnes.

'Widnes finished third from bottom of the Premier League,' he's saying, 'but they were still relegated because they had it in for the town. The two teams below them stayed up, but Widnes were kicked out because Murdoch wanted to open the game up to other areas. Teams from London, Gateshead and Paris were expected to join and it was hoped they'd create more national interest in the game . . .'

'BERT!' barks Marian. He looks round. 'Stop *boring* Ben!'

After the first course, according to the instructions on our name plates, a certain number of us switch tables. Dinah and I stay put, but where Gus was, it's now Anna from MI5. Anna's pretty, mid-20s, with long, dark hair, and says, as she sits down, 'I've just learnt a lot about birds of prey.'

'Was that the highlight of your table?'

'Yes,' she says.

'Here, we talked about elves,' I say. 'Who were the people into birds of prey? No, let me guess. Are they on this table now?'

She nods. I stare at someone. She shakes her head.

'You talked about elves?' she asks.

'And orcs.'

Anna nods as I look at someone else. 'And?' I look around at another new arrival with a beard. She nods. Within minutes, this man's telling the whole table how to attach a falcon to a handling glove.

'Told you,' says Anna, leaning over. 'Very weird.'

I've drunk quite a lot by now and I say across the table to this guy, 'What's your favourite bird of prey?'

'Falcon,' he says, immediately.

I nod and look at Anna. 'I didn't think he'd have a favourite,' I say to her.

'What's yours?' the guy shouts over to Anna.

'Kestrel,' she says.

'Quick on your feet,' I say. 'Owl,' I say in response to the inquiring expression of the guy across the table. 'Do you think he does this everywhere he goes?' I ask Anna.

'Straw polls of favourite birds of prey?' she says.

'They're taking the piss out of you,' the guy's wife says to him.

'I don't mind,' he says. Then to me, 'Owls are very stupid, you know. They're the stupidest bird of prey. Their eyes are so big, there's not enough room for a brain.'

'Sparrows have tiny eyes,' I say to no one in particular. Then to Anna, 'I'm not really sure what I'm saying. I've had two daiquiris and some wine. I thought daiquiris were red. Mine was brown.'

'You get different sorts. Strawberry daiquiris . . .'

'And sludgy daiquiris.'

'Yes,' she says.

'I had a sludgy daiquiri.'

'You're making me laugh!' she says.

'So what do you do?' I ask.

'I'm a civil servant,' she says.

'That sounds dull.' She smiles. 'I'm baiting you into revealing what you *really* do.'

'I know,' she says. She sweeps hair away from her face and I think she's about to turn away and talk to the person on her other side when she says to me, 'OK, there's M15 and M16, which is international, and then there's MOD Intelligence.'

'And you're MOD Intelligence?'

'Yes.'

'And can you say what it is you do there?'

'This and that.'

'No, in other words.' She dips her head slightly, to let me know I've cottoned on. 'You have the most interesting job here and you can't talk about it.'

'It's not that interesting,' she says.

'Can I ask closed questions and you say yes or no?'

'Yes.'

'Does it give you an insight into how the country is run that is shocking?'

'No.'

'It is how you expect?'

'Yes.'

'UFOs that abduct people from market towns in the dead of night?'

'No.'

'Secret societies of benevolent lizard-based life forms secretly ruling the world?'

'No.'

'So David Kelly and—'

'If you saw the red tape involved in doing just very minor things . . .'

'So do you tell anyone anything?'

'My mum.'

'Boyfriend?'

'Single.'

'And friends are vetted?'

'Every two years.'

'In case you're friends with a Russian oligarch or are in debt and bribable?'

'Yes.'

'And what does that involve? Waterboarding?'

'No.'

'Truth serums, beatings, sensory deprivation, Marillion at an ear-piercing volume?'

'I wish it was *Spooks*. Six people saving a city each week from a small office, but no.'

'The office is bigger?'

'Much.'

'And you have more colleagues?'

'Lots of colleagues.'

She asks what I do and I tell her I'm a writer. She tells me about the first book she read. It was *The Silver Arrow* by a Polish writer.

'From then on . . .' she says.

'You loved books?'

'Yes.'

'Do you read much now?'

'No.'

'Do you always answer just yes and no?'

'Yes.'

Dinah, who's been hovering, jumps in. 'I'm sorry, Anna, isn't it? Can I ask you a really boring question?' Anna looks up. 'Where are the coats?'

I look at Dinah.

'I can't find Charlie's waistcoat. There's a toy in the pocket he wants.'

'I'll show you,' says Anna. They disappear.

'I do one spy-ish thing,' I tell Anna, when she's back. She tilts her head questioningly. 'Rather than walk past a parked van – especially a Transit van – I always cross the road beforehand, to walk on the other side of the pavement. In case I get bundled into the back of it by kidnappers.'

'I see.'

'Actually, two things. I do two spy-ish things. Sometimes, when I unexpectedly have to tie my shoelaces in the street, I like to imagine that by bending down at that very second, I have unwittingly thwarted a rooftop sniper's perfect headshot. And now you're going because I'm boring you.'

'You're not, but I am going,' she says.

'Another daring mission to thwart a terrorist strike at the heart of our democracy?'

'No. The tables are swapping again.'

Marian sits beside me this time. 'Dinah told me the bad news,' she says. 'I am sorry about your book.' She rests her hand on my forearm. 'Can I say this without sounding like an interfering mother-in-law? Now, this is just an idea.' She laughs. 'Have you thought,' and she taps my arm five times, once for each of the following words, 'about retraining as a plumber?' She leans back, as if to better take in my reaction. 'Or an electrician? Only,' she leans forward again, and hands me an article from the *Mail* about the shortage of plumbers and electricians, 'they're crying out for them.'

After the speeches, Alex and Zoe cut the *pièce montée*, the French wedding confection, a sort of pyramid of profiteroles, and we go outside to release the sky lanterns. They look too heavy for flight, but once the flames are strong enough, they take off, narrowly clearing a bank of trees.

'It's like a Chinese V2 raid,' I say, sidling up to Anna.

'To burn down thatched cottages in the Lot-et-Garonne. Found out any more about elves?' she asks.

'No, but I've learnt a lot about plumbing,' I tell her.

Gus approaches. He shows me a reefer cupped inside his palm. 'Of course, if you want to write about elves and orcs, this stuff also helps enormously,' he says. 'Come with me.'

'And we come at it from two angles. You try to discover the meaning of life through religion. I try science. The book's about our different approaches. What do you think? We write alternate chapters.'

I have no idea what time it is when Buster calls.

'And that's it?' he says. 'I broke off my spotted dick in the cookhouse for this?'

'Listen, what we do is, we go back to Chesham High and I interview Mr Welch. That's how we start it. It's a bet in a pub. You bet me I can't get closer to solving the meaning of life through physics than you can through religion.'

'And why are you interviewing Mr Welch from physics?'

'Because that's where it starts. I interview Mr Welch from physics and you interview Miss Place from RE. Then we get a recommendation from each of them and speak to whoever they suggest next. It's a chain, you see. The aim is to get all the way to, say, the Pope. And for science, I don't know, Stephen Hawking. They're top of the chains.'

'So why don't we go to them first then?'

There's a pause. 'Er . . . I don't know. After each interview, we write it up. We take the piss out of each other. Buster's getting on my nerves talking about Miss Place. I might get on your nerves talking about Mr Welch.'

'You already fucking are,' he says. 'I've got a show in an hour. Have you taken something? You sound weird.'

'A story would evolve. The story about you and I. Being brothers. That's the problem with the last book; it was too contrived.'

'But *this* is contrived, and what if Miss Place recommends Mr Earnshaw from technical drawing?' says Buster.

'That's unlikely. But it would be funny.'

'And Mr Welch recommends Mr Windle from chemistry.'

'Funny again. But we'd have to be pure at heart. We'd have to be serious, believe we were really searching, otherwise they wouldn't take us seriously. Imagine it.

What are you doing this weekend, Ben? Er, Buster and I are off to the Vatican to see the Pope.'

'And then the Pope recommends Miss Place from RE,' says Buster.

'And Stephen Hawking recommends Mr Welch,' I say, and then it hits me. 'Fuck, it's a shit idea, isn't it?'

Buster laughs good-naturedly. 'It's not shit.'

'It is, it's fucking shit.'

'Actually, you're right. It is shit,' he says.

'Christ, look how desperate I am. What am I talking about? Miss Place from RE!' I start to laugh wildly, but then my stomach cramps up. I double up in agony and a great searing pain shoots through my abdomen like a sword.

'You alright?'

'No, I've got to go.'

It's later, and I'm sat outside our tent on Dinah's foldaway chair, with a towel wrapped around me, a washing bowl at my feet. 'I just don't think you love me enough,' Dinah's saying. Ugly scenes had ensued when we'd left the venue at the same time as Anna. On the steps outside the hotel, I'd made some sort of a joke about doing up my shoelaces to evade a marksman's bullet. I'd somehow lost my balance bending over and had fallen down some steps and skittled over both Anna and an aunt of Alex's. In the end, Bert had had to drive us home in our car.

Dinah's grimacing and holding her head up and baring her teeth with despair. Her face is red from crying. Her make-up's run and has blackened her eyes. 'Tonight's made me realise it. You don't love me like you should, Ben.'

'Why are you saying this? Of course I love you.'

'No, you don't,' says Dinah.

We go over some specifics. Knocking her into the Atlantic with the paddle. My behaviour in front of her mum and dad. The thoughtless idea about travelling round the world.

'Do you know how hard it was getting on that GTP course, how many interviews I had to have, how many conversations I had with other teachers? Then you come out with an idea like that. And do you know how else I can tell? You're so loving to the kids. That's how you'd be with a wife you loved.'

'It's not true,' I keep saying.

'I want someone who's devoted to me,' she says. 'You're not devoted to me. That's because you don't love me.'

'I *am* devoted to you,' I say. 'And we've been together 20 years. Of course I love you.'

But she carries on in the same vein, going through everything I've ever done wrong and even bringing up my reluctance to get married, before she adds, 'My mum and dad felt sorry for me tonight, Ben. I could see it in my dad's eyes. And you smoked dope in front of them. In front of my dad, who's 75 years old! Someone who's devoted would not do that.'

'I didn't do it in front of him. He didn't see me. It was one joint, and it's a reaction. Can't you see?'

I remind her I had some bad news. It's a reaction. I needed to let off some steam. Of course I love her. I *am* devoted to her. But then a sudden thought crosses my mind. 'Are you leaving me?'

'No,' she says, contemptuously, 'but I am hardening to you. When I first met you, you were very selfish, Ben. Then when your mum died, it changed you. Since then, you've improved, but I've still had to deal with all your selfishness. Poor old drudgy Dinah has had to deal with it.'

'Drudgy?'

'I'm 40,' she says. 'And I'm drudgy. I know I'm drudgy.'

'You're not drudgy.'

'Yes, I am. I'm the one who does the unexciting jobs. I'm the drudge. I earn the day-to-day money. I tell the kids off. I make the dinner. I support us. Do you even still fancy me? Be honest.'

'If you're talking about last night, you were shining a torch in my face, talking about albumen.'

'I'm overweight, my boobs sag and I never lost my baby fat, but I can't be bothered to exercise and I'm not going to.'

'Has this got something to do with tonight? With Anna?' She looks at me, then turns away. 'I was chatting to her. She was sat next to me. What was I supposed to do? And she's a spy.'

'Who happens to be very pretty. Anyway, it's not about her. Although you were a bit obvious, Ben.'

'What?'

'Lunging at her on the steps.'

'I didn't lunge, I told you what happened there.'

'Oh yes, that's right, you were pretending to do your shoelaces up to avoid a marksman's bullet!'

'It was a joke from earlier. If you'd heard what we talked about . . .'

'Sorry, private joke, was it?'

'Stop it.'

She looks up at the sky.

'I had a moment at the wedding.' Dinah says. 'I was talking to Zoe. She was telling me about her first marriage.

How awful it was when she split up with Dan. Some of the things he used to do to her. Bullying, intimidation. It took her ten years to recover her self-esteem. She only realised how awful her first husband was when she met Alex.'

'Jesus! I'm not that bad, am I?'

'No, but you're hard to live with, Ben.'

She talks about the builders – how I should've taken some responsibility off her shoulders and got a job to bring some money in.

'But no, you went straight back to your book. Straight back into the study to work on the book that you'd already wasted seven years on.'

'It's not seven years. And I thought that was our best chance of getting money in.'

'Really? Honestly?'

'Yes. And it hasn't been a solid seven years. After Phoebe was born, you went back to work. I was the main child-carer. I couldn't write then. And I'm not saying that wasn't the best thing that ever happened. It was. I know it's taken a long time and I'm sorry . . .'

'Ben, I *had* to go back to work because you weren't earning any money.'

'I made money writing the guidebooks. I switched to guidebooks. I have an idea about that actually. I was reading about the Bradt guides. You know the ones I mean?' She nods. 'It was started by a husband and wife team. They wrote their first one about a barge holiday down the Amazon River. Now they cover 120 countries. We could do something like that.'

'The Hatch guides?' says Dinah.

'The brat guides. You know, because we write about kids' stuff.'

She stands up. 'I'm going to bed,' she says. She walks into the tent. A few seconds later she comes out and throws my sleeping bag and pillow at me. 'And the reason I'm too old for another child, by the way – a third child I'd really love as well – is because you were so bloody thick you didn't know kids were what you wanted. I am so tired of leading you, Ben.'

CHAPTER 13

For a moment I can't work out where I am. The sun's cooking me through the windscreen and I have a blinding headache. I kick off my sleeping bag. Through the passenger window, I can see the remnants of devastation – the foldaway chair, the bowl I was sick into. Then I realise my phone is ringing in my pocket. It's Jake, my guidebook editor.

'Wotcha,' he says. Jake's one of the few people in the world who still use the word 'wotcha'.

'Wotcha,' I say.

Jake asks about the trip. Ignoring the fact that I've got sick down my top, recently upended a spy, smoked dope in front of my father-in-law and slept in the car, I tell him it's going really well and talk up some of the highlights.

'Any news on your novel?' he asks.

'Random House are taking a close look,' I lie. 'It's with the marketing people. Sales need to have their say, but fingers crossed. It's taking a while though.'

'Same with travel,' bemoans Jake. 'It's the way it's going. It's getting harder and harder to get stuff commissioned.'

I detect a change in his voice. 'Mate, that's why I'm ringing actually,' he says. There's a small pause. 'You know I really like what you do. I've enjoyed the entries you've sent me. I never knew that about Camembert. And we've always worked well and we get on. But unfortunately that doesn't matter with the bean counters upstairs.'

I laugh. Jake doesn't.

'I'm under pressure. It's hard because everyone liked your book in-house. The copyeditors, Hannah and Steph, were coming up and saying, "I like this." They almost never do that.'

There's a pause.

'We've had the sales figures through for *Britain With Your Family*. I can't lie. They're not great. It's kind of what I've been waiting for. It's left a big hole in my figures. And on this basis, it's hard to get positive feedback on the France book. It makes it difficult to go in there and pitch for you. They just look at the numbers. I don't know, travel's getting more event-based. More niche. Maybe we got behind that curve. But it's a good book and it went down well on Amazon Vine.'

Jake carries on in this vein. It's not my fault. We'll speak in more detail when I'm back. He's sorry. Hopes we haven't been too inconvenienced, wanted to tell me now before we were any further into the trip.

'But if any stuff for the website comes up, you'll be in line for that.'

He talks about other things and I can tell he feels bad. He's a nice guy, finding it hard to say goodbye. So I help him out.

'OK, thanks for letting me know, Jake.' I hang up, and it's like I've been dumped. It's not you, it's me. Let's still be friends. I sit back in the seat and try to absorb this new shock. It strikes me quite forcefully that I'm 42 years old. At my age my dad had already been the first producer of *I'm Sorry I Haven't a Clue* and *Just a Minute* and was running BBC Radio 4, about to get an OBE. I can't hold down a job reviewing prune museums.

I sit for several minutes, picturing myself breaking this news to Dinah, and in the end I take the coward's way out. I write Dinah a note on the flyleaf of the Rand McNally road map. I roll it up and wedge it between the teeth of the tent zip. Then I get back in the car and I turn the key in the ignition and wait a few seconds, half expecting to see Dinah emerge. She doesn't.

I only mean to go on a short excursion, but at the top of Zoe and Alex's driveway, I take out the sat nav. I don't know where I want to go, but at the same time I want to be told how to get there. There's a P sign for parking across the road, so I type in a P. Randomly, I add an A and an M, and destinations pop up on the scroll-down menu. The first of interest is Pamplona, over the border in Spain. I select a Bruce Springsteen album for the CD player, turn the music up and open the windows. As I pull away, the cross-wind blows Zoe and Alex's wedding invitation, which is on the dashboard, out of the window. It feels like the first fresh air I've breathed in days.

I drive through tunnels cut into the hills and catch my first sight of the Pyrenees on the other side of Landes de Gascogne Natural Park. Pretty soon the road signs change from French to French *and* Spanish, then finally, beyond Biarritz, to just Spanish. I've never been to Spain and always imagined it to be hot and dusty. But round here it's lush, with fields of wild flowers and beautiful green hills.

At lunchtime I stop at a sheep farm on a country road off the E80. The farmer speaks no English and my Spanish is worse, but I manage to buy a small wheel of his sheep's cheese. I lie on a grassy bank by the roadside, eating it from my hand. For 20 minutes nothing passes except a flock of lost sheep zigzagging down the road. An email comes in from the Hautes-Pyrénées tourist board. It's about a section of our itinerary entitled 'Caves, chasms, spas, walks and castles' that we'll now never do. I've also received three messages from Dinah. The first: 'Where are you?' The second: 'Where the fuck are you?' The third: 'Stop being a twat.'

In San Sebastián I find the tourist office. Here I sort out some accommodation in the village of Lumbier, an hour outside Pamplona. I can't stay in the city itself, as tomorrow is the final day of the bull run and everywhere's booked. Lumbier is tiny. There are eight houses and one church. José and Marcia are a young couple. Their house is tiled throughout and has a huge Mexican-style front door. I pay José 120 euros for two nights and another ten for an evening meal. My bedroom's in the middle of the house. It's dark, has shiny wooden beams and a small shower next door. I have my own dining room with a shuttered balcony overlooking their garden, where I eat my *pintxos* – little dishes of meat, cheeses and fish on half slices of baguette. There's also a bottle of Rioja, a giant Spanish melon, serrano ham and a bowl of olives.

After I've eaten, I feel restless. I want to go somewhere, but I can't think where. I want to talk to someone, but I can't think who. I pull my sandals on to take a wander round the village, then change my mind, so I take them off.

Except I preferred it with my sandals on – it created a sense of urgency – so I put them back on again. This happens three times. They go on. They come off. I try to read, but I can't concentrate long enough to reach the end of a sentence. And I start to wonder: is this what a breakdown feels like? A total inability to make even the most minor decisions or complete the smallest tasks? For the next 20 minutes, I check my phone for life-changing emails. None. For life-changing texts. None. For life-changing voicemail messages. None. I switch the telly on and find CNN and I look for life-changing news events. There aren't any. Now I feel like I'm waiting for something, but I don't know what.

There's an oak games cupboard in the bedroom here, and inside there's a pack of cards. It reminds me of this weird thing that happened after Dinah and I split up. Basically I was making such shit decisions that I decided to outsource them to fate, using a pack of playing cards. What I'd do was assign cards in the deck to women I'd once had feelings for. Nikki, who I was in love with in the fourth form, was the ten of hearts. Smith, the four of clubs. Dinah was the seven of diamonds, and there were others too. The way the suit was arranged on the card, the pattern of the diamonds, clubs, spades and so on, influenced who was which card because, if looked at in the right way, they resembled a woman's body shape. How a ten is stacked, for instance, sort of looks like a woman with swimmer's shoulders. The colour of the card was important too. Red cards were fair-haired girls. Black cards, darker-haired girls. Also, the number on the card sometimes fitted a face. Dinah's aquiline nose made her a seven for this reason. I'd drink a bottle of red wine and stare at a picture of my mum. As I did so, I'd try to conjure her up in my mind. I'd remember Mum's voice, how her face moved when she pulled certain expressions, then, keeping this in my head, I'd cut the pack. I'd feel through it with my fingertips, not looking, but trying to sense where Dinah's card was, believing as I did this that my mum was guiding me, helping me find the right card. Weirdly, I beat the odds more than I should have done.

There was one time in particular when I did this that stands out. My dad had met and fallen in love with Mary. He was moving in with her, so was in the process of selling the windmill. One day, before he sold it, I decided to drive there in my mum's old Peugeot 205 that I'd inherited. In it, I found a single glove of hers that I used to wear when I drove. On the way, the song 'I Love You Always Forever' by Donna Lewis (big in the charts when Mum died) came on the radio. That set me off straightaway.

Inside the windmill, it was cold and empty. Dad had already cleared it out. When I'd set off, I wasn't even sure I'd go inside and now I was, I still wasn't sure why I was there. I found one of Mum's old ironing receipt books in a drawer and I took that. But it didn't seem enough. I must have seen a detective on TV do it, because in Mum and Dad's old bedroom, on an impulse, I reached down the back of Mum's dressing-table mirror. Behind it, I found a photo. It was of Mum in her brown duffle coat, her hair in a beehive. I recognised New York. It was taken on her honeymoon. It was perfect.

When she died, my mum's ashes were scattered over the rosebushes in the back garden. On a windy day I'd helped Dad stamp them into the soil to stop them blowing away. There was a bench beside them. Dad had had it inscribed:

'Roses, roses, roses all the way.' It was what he'd told Mum on their wedding day. Sat on the bench afterwards, with the photograph, saying goodbye to my mum, it occurred to me that I should take a rosebush as well. I used her driving glove to uproot it.

Back in my flat, after replanting the bush in the garden, I picked up an answerphone message from my dad. He'd completed on the windmill that morning, 'So please don't go back.' That night I cut the pack of cards, staring at this new picture of my mum, and I got the seven of diamonds, Dinah's card. Fluke? I cut it again. Seven of diamonds. When I got it the third time (the odds: 1 in 140, 608), I called her. I still went travelling for five months, and maybe I'd have called her anyway, but it was the start of our reconciliation.

Now, I sit on my bed with the cards, but I have no pictures of my mum, so instead I Google my dad and find a picture of him alongside his obituary on a BBC news page from 2007. I cut the pack, staring at his photo, but it doesn't work. I try ten times, but I can't cut the seven of diamonds.

In the end I call Mary.

'The sun's splitting the rocks and I'm sat on the balcony in Cape Town, sipping a rather nice glass of white wine. How are you, my darling?' she says.

'I'm OK,' I lie.

'How's France? They eating baguette yet?'

'Actually, I'm in Spain.'

'Oh.'

'The French guidebook was cancelled.'

There's a pause. Mary makes a hmm noise. 'I did worry, my darling, that you were leaving without a contract.'

'I know you did. I'm trying to get a commission to write about Pamplona.'

She makes the hmm sound again. 'And what about the hotels you've stayed in, my love? I'm not being funny, how are you squaring it with them, or are you leaving that to Dinah?' She laughs. 'Didn't a lot of places put you up for free?'

'Yes.'

'Oh dear,' she says. 'And any news on the novel?'

'My agent wants me to self-publish it.' She doesn't say anything. 'Apparently you can do that on Amazon and make almost as much. Or I could blog it.'

There's a pause. 'And Dinah?' she says.

'Still in France with the kids.'

'Is everything alright?'

'Yeah, fine. Good. Really good.' There's a pause. 'Actually, not very good.'

I tell Mary the situation, leaving out the more gruesome details.

'The second happiest day of his life, your dad called your wedding,' she says. 'He was worried you'd never settle down. You have your plus points and you have your minus points. It's no fun without Punch, but you're an awkward so-and–so, Ben Hatch. Goodness knows, you drove your dad half mad. I'm sorry about the novel and the guidebook's a shame, but these things, they come and they go. Your wife doesn't. She's a good girl, that wife of yours. Are you catching my drift?'

'I thought you might call me an eejit.'

'Well, you are an eejit.'

'Thank you.'

'Love you, my darling,' she says.

'Love you too.'

And in a funny way, getting bollocked by Mary is as close as I can come to talking to my dad.

I call Dinah afterwards. She's with her mum and dad at Zoe and Alex's.

'Where are you?' she asks.

'Spain.'

'Hold on.' There's a pause. I hear a pan sizzling. Phoebe shouts something. Dinah comes back on. It's quieter now.

'How are the kids?' I ask.

'Fine.'

'Did you get my note?'

'Yes.'

'I spoke to Jake.'

'You said. What are you doing in Spain?'

'It's the Pamplona bull run tomorrow. I'm going to write about it.'

'Who for?'

'I don't know.'

'I love the way you think my job's so easy. You can't just get travel commissions like that. You have to know people. It's been done to death. Nobody will take a piece on it.'

'They would if I ran in it.'

There's a silence. 'Are you serious?'

'Why not?'

'Because every year people get killed. Do you even know what happens?'

'I've read about it.'

'They release enraged bulls into crowded narrow streets. Massive bulls. People get trampled, crushed, impaled.'

'I'll be fine. Most people are drunk. That's why they get hurt. I'll be sober. What you mustn't do is hide in doorways. Or come between an angry bull and the rest of the pack.'

'I've phoned the agency,' she says.

'Have you?'

'We have to pay a 20 per cent surcharge on every cancelled booking on the house. There are six of them. It'll cost a grand. That's still cheaper than carrying on. Now I've got two children to feed and put to bed. Please don't get gored. It would really upset the kids.'

'Can I say goodnight to them?'

'Phoebe!' calls Dinah.

Phoebe comes on. 'Hello, Daddy.'

'Hello, Pops. Are you having your dinner?'

'I love you, Daddy.'

'I love you too, Pops. So what's for dinner?'

'Pasta, Daddy?'

'Yes.'

'I *love* you, Daddy.'

'I love you too, Pops.'

'Daddy?'

'Yes, Pops.'

'When are you coming back?'

'I'm not sure.'

'Daddy?'

'Yes?'

'Are you sorting your life out?'

'Is that what Mummy said?'

'Yes.'

'Yes, sweetheart, I am.'

'Daddy?'

'Yes.'

'Charlie wants to say something. I love you, Daddy. Here's Charlie.'

'Hello, Charlie. Are you having your dinner?'

'Yes.'

'What are you having?'

'Pasta.'

'Is it nice?'

'Bye, bye, Daddy.'

The phone clunks down. Dinah comes back on. 'Remember what I said.' And she hangs up.

CHAPTER 14

I get up at 5 a.m. It's an hour's drive to Pamplona. When I reach the city, it's already busy, with thousands more people streaming in. Everyone's dressed in white and red. White trousers, white shirts, red hats, red sashes. I park in a multistorey near the south bank of the River Arga and follow the crowds through the pedestrianised town centre, past the Monument to the Running of the Bulls in avenida Roncesvalles. It's like a cup-final football crowd in fancy dress. New Year's Eve with bulls. The streets stink of piss, beer and trash. The police, in red berets, grey trousers and boots, look like something out of the West End.

The plaza de Toros is just outside the bullring. There are two tiers of wooden-gate-style fencing, a lower front section and a higher one behind that people have already clambered up to get the best views. Between these fences is a three-foot-wide no-man's land patrolled by police. People have lined the route and are hanging off balconies, waving flags, over the narrow cobbled streets the bulls will run down. Many have been partying all night. There's a man next to me doing an impression of an emergency vehicle over and over again. He throws his head back like a wolf as he howls. Men lie in gutters asleep. Others are pissing up alleyways, and there are two young guys physically propping each other up, like bookends. Brass bands occasionally strike up. There's chanting and an American girl's wondering in her lazy drawl if they 'like, slaughter all the bulls at the end and stuff?' I watch a policeman direct an Aussie guy to the start line, and I follow him.

Before the race begins, a line of police in peaked hats and black uniforms fan out in a line, within touching distance of each other, in front of the runners. We bunch up behind them. There's an air of expectancy and excitement around me. But it feels like I'm watching this from afar, that I'm not really here.

In New Zealand, backpacking alone after I split with Dinah, I did a tandem skydive over Lake Taupo. It wasn't until I was sat on the edge of the plane, staring 10,000 feet below at the abstract-looking ground, with the instructor banana-d to my back, that I realised how frightened I was. That jump came out of an urge to feel something because the rest of me was so numb. It feels the same now.

At the start line someone occasionally bottles it and climbs quickly through a gap in the barrier and, while the police roughly help them through, the crowd whistle their contempt and try to push them back out on to the course. Nobody speaks to me. I speak to no one. I'm conscious that I'm not dressed correctly. I'm wearing sandals and my bumbag, which I've tightened so it doesn't bounce when I run. The runners chant now as they gird their loins. They limber up, stretch their calves and touch toes, like they're about to do the 200 metres.

When the first rocket's fired, the atmosphere visibly tightens. Slowly people move forward. It's like the start of a marathon. The rocket means the first bull's been released. Somewhere behind us, a bull's heading our way and nobody wants to be seen to be too eager to get out of its way. There's a mix of women and men, the young and middle-aged. Many have loose, glossy-eyed, drunken faces. A few look scared.

After the second rocket, the buzz increases. The pace quickens, voices rise. I hear a loud rumble. It's like the sound of a heavy wheelbarrow being pushed through the streets. People overtake me now. The crowd's so thick that when the bull passes me, it feels surreal. In fact it seems so much a part of this crowd, it's as if it too is running away, running from something even more scary behind it.

I trot along on the edge, avoiding doorways, and I've been running for about two minutes when I stumble on a cobblestone and trip up on the flap of my sandal. I fall forward into the back of the man in front of me. As I go down, someone stands on my hand. I hear the wheelbarrow rumble again. Others have tripped over me. They're scrabbling to get up. One man's dribbling, his eyes on stalks. I get up and notice a gap ahead in the fence. I shimmy through the runners to my right and duck through the barrier. A policeman manhandles me through no-man's land and past the second barrier, almost throwing me through it into the empty street. People on the second-tier fence drum their feet on my back as I pass beneath them. I'm slapped in the face by a woman with a painted red face, kicked up the arse and punched on the side of the head. Almost immediately, I hear the third rocket and the atmosphere loosens. It means the bulls are all safely in the ring. People jump down from the barriers and mill in the street, laughing and talking. But then I hear the rumble again. Voices around me become high-pitched. People run. A policeman jumps on to the barrier and tucks himself in. An ox runs through the thinning crowds towards the ring. There's laughter after the panic. The stench of rubbish and piss re-assaults my nose. My sandals have split from standing in broken glass. There's a lump on my head and my hand hurts. Just like after my skydive, I don't feel anything. No adrenalin rush at all. I just feel sleepy and angry with myself for doing something so needlessly reckless.

In the main square, at Café Iruña, Hemingway's old haunt, I order a hot chocolate and *churros* caked in sugar. Beside me sits a man who intermittently wakes to chant, 'Xavi, Xavi, Xavi!' before falling back to sleep, his head lolling forward. Euro pop blasts out of the café, whose tables and chairs have been removed from its ornate interior to allow for dancing. There's a crash. A two-litre bottle of mineral water lands a few inches from my head. Three lads, their eyes barely open, apologise and pick it up. There's shouting in the square. A crowd of boys are ripping shirts off each other's backs. They tear at them like dogs. When the shirts are in rags, they laugh, drape them over their shoulders like towels and walk on. I watch another man punch his friend in the face. He just turns and whacks him. Friends haul the puncher away. Within seconds, both men are bundled into a police car. Bin lorries whine up the narrow streets. The fence barriers that lined the route are removed by men in high-vis jackets and chucked into the back of flatbed lorries. People march towards their cars and coaches, parked on the city's edges, and slowly, as early morning becomes late morning, the atmosphere in the city changes.

I have a sleep on a bench in the main square and, at midday, the procession of Giants and Big Heads (Gigantes y Cabezudos) starts outside the town hall. Huge, beautifully painted puppets, larger than a two-storey house, enter the packed square behind a brass band, accompanied by nineteenth-century-style courtesans on hobby horses, who whack children in the crowd with foam balls tied by string to the ends of sticks. The puppets represent the kings and queens of Spain and are set on wooden frames. They're operated underneath, so elegantly that you can perfectly imagine how a 20-foot person would dance. City dignitaries are surveying the crowd from the town-hall balcony, dressed in tuxedos, the mayor in his sash, checking his phone, reading messages, laughing, showing them to those around him.

I bump into the American girl again later in a bar, the one who wanted to know if they'd be slaughtering all the bulls at the end. She's playing draw poker on a bar-top machine. I order a beer and ask if she's having much luck, and she says 'N-ah-t really', and when her change runs out, as she waits for more from the barman, I ask where she's from.

'New York,' she says, 'but now Hollywood.' She's here with friends. She receives her change and feeds the slot and I ask why she moved to Hollywood.

'It's a place,' she says.

'Why Hollywood, as opposed to anywhere else?' I ask.

'Never been to Hollywood,' she says.

'It's quite hard talking to you when you play that. You must be winning a lot,' I say. She says no, she just has a problem, that's all. In the end, her coins run out and she becomes more friendly. She asks what I'm doing in Pamplona. I tell her I'm hoping to land a writing commission.

She doesn't like the bar. 'The music is like . . . blergh,' she says, and flops her hand over dismissively. 'But then I'm, like, pr-ah-bly totally jaded because I'm from New York.' She does the thing with her hand again then tells me, 'I'm in the movie business and my boyfriend's in the music business.'

A guy comes up. He has floppy golden hair, a Hawaiian shirt and an expensive gold watch. He says something I don't hear and laughs, 'You know?' he says, and he laughs again, so I laugh, even though I have no idea what he's talking about.

After he's gone to the bar, the girl says, 'That's Patrick. Don't mind him. His parents own Campbell's soup and he's seriously loaded. I'm talking millions. Really! Billions probably. But he's just, like, a real cool guy.' She and her boyfriend met him in San Sebastián, she says. 'He takes a lot of pot, but he's alright. He owns magazines. You oughtta stick around.'

After this, they kind of adopt me. The bar's incredibly noisy and occasionally a brass band marches in. Everyone stands when they do and sings, 'Xavi, Xavi, Xavi', with their hands over their hearts. Then the band marches out. We sit down and I start telling Patrick about France, but he cuts me off to say how he was busted for pot in the Bahamas. He travelled there on his yacht, but it was a set-up.

'The cops are, like, banging on my door and I didn't know who they were and they searched my bedroom and found two ounces of pot. I was narked. My broth-ah prob-ah-bly. We don't get on.'

In fact, he only asks me one question about myself, which is whether I am on my own in the city. I tell him I am. 'You must have balls,' he says. 'You ran with the fuckin' bulls, man. That's so cool.'

The girl's boyfriend is very tall and sort of Native American-looking. I can barely hear what the others are saying, but it's even worse with him because of his height. He says things and pulls the face you make after a joke, so I laugh along. When I've finished my beer, Patrick buys me a vodka with cranberry juice and starts talking about Campbell's soup. There are about half a dozen products he mentions, but they're American, so I haven't heard of any of them. I say 'Really?' a few times and the girl leans over and says, 'He's n-ah-t normally like this.'

Patrick tells me a bit more about being busted in the Bahamas, how he spent a week in jail but paid $3,000 to get off on a charge that would've put him away for nine months.

'I had a good lawyer,' he says, laughing, and he puts his hand up very slowly for me to give him a high-five, which I do.

Outside, in the bright sunshine, he shakes my hand. He does it in that clasp way stoners do and I'm about to head for my car when he says, 'Hey, wanna come back and smoke some pot? I'll show you my magazine.' So then I'm climbing into his Chevrolet Blazer, which is parked outside.

'Nice car,' I say.

'Oh, this is a hire car. I drive a Mercedes, a Porsche, and a BM, but I flew over,' he says.

In the car the Native American-looking guy asks Patrick to put on a CD of their band and, although they said his place was across town, the drive takes 20 minutes. It's up in the hills, set back from the road, so you can't see the house from the street. There are security gates that the girl uses a remote on the dashboard to open. We travel up a curved, palm-tree-lined track that opens on to a gravel driveway dominated by a fountain. Behind this is a white house with sweeping stone staircases either side of it. Inside, there are parquet floors, and one room is a huge aviary with white cockatiels flying around the domed glass ceiling. Another room has a white grand piano in it. Apart from this, it's almost bare, with no pictures on the walls at all.

In the kitchen, Patrick sits on a stool at the island with a bong. He draws on it and passes it along. When it's my turn, I forget to put my mouth wholly over the hole and don't get anything.

'Did you get a hit at all?' he says.

I say no and he reminds me what to do. This time I cough afterwards. Nobody laughs. The Native American-looking guy puts the Rolling Stones on the stereo and says 'Mick is the best', and the girl's now stroking a cockatiel.

'This is my burrd,' she says. 'I love this burrd. I don't need you guys. I got a burrd.'

Patrick passes long-stemmed wine glasses around, then gets a magazine out. It's nature-themed, with fashion adverts in it. Patrick says he helped finance it because he's very into the 'invironmint'.

'Like, these burrds are all native Spanish. I wouldn't take burrds from Orstraliah because, like, that's their native burrds.'

The girl and the Native American-looking guy scratch pictures in the magazine and sniff their fingers afterwards. She does it to a picture of a black guy water-skiing. 'I like the smell of black men,' she says.

The tall guy does it to a picture of a speedboat. 'Speedboat smells good,' he says, and she does the same and agrees. Patrick scratches the nipples on a picture of a woman standing up at a party, then her crotch, and he laughs. I'm conscious I haven't said anything for a while, so I mention the sort of comedic slant I like to take in my writing.

'Wow! British comedy is the most sophisticated in the world,' says the Native American-looking guy. He pretends to pick his nose and eat it. He does it very fast and a couple of times, with his hands cupped to his face in a shovelling movement.

'You're right,' I say, thinking he must be talking about Benny Hill. 'There is lowest common denominator stuff as well.' And now I get an irresistible feeling, through the fog of alcohol and dope, that these people are alien to me. They don't want to have conversations. Everything is simply sensations. The Native American guy starts drumming the table. Patrick does too. Mick Jagger's now singing about women taking it from behind. The girl leans on the island, gyrating her hips, doing explicit actions to the songs.

'You like this?' says the Native American guy.

I don't reply, and the girl asks if any of us want a slow dance. Again, I don't say anything. A Doberman walks in and out of the room. Patrick tells me there are five more patrolling the grounds.

Then it gets really weird. The girl asks if I want to go outside to smoke a cigarette, and when I hesitate, she says,

'You thought I was comin' on to you! He thought I was comin' on to him!' Nobody seems interested in what she's saying and everyone's now petting 'burrds' except me.

At this point, Patrick opens the door that the dog came through. It leads into a double garage. There's a dog rug in the middle of the floor. We move in here and stand around it.

'Hands and knees,' says the girl, and she smacks me on the arse with the rolled-up nature magazine.

I laugh and she does it again, more insistently. In the corner of the garage, I notice a video camera on a tripod stand.

'On yer hands and knees,' she says.

I look at her.

'Am I weirding you out?' she says.

I say 'A bit', and she does it again, and everyone's looking at me, and I can feel the danger now. It's clear to me – they've picked me up because I'm on my own, for the express purpose of procuring me for Patrick. They're in the movie business. The porn business. Nobody knows I'm here and my phone's out of juice. They're going to film me getting raped by Patrick on this dog rug, then they're going to kill me and feed me to the Dobermans.

The tall guy picks up a rolled-up tent, puts it between his legs and starts swivelling it around. Patrick does the same with a broom handle.

'Every man in Hollywood is gay,' says the girl. 'I'm sure of it. They just don't know it.'

I go to leave the garage. The girl blocks me, teasingly, holding an arm across the doorway. I duck underneath it playfully. In the downstairs toilet, I try to think of a plan, but I don't know where I am and, anyway, Patrick mentioned dogs patrolling the grounds. I sit on the toilet, ripping off paper and scrunching it up and throwing it into the bowl, in case they're outside, listening. I go through scenarios. But I can only think of one viable escape route. The front door we came in through is a few feet away from the toilet. I flush the loo and leave the room. There's nobody in the hallway. I try the front door catch, but it's locked. Back in the kitchen, as calmly as I can, I ask Patrick if he'll call me a cab. I have a flight in the morning and my wife and kids are expecting me back at my hotel. Patrick doesn't connect with this new information, so I repeat it. This time, he opens a drawer and finds a directory, but he's too out of his face to find the letter 'T'.

'This is very un-Mick-like behaviour,' says the Native American guy.

When I mention the early flight again, Patrick says he'll drive me tomorrow. I can stay over. When he leaves the room to fetch another cockatiel, I ask the Native American guy if he'll call one. He picks up the phone, dials a number and looks at me as he speaks into the receiver. For the next half an hour, I keep them all in my line of sight. For a while, they make out that Patrick's wife, Wendy, is upstairs. They make jokes about how she's always 'so tired'.

Some time later, there's a loud barking sound outside. Patrick's out of the room, and the Native American guy leans across the island and whispers 'Run'. I stay rooted to the spot. I'm not sure what to do. He says it again. This time, he points at the garage. Something in his face tells me to obey. I dash through the doorway to the garage. There's a side door in it, leading outside. On the second go, I force it open. There's no cab there, so I run round the side of the house to the front. The taxi's by the fountain. I hear loud barking. I jump in and slam the door, just as two Dobermans leap on to the bonnet. They snarl and slaver over the windscreen. The driver wildly slams the cab into reverse. The dogs jump or fall off and trot beside us as we head for the gate. The last thing I see as they open is Patrick, standing at the front door, the tent pole between his legs.

It's 3 a.m. when I reach the car park. I flop into the driver's seat, my heart beating hard. I feel like I've just escaped from the Titty Twister bar in *From Dusk Till Dawn*. I feel jumpy, too wired to sleep. I put my phone on charge, wind the seat down, and I wonder if I should drive to a police station to report what happened tonight. I'm still wondering this when I fall asleep.

CHAPTER 15

In the dream, I'm in the middle of a huge park. I'm putting my sandals on. It's dark. Night-time. I don't know where my children live, or how to contact them. I walk through the park, through bracken and clearings and I'm lost, calling their names, tripping and falling.

I wake like a junkie given an adrenalin shot to the heart. Sweat's dripping off my forehead. My shirt's soaked. I open the driver's door, but the burnt smell of diesel is worse than the heat. My eyes feel sticky and my mouth's so dry opening it feels like unfastening Velcro. I piss behind the car. It's the dark, unwell piss of the sort you see in unflushed public toilets. I find a vending machine in the multistorey stairwell. I drink a bottle of Vittel and eat a Bueno bar. Back in the car, I call Dinah. She doesn't answer. I call her dad. He doesn't pick up. I try Zoe and Alex's house. It goes to answerphone. I text Dinah and say I'm very, very sorry. Then I call Buster.

'Right! So, you smoked some dope at a mansion owned by the heir to the Campbell's soup fortune and there was a

Native American there and cockatiels were flying around.'
He snorts.

'What?' I say.

He laughs. 'You were stoned, you knob. I never do
dope. It makes me paranoid. You were paranoid. I bet
there was a catch on that front door you just didn't
see.'

'You don't believe me?'

'Of course not.'

'So what about the dog blanket?'

'Yeah, and there was probably a bowl of Winalot there
too, so what?'

'And the video camera?'

'People store stuff in garages.'

'There're other things I haven't told you. They were
listening to this Rolling Stones song about taking it up the
bum and the girl was slapping me on the arse with a rolled-
up magazine.'

'What song?'

'I don't know. I wasn't in the mood for Shazaming.'

'I play records every day. I've never heard of it.'

'To be fair, you're unlikely to play a song about taking
it up the bum on forces family radio. What about the
Dobermans?'

'OK, Google Campbell's soup and . . . what was his
name?'

'Patrick. OK, I will.'

So I do. And nothing comes up. The heir to the
Campbell's soup fortune is a guy called Bennett Dorrance
who's on the *Forbes* Rich List at number 250 in the US.
There's nobody in the family even remotely the age or
appearance of Patrick.

He laughs. 'Told you.'

'They must have changed the story. They're hardly likely to tell me his real name, in case I escaped.'

'What, you think he might really be the heir to the Knorr soup fortune?'

Buster laughs. 'Or maybe he was a Jaffa Cake millionaire. Or a Yorkshire pudding mogul. You were paranoid, you berk. Although the big question is why you went back there in the first place.'

'The girl said he owned a magazine. I thought I might get some work out of it.'

'Ah, a girl. I see. Did you fancy her?'

'No.'

'You did, didn't you?'

'She had a boyfriend.'

'Oh yes, that's right, Sitting Bull. I bet she was good-looking.'

'She was quite good-looking.'

'And what were you doing running with the bulls? You're normally scared of labradoodles!' Buster says he thinks I'm having a midlife crisis. It's what happened to him when he turned 35. In the end he was lucky – he upended a Mazda 323 in the poor man's Dakar Rally, the Red Lion Foods Great Escape car rally to Barcelona – and came to his senses. He points out the irony that he's in Afghanistan, at the focal point of the war on terror, where soldiers are losing their lives every day, yet still a volley of international phone calls have been exchanged about my safety on my summer holiday.

I tell him what Dinah said, although he knows about it already as Dinah's spoken to Holly.

'What do you expect? You smacked her into the Atlantic

with an oar. And what else? Lunging at a spy at her cousin's wedding.'

'I didn't lunge. I fell on to her.'

'You fell on to her?! What's this, *Carry On Up the Champs-Elysées*? Smoking dope in front of her dad then.'

'It wasn't in front of him.'

'He had to carry you to your car.'

'He helped me to the car yes, but . . .'

'When I last saw you, you were watching *Downton Abbey* in your stripy PJs, eating Kettle crisps. You've turned into Charlie Sheen.'

'Did Holly tell you I lunged?'

'The word "lunging" was used.'

'Will you ring Dinah for me?'

'Me?! Don't get me involved.'

'You're already involved. I'm driving to Biarritz. Can you tell her I'll meet her there at the train station? She's not answering me.'

'Biarritz?'

'Yes.'

'Sure you don't want to drive to the Tomatina Festival in Valencia? See if you can get bummed by the owner of Alphabetti Spaghetti?'

He laughs at his joke. There's a pause.

'Listen, Dinah loves you to death, you knob, and you feel the same about her. Just show her that once in a while. That's why she's saying this. And your novel – it's hardly a shock. What did you think was going to happen after seven years out of the game? You've got to work your way back up there.'

'You sound like Dad.'

'I feel like him, talking to you. And you're supposed to be the bright one.'

'Do you ever think it's weird, what we still do to impress Dad? He's been dead five years, but there you are, a perimeter wall away from the Taliban, broadcasting. And I'll get in a Chevrolet Blazer and risk my life at the hands of some soup or jelly or Yorkshire pud fucking psycho, or whatever he was, just to write 1,000 words about tripping over my sandal on the bull run.'

'Is that what happened? You tripped on your sandal?'

'Yeah.'

He laughs. 'It's in our DNA now,' says Buster. 'Nothing we can do about it.'

'I hope he fucking appreciates it up there.'

There's a whoosh of a helicopter coming in to land.

'Alright, I'll ring her,' he says. 'But do you know what I do these days with Hol? I do what Dad did with Mum. I apologise, whether I think I'm in the right or not. It saves a lot of time in the long run.'

I think back and laugh. 'He did do that, didn't he?'

'Right, I'm off for my syrup sponge now. Try and stay out of fucking trouble.'

I'm zipping my phone into my bumbag after another attempt at reaching Dinah when I find the article Marian gave me. At the bottom of the page, it lists universities that run plumbing courses. It makes me think of something my dad said to me once. 'My son, Dinah married a writer.' It was on the point of abandoning my novel. I was three years into it and it was still going badly. At the time I thought what my dad meant by this was Dinah will look down on you if you're not a writer, if you do something else she won't respect you. My dad over-valued creative people. He elevated them. Telly people, actors, writers and performers. The people he worked with. They were a breed apart to him. I also thought what he meant was he might lose respect for me too. But then later I started to doubt this and I began to wonder if he meant something else. 'Dinah married a writer.' Was he saying this, as in: Dinah married a writer so she knew the deal? In other words that there'd be ups and downs and she'd have to take the rough with the smooth. Either way it had made me determined to carry on writing. But right now I'm thinking Dinah didn't marry a writer, she married me and I don't have to be a writer. I ring the number in Brighton and ask the woman who answers if she can post me an application form for a City and Guilds course. After this, I call Louise Winfield from ITV's *Tonight with Trevor McDonald* on the number Busta gave me. She's lovely and makes notes as I tell her the story, saying the word 'bastard' under her breath every now and again. Afterwards she asks me to email her the details because she thinks it might also make a *Homes from Hell*. She'll contact the producer there, and is happy for me to tell Builder Nick that they're looking into the case. Armed with this, I ring Nick. I channel my dad at his most businesslike and add in a dollop of Tony Soprano.

'Hello, Nick, it's Ben. Long time no hear.'

'Ben?' he says.

He clearly can't remember me.

'The guy you stole £20,000 from? I was just wondering if you've been contacted by someone from ITV yet?'

I let that sink in.

'Only, I just passed them my file on you. You're going to be on the telly, Nick. Oh, and I'm also going to pay

£150 to get leaflets printed with a picture of your face on them, with "conman" written underneath. I'm going to post them on lamp posts outside your house and where your wife works.'

He starts to mumble about cash flow and how there's no need for this.

I laugh. 'No need! There's every fucking need. You've caused my family no end of grief. Do you know where I am right now?'

He says he doesn't.

'I'm in Spain. I've just run with the bulls in Pamplona, Nick. I almost got myself killed trying to earn back some of my money that you stuck on a roulette wheel in a casino to feel like a big shot for five minutes. First, you're going to be on *Homes from Hell*. That's already sorted. Then, when they pass on your details to the police and Trading Standards and the Inland Revenue, which they have to do, by the way, you're going to jail.'

He tells me to calm down.

'I'm very calm, Nick. And you've got one chance of avoiding all this. Come to our house on 6 September at 1 p.m. I want £200 from you as an act of good faith, but more importantly, I'll want to hear you tell me how you're going to pay me back. Because that's what I've decided – you're going to pay me back.'

'Fine, I'll be there,' he says quickly.

'Good. Enjoy the rest of your summer.'

''Tend I was asleep.'

''Tend I was dead and you were sad.'

''Tend I am in love with you.'

''Tend we cry ourselves to sleep.'

''Tend we didn't cry, just rubbed our eyes.'

I hear my children's voices before I see them. I'm in the waiting room at Biarritz Station, in front of a glass wall showing a map of towns and cities near Biarritz, with white lines linking them.

''Tend we slept together because we were sad.'

''Tend I was sick.'

''Tend I was dead. It's Daddy,' shouts Charlie, seeing me first. 'He's in here!'

Charlie looks electronically tagged. He has one Ben 10 wristband on his left wrist and another round his right ankle. I pick him up. He squeezes me as hard as he can. Phoebe enters the waiting room and rises to her tiptoes when she spots me. 'Da-dd-eee!' she says.

'Pops!'

I scoop her up too and kiss her head.

'Your face is itchy, Daddy,' she says.

'I haven't shaved, sweetheart.'

And I feel like a wilted plant receiving its first drops of water in weeks, as they press their beautiful, smooth faces into mine. When I look up, Dinah's standing in the doorway. She's wearing my Panama hat, carrying two squishy bags. I put the kids down, Dinah drops the bags and we hug in the doorway.

'I'm sorry,' I say. 'I'm so, so sorry.'

She starts to cry. I wrap my arms round her. We sway from side to side. The kids jump around us.

'Daddy!' says Phoebe.

'I've had such a terrible time,' I say.

'Me too,' she says.

'Daddy!' says Phoebe.

'Honestly, when I tell you what happened!'

'Daddy!' says Phoebe.

'Phoebe's got something to show you,' says Dinah, breaking away. 'Let her show you or we won't get any peace.'

'What is it, Pops?'

She jabs at me with her index fingers. In her American accent, she says, 'That's another fine mess you've gotten me into.'

'That's grcat, Pops.'

'She's been practising it the whole way here. And Charlie, show Daddy what you've learnt.'

He grins and beckons me with his hand to follow him.

In the men's, he stands on tiptoe at the urinal.

'Wow! You can do stand-up wees!'

He looks round. '*And* I do them outside too,' he says. 'On trees and in the grass.'

'Careful, you're also doing it on the floor right now.'

'Oh yeah,' he laughs, and swivels back to face the wall.

He washes his hands.

'But you mustn't do them on tents,' he adds, looking up at me, as we walk outside.

'Did you do one on a tent?'

He nods solemnly.

'I like the way he leans forward,' I tell Dinah outside.

'I know. The drunk-in-an-alleyway-at-last-orders look. A proper smelly man now. Which reminds me . . .' Dinah reaches into her handbag and takes out a packet that she slaps into my hand.

'Peace offering,' she says. And I don't have to open it to know what it is. I can smell it.

'Munster cheese. Thank you.'

'The smelliest one I could find.'

I pick up the bags.

'And, want to hear my news?' says Dinah. 'I've landed a column in the *Telegraph*. Six pieces on what to do with kids this summer in France.'

'Wow! That's amazing. That squares it with the hotels. So we can carry on?'

'Yup.'

'But do you want to?'

She pops the Panama hat on my head. 'Of course I bloody do.'

'Daddy, what are we doing today?' asks Phoebe.

'Well, it says in the Master Document here that Sephardic Jews fleeing the Spanish Inquisition settled in Biarritz . . .'

Phoebe slumps her shoulders forward.

'. . . bringing with them the secrets of chocolate.'

She straightens.

'Soooo, we'd better go . . . to . . . a . . . choccy museum!'

'Yay!' says Phoebe.

'But first, guys, we're going to check in to our new place, then have a surfing lesson.'

In one of France's coolest cities and Europe's surfing capital, we've somehow found the least fashionable B&B. It's run by an Englishman from the Wirral called Peter. He manages the place with his wife, Alison, who has a lazy eye and sells laminated poems about injured cats behind the reception desk. We have two rooms: a bunk-bed room for the kids and a small bedroom for us, where the bed fills the room so entirely there's only enough space round its edges to get changed if you stand on one leg and throw your other leg over the expanse of bed, in the manner of Colin Jackson hurdling. The beds have orange quilts, the curtains are brown and the floor is a sticky lino that lifts when you walk across it. Our bedside tables hang by loose metal brackets and slope forward. But it's still a massive improvement on sleeping in the car.

We sling our bags in, lock our valuables in the safe and I'm changing for surfing when Dinah asks, 'So did you do it then? The bull run?'

'Yes.'

She nods.

'But I bottled it after 100 metres. I got kicked up the arse and called a coward.'

She laughs. 'Good,' she says.

'And something terrible almost happened to me afterwards. Did Buster tell you?'

'Yes. And I don't want to hear it,' she says. Dinah touches my arm. 'Look, I'm sorry I said what I did, but I felt it needed saying. We'll talk tonight. The kids have been dying to see you. Let's give them a nice day.'

The beach is a small rocky cove down three flights of stone steps, and the surf centre is full of tanned, blue-eyed dropouts with dreads, bongo drums, frayed short jeans and thick, leathery feet. Bernard, the manager, is an ex-boxer. He's stocky, with a lined face and the watery blue eyes of a husky.

We change into wetsuits and, on the beach, the sea is the temperature of bath water. Large Atlantic waves roll in. Bernard gives us safety advice. He tells us not to wrap the board cords round our wrists or it might hurt our hands, and we must dive underwater if a loose board comes our way. He lies face down on a board in the sand, showing us how to approach a wave. We copy him on our Malibu MacB longboards, hands under shoulders in the push-up position, legs extended behind. Half an hour later, I've more or less given up, after being knocked on the head so many times, and I'm playing with the kids in the sand, while, knee-deep in the water, Bernard's asking where Dinah's surfed before.

'I've never surfed,' she beams.

He asks about windsurfing and snowboarding. She shakes her head. He asks where she's from.

'Brighton.'

'Ah,' he says, as if this explains the natural ability that's enabled her to coast in on three consecutive waves, 'you know the ocean.'

An hour later, when I emerge from the changing room back in the surf centre, Dinah's already outside, talking to Bernard in French. Though not about surfing. He's standing very close to her, showing her pictures of his kids.

'A man like you, you will find another wife, Bernard,' I hear Dinah say.

Bernard's wetsuit is open, revealing his hairy chest. Ray-Bans dangle from his neck. After a long conversation together, during which time I've fussed around the kids, trying not to look like a spare part, he kisses Dinah on each cheek. Then, as if only just noticing I'm still there, he pats my cheese-bloated stomach with a curled, sparring fist.

'*Maintenant on mange*,' he says.

Dinah laughs, which is fine until she apologises for laughing, which is not so fine. Bernard asks her whether I'm '*sportif*'. Dinah laughs at this absurd suggestion, although, actually, back in England, I do run sometimes. Before we leave, Bernard again pats my stomach playfully in a way that either means a) I wish I could do this for real and damage your kidney or b) I am so sorry I cannot stop flirting with your wife. Please accept this matey gesture as recompense.

As we walk back to the car, Dinah tells me Bernard's tale. He used to live in a tiny Pyrenean mountain village with his wife and three children. They went to school on quad bikes. He kept goats. But his wife left him because of the isolation. She had no nice clothes to wear. In the winter they were snowed in and she missed her friends and hated wearing muddy boots all the time. To win her back, he'd moved to Biarritz, but it made no difference. He now saw his kids once a month and had retrained as a surf instructor.

'So, what you're saying is: substitute boxer for writer, surf instructor for plumber, three children for two children, an inaccessible mountain village for the back of VW Passat, and a lack of nice clothes for you and . . .'

'We're left with you when we're back,' she says. 'Divorced, coming on to housewives when you're mending their ball-cocks in Ditchling Beacon.'

On the top concrete step now, Dinah stops and puts her arms round my neck.

'You look frightened,' she says.

'Do I?'

'Yes.' She smiles. 'Did you think you'd be in more trouble than you are for storming off to Spain like a nutter?'

'In all honesty, yes.'

'Is that why you contained yourself back there with Bernard?'

'No, that's because he's an ex-boxer.'

She laughs. I kiss her.

'I don't get enough kisses from you,' she says.

'Me neither,' I say, and we kiss again.

'Are we OK?' I ask Dinah.

'I don't know. Why did you drive off?' she asks.

'I thought that when you were accusing me of not loving you, what you really meant was that *you* didn't love *me* any more.'

'Is that true?'

'And I didn't want to have to tell you about Jake. I feel I've disappointed you lately.'

'You know I love you,' she says. 'I show you that all the time. And I'm never disappointed in you; I was disappointed *for* you.'

'That's nice.'

I kiss her again. 'And I'm sorry I made a tit of myself in front of your mum and dad.'

'My dad was quite understanding actually. In fact, he told me off. He told me you had to let a man blow off steam once in a while.'

I laugh. 'Did he?'

'Although I think he came home a bit drunk from the golf club the other day, so he might have had his own agenda there. The kids really missed you.'

They come past us now. They're fighting over which one of their teddies – Waddles (hers) or Simba (his) – has diarrhoea.

'Waddles *always* has diarrhoea,' says Charlie. 'It's not fair.'

'I know, but she's eaten a bad thing, Charlie.'

'Simba's got diarrhoea,' he says.

'They can't both have diarrhoea, Charlie.'

'But you *always* choose who has diarrhoea,' says Charlie.

'Charlie, Waddles has diarrhoea and Simba's looking after her.'

'*Not* playing.'

'Phoebe,' I hear myself saying, 'let Simba have diarrhoea too.'

'Okaaaay, Simba's got diarrhoea as well,' says Phoebe.

'I've missed them too,' I tell Dinah. 'And I missed you.'

We walk towards the car, hand in hand. 'It's awful not having anyone to joke around with, isn't it?' she says.

'I know. Let's blow the budget and get some lunch, shall we? I've got some news for you as well.'

Like our mini personal scribes, recording all that happens in highlighter pen, Charlie and Phoebe are perfecting their surfing pictures. Charlie draws me like a cartoonist. In his pictures, I always have just three hairs sticking up from the top of my head, like a tuft of grass. Phoebe's depicts us standing beside our surfboards in front of the Hotel du Palais, a former castle belonging to Napoloen III that overlooks the beach we're in front of now, eating Spaghetti Bolognese in the midday sunshine.

'Basically I need him to admit he's abandoned the job. Otherwise, legally, he can just claim he means to finish it.'

Dinah and I are talking about Nick the builder and my chat with Louise Winfield, while at the same time, we're watching the son of the café owner, who's about nine, swinging between the backs of two metal chairs by his upper arms, mesmerised by Phoebe.

'And so he's agreed to come to the house?' says Dinah.

'Yeah honestly, you should have heard me. I scared myself. What I thought I'd do is go in heavy about Trevor McDonald. Really shit him up with that. Then I'll be all reasonable and tell him I know he hasn't got any money. I'll suggest a deal. "Forget the £23,000, Nick, let's make it £15,000." I'll draw up a letter and make him sign it, where he admits he can't finish the job and that he agrees to repay the £15,000.' I pause and look over at the boy. 'He's still staring at her,' I say.

'I know and what gets me is, she hasn't even noticed,' Dinah says.

'Anyway, I'll also secretly video it all, so he can't claim I forged his signature.'

'Was that her idea?'

'Yeah.'

'Well done, love.' She rests her hand on mine.

'I should have done it ages ago. And I haven't told you. I've also got an application form for a City and Guilds course in plumbing coming to the house.'

She widens her eyes. 'Really?' Then she laughs.

'What?'

'Now I'm imagining you as a plumber.'

And as she says this, one of the chairs the boy's swinging on gives way. He crashes to the floor, knocking a table over. He gets up comically fast, rights the table and places his arms back over the chairs as if nothing's happened. He continues to stare at Phoebe. Dinah has to stop herself laughing.

'That sort of thing used to happen to me a lot,' I say.

We both look at Phoebe, who's still oblivious.

'I don't know whether I like it,' I say.

'And what about those two boys on the beach?' Dinah

says. Earlier, two young French lads had sat next to Phoebe on the beach when we were surfing. They'd asked her name and when it became clear she didn't speak French, they'd had a sand fight to impress her.

'It's the adult front teeth. They make her look older,' Dinah says.

'What age were you when you started noticing boys?' I ask.

'Even at 14, I wasn't interested,' she says. 'I was so square. I remember a boy calling for me and I got my mum to send him away because I was up to a good bit in *Swallows and Amazons*.'

I laugh. 'I kissed Justine Harvey when I was 10.'

'Did you love her?' asks Phoebe, looking up from the lemonade she's drinking through a crooked straw.

I laugh. 'Ah, so you *are* paying attention.'

Phoebe smiles.

'I thought I did,' I tell her.

'Did you want to marry her?' says Phoebe.

'I didn't know about marriage then.'

'And what about when you met Mummy?' she asks. 'Did you feel all funny and in love?'

I look at Dinah. 'Mummy and Daddy were friends first,' she says.

'Sometimes it happens that way,' I say.

'What did you feel?' Phoebe asks.

I look at Dinah again. 'Well,' she says, 'Daddy made me laugh, and I made Daddy laugh.'

'And we grew to love each other,' I say.

'Then you got married?'

Dinah laughs. 'Not quite. After about ten years, Daddy asked me.'

'Why?'

'Because—' I start to say.

'Sometimes it takes a long time for people to decide to get married,' says Dinah.

'Why?'

'Because life is complicated,' she says.

'How did Daddy ask you, Mummy?'

'It was early in the morning,' she says.

'Was it on a lovely balcony?' says Phoebe. And Dinah and I laugh. 'Why are you laughing?' she asks.

'Because Daddy asked me on the doorstep, in an egg-stained dressing gown.'

'Ugh! Daddy!' says Phoebe. 'That's not very romantic.'

'Actually,' says Dinah, 'it was. It was very romantic.'

'And were you worried Mummy would say no?'

'I was a bit.'

'I think Daddy was pretty sure Mummy would say yes.'

'I hoped she would.'

'And then, after you got married, you had children?'

Dinah laughs again. 'Not quite.'

'Why?'

Dinah looks at me.

'Was it complicated?' asks Phoebe.

'It's always complicated with Daddy,' says Dinah, getting up to pay.

As we leave, the boy – unable to contain himself – waves at Phoebe. Again, she doesn't register this.

'Wave back, Pops,' says Dinah. 'He's put his back into impressing you for an hour.'

But she doesn't want to. The boy says something to Dinah in French.

'What did he say?' I ask, as we head back to the car.

'He said, "I like her, does she speak French?"'

'He's in love with you,' says Charlie.

'Really?' asks Phoebe. 'He said that?'

'He wants to marry you,' says Charlie.

'You've got a little admirer,' says Dinah. 'Do you like him?'

She shakes her head, thinks for a minute and says, 'I don't know.'

'Is it complicated, Pops?' I ask.

And she nods and goes into her shy walk, the one where she moves her hips stiffly, jerking her legs out like compass needles.

It's been a fun day. The chocolate museum, the Biarritz aquarium. I've just bathed the kids, read them stories, and I'm leaving their bedroom when Phoebe says, in the same voice you might use to remind someone to shut a door they'd left open, 'Cuddle, Daddy!'

'Oh yeah, sorry, sweetheart.'

I walk back into the room. Against the perfect white around them, Phoebe's chestnut-brown eyes look like freshly fallen conkers. We go through our bedtime ritual.

'Stand-up one,' she says, standing on her bed. I hug her.

'Sit-down one,' she says, sitting down on the bed. She throws her arms wide. I cuddle her

'And lie-down cuddle.'

She climbs under the covers. I cuddle her. She puts her index fingers together and draws eight hearts in the air. She counts them out. I do the same. 'One. Two. Three. Four. Five. Six. Seven. Eight.'

'And, Daddy,' she says, 'one for luck.'

'One for luck.' I copy the final heart.

'Night, night, Daddy. I love you.'

'Night, night, Pops. I love you too.'

I turn to Charlie in his bunk. For three years, he and I have been having The Trap. On the lower bunk, his covers are thrown back, his legs are open. New Simba's taut between his hands like a garrotte. (New Simba's the back-up soft toy I cleverly bought in case he lost his all-important Original Simba, but which has now assumed an equal importance with Original Simba, meaning they both now travel together, doubling the risk of catastrophe.) Charlie places Original Simba on his pillow, beside his head.

'OK. Look at Simba and say, "What's that?"' he says, going into the drill, which, for some reason, he still feels the need to talk me through, after all this time. I lean forward between his legs and look at Original Simba. Charlie gently circles my midriff with his legs. Then he clamps his legs tightly round me and cackles.

'Got you!' At the same time, he wraps New Simba round the back of my neck and tightens the garrotte.

'Oh no, I'm trapped,' I say, noosed by Simba. 'A deadly snake has got me.'

'A deadly crocodile,' he says.

'Oh no, I'm trapped. A deadly crocodile's got me.'

'Actually, I *do* want a snake.'

'Oh no, I'm trapped. A deadly snake has got me.'

'No, no, no. A crocodile, I want a crocodile!'

'Charlie!'

'OK!' he shouts. 'A *deadly snake*!'

At the end, he says what he always says, 'I'm so strong, aren't I?'

'You are.'

'Tell Mummy how strong,' he says.

'I will. Night, night, sunbeam.'

* * *

'Are you a golf fan, Ben?' says the manager, Peter, in the restaurant later, and before I can answer, he's placed a card on top of the menu that says 'Golf-Buddy' on it. Underneath this is his name and address, and on the other side, which he flips over, it demonstrates a product. The product is a yellow plastic strip with an arrow on it.

'You place it on the fairway, ahead of your ball,' explains Peter. He pretends to hold a golf driver. 'The arrow indicates where you want to hit the ball. Little business of mine.'

'And there's also Putting-Buddy,' says Peter, a few minutes later, when he returns after waiting on a nearby table. He now takes out a small laminated arrow from his wallet. 'You place this one on the green. You use it to . . . well, you get the idea.'

Peter's basically invented an arrow. He could, of course, apply it to anything, if it hadn't already been applied to everything, but he's chosen to apply it to golf. He tells us their story in between waiting on other tables. Peter and his wife initially planned to move to Spain to set up Golf-Buddy, but fell in love with Biarritz on the drive down. The idea was that Alison would run the B&B, while Peter worked on Golf-Buddy. But they hadn't realised how much work the B&B would involve. It meant Golf-Buddy had been delayed. But now that a fast road's opening to Pau, they're hoping to attract the RVs. The extra bookings will mean they can hire a member of staff, freeing up Peter.

'Any road,' says Peter now, taking out his pad, 'the website's on the card. Have a look. Now, what was it, two plates of charcuterie?'

'Dinah, I've changed my mind about plumbing,' I say, when Peter moves away. 'I'm going to work on Golf-Buddy with Peter. It's brilliant. It's the simplest, most effective golfing aid on the market. It's changed my game and it can change your game.'

'But, love, what if it doesn't succeed?' says Dinah, playing along. 'It's just an arrow.'

'It isn't just an arrow. It's a golf-alignment tool.'

'And, naturally, at some point, you'll force Peter out as chief executive,' she says.

'He doesn't think big enough, Dinah. Peter hasn't grasped the global market. He's not a visionary. The shareholders aren't happy. And that last batch of arrows he produced, they were fucking CROOKED. I'm showing him the door.'

'With one of his own arrows?'

'Yes! Then I'm going to apply the ampersand to squash.'

'Do you know what I've decided?' I tell Dinah when the plates of charcuterie arrive. The meat's hilariously arranged, in a higgledy-piggledy, crushed fashion that suggests someone's thrown each slice high into the air, while someone else had the job of attempting to catch them on the plate.

'What?' she says, rolling up a piece of salami.

'I'm going to accept that you're always right whenever we have an argument. I'm never going to row with you again.'

'Have you caught the sun?' she says.

I laugh.

'Actually, I meant that,' she says. She touches my face. 'You're hot and very red.'

'I'm going to be like some sort of Mormon bride and always do what I'm told.'

Dinah passes me some face cream from her handbag.

'I'm going to be a very obedient plumber. You'll just have to be careful not to abuse your power.' I rub cream into my face. 'I think the confusing thing's been, you're always right, but often not for the reasons you claim. That's what's caused us problems.'

'I see. So even though I'm in the right, I'm still to blame. Put some more on or it'll sting later,' she says.

I rub more in. 'In fact, my superior arguing skills have almost caused some terrible kinks in our relationship.'

'Give me an example.'

'Do you know what really put me off having kids?'

'There is no more sombre enemy of good art than the pram in the hall.'

I close my eyes.

'Ashamed of yourself?' she asks

'Did I really quote that?'

'Yes. Or is it that maybe you wanted a few years of being married first? Of it just being us?'

'Did I use that one?'

'That was one of your sweeter excuses,' she says.

I sigh. 'I did make quite a few, didn't I?'

Dinah rubs her face to imply I should apply more cream.

'But actually, the real reason was that I thought kids would bore me. I've never told you that. I had no idea how much fun they'd be.'

Dinah shakes her head at me.

'I think it's more about how much time you spend with them. It's like when I used to collect stamps. To start with, collecting stamps seemed boring. I was even a little ashamed of it.'

'No, surely not?' laughs Dinah. 'A boy of 16, collecting stamps. How much more normal can you get at puberty, when your hormones are raging, than collecting tiny pieces of coloured paper?'

I laugh. 'But then you get interested in the different types of printing, the gum – you see the intricacies and the character of each stamp. The world of stamps opens up. My dad couldn't spend that much time with us when we were small. He worked too hard. The world of kids never opened up for him.'

'Unless, of course, you actually were just *really* boring,' says Dinah. 'Like, say, you were a stamp geek.'

I laugh. 'It's weird. You're the same person I first met,' I tell Dinah. 'You seem the same. But I can't relate to how I used to be. When I talk about myself in the past before kids, I feel like I'm sticking up for an old friend. Some old friend I probably wouldn't like much if I met him now for the first time.'

'Come on, Stanley Gibbons, bedtime now.' She stands up.

'Because I'm boring you?'

'Exactly.'

On the way upstairs, we pass the guestbook. I add a comment, pretending to be British pro-golfer Nick Faldo, praising Golf-Buddy, crediting it with helping me win the Open Championship in 1992. 'I had no idea in which direction to aim my golf ball before Peter's arrow helped me out. My game is now back on track and I'm climbing the world rankings. Thank you, Peter. And can I also recommend the delicious plate of charcuterie?'

In bed, we have just a sheet and some scratchy tartan blankets.

'It's cold,' Dinah says. 'We'll have to snuggle.'

She rolls towards me and rubs her cold feet on my leg. 'Hey!'

'What? We're snuggling,' she says.

'You're stealing my heat, you mean.'

She laughs and rubs her freezing foot quickly up and down my leg. I try to push her away. 'How come they're so cold? Weren't you wearing socks down there?'

'No,' she says, doing the same thing again.

'Then that was very silly, but you're not having my heat. I worked hard for it.'

And now both her feet are rubbing up and down my legs like a demented cricket. 'Although I have other ideas, if you really want to get warm,' she says.

'Seen some albumen, have you?'

Dinah laughs. 'Has albumen entered our private vocabulary?' she asks, when she's recovered.

'I think it has. Although you'll have to be gentle with me because of my sunburn. You'll have to treat me like porcelain. In fact,' I say, 'maybe I could get some device to suspend you from the ceiling, a pulley system, to lower you on to my knob.'

'That's awful,' says Dinah, laughing.

I cross my hands over, to pretend I'm tugging at a pulley.

'Especially if I had to go right back up to the ceiling each time,' she says.

'Imagine asking Alison for it in reception. "Alison, I would like to borrow the B&B's sexual pulley system, please."'

CHAPTER 16

'*Combien pour le chien?*' asks Dinah, indicating a dog doll, standing up in a toreador's outfit, with a prayer in Latin to the Virgin Mary written on its wooden plinth.

The woman in the souvenir shop says she'll have to look it up.

'Dogs dressed as matadors have gone through the roof,' I tell Dinah. 'So many are traded, it has its own commodity market. It's like tin or grain.'

We've spent a week in the Midi-Pyrénées, where we've walked to Cirque de Gavarnie, the tallest waterfall in Europe, and taken a cable car to the Pic du Midi, to see the telescope that helped NASA map the surface of the moon for the Apollo missions. In the pink granite city of Toulouse, at the Cité de l'Espace, we crawled through a replica of the Mir Space Station. We've scaled the medieval walls of Carcassonne, hunted for the lost treasure of the Cathars in Montségur and Rennes-le-Château and celebrity-spotted Clive Swift (Richard in BBC sitcom *Keeping Up Appearances*) in the fortress town of Minerve, licking a Cornetto.

We even stumbled, by chance, on the Tour de France in Ayzac-Ost, after we took a wrong turn heading to the Pyrenean Animal Park and ran into a police roadblock. As we got out to see what was going on, seven helicopters whirred overhead and PR girls in cars shaped like Vittel bottles drove past, chucking sweets and fridge magnets and key rings into the crowds lining the road, followed a little while later by the riders themselves.

Though our highlight was still probably the town of Pézenas, where we listened to perhaps the most incongruous soundtrack to a turn-of-the-century fairground carousel ride of all time: Charlie and Phoebe waving innocently to us, while gently rotating on bobbing, prancing horses to the strains of NWA's single 'Fuck tha Police'.

Now we're browsing the tacky souvenir shops down rue de la Grotte in Lourdes, where you can buy almost anything with a picture of Christ, the Virgin Mary or St Bernadette on it. Condiment sets, oven gloves, barometers, key rings, snow-shakers, rosary beads, thimbles, mugs, place mats, teapots and even this magnificent dog doll dressed as a Spanish matador.

The woman returns from the back of the shop. '*Quarante-cinq*,' she says.

'Thank you,' Dinah says. Then, raising her eyebrows at me, 'Forty-five euros!'

'Told you. There's a trading bubble.'

'In dog dolls dressed as matadors?'

'The price will come down.'

'You think I should wait?'

'I'd wait.' I look at the old woman. '*Combien pour le* wooden statue of the Regency man playing a violin beside

St Bernadette?' I ask. She goes to the back of the shop again to check the price.

Earlier, we'd parked beneath the tourist office in a multistorey which had religious arias piped into it. 'It makes you feel we're in the opening segments of *Morse* and are about to be stabbed,' Dinah said. The lifts to street level didn't ding, they donged, like church bells. Outside, the local cinema was showing *The Miracle of Lourdes* and the red lanes we at first mistook for cycle routes are, in fact, wheelchair paths reserved for the disabled who are pulled around Lourdes on special blue canopied chariots by the thousands of white-tunic-wearing helpers who volunteer here.

The Domaine de la Grotte is a sort of annexe to the town. Every approach to it is thronged with souvenir shops, some the size of supermarkets. The Domaine's focus is the grotto where Bernadette Soubirous, a 14-year-old miller's daughter, saw 15 apparitions of the Virgin Mary over the course of several days in 1858. Hungry, suffering from TB and cholera and living in a disused dungeon, she convinced her parish priest and then the rest of the Catholic world that the Virgin Mary had spoken to her and had asked her to found a church in Lourdes. Now there are several, including the 1866 underground crypt, the Basilique du Rosaire et de l'Immaculée Conception, and, newest of all, the underground Basilique St-Pie X, a concrete church with a capacity of 25,000, roughly equal to that of Brighton's new Amex Stadium.

The Grotte de Massabielle, where St Bernadette experienced her visitations, is less of a cave and more of a small rocky overhang by the Gave de Pau River, beneath the Basilica of the Immaculate Conception. It's a 20-minute queue to get in. The opening's stewarded by helpers in red shirts and we file in at walking pace. The atmosphere's funereal yet relaxed. When the kids make a noise, they're not shushed, as they are in museums. Instead, helpers smile at them. There's a pane of toughened glass at the entrance, over the source of the spring, and soon after this, we touch the cave's damp wall with our left hands. It's at this point that you're supposed to make your prayer.

'What did you wish for?' I ask Charlie outside. The smell of crème brûlée fills the air now – it's the votive candles (the *bruloirs*) burning in enormous braziers all around.

'A Lightning McQueen set,' Charlie says. He isn't sure there's such a thing as a Lightning McQueen *set*, but he's a veteran of enough birthdays and Christmases to know that adding the word 'set' vastly increases the scale of a present and its worth.

Nuns beetle about, swallows dart in and out of the trees and brown-robed monks in pairs, like Eric Sykes in *The Plank*, carry vast candles the size of tree trunks over their shoulders.

'Phoebe?'

'Some of the best cheese in the world for my sandwiches.' That's how Phoebe now refers to Roquefort cheese.

'I think we can arrange that one ourselves,' I say. 'Dinah? What was yours?'

'A nice cup of tea,' she says.

'Of course it was.'

In the underground basilica, after our tea stop, there's a service going on. Inside the church, it looks like the interior of the Death Star. The high roof's supported by enormous slanting concrete pillars and the space is truly vast. The first few front rows are full of wheelchair users. Whitecassocked priests walk along the lines of worshippers, offering the sacrament.

'That man's got something dangling from his chair,' says Charlie.

'It's called a drip, Charlie.'

'A drip?'

'If someone is so ill they can't eat, they receive food directly into their body from tubes coming out of bags like that.'

'Can they get treats like crisps down the tube?'

'No.'

'I feel sorry for them,' he says.

La Petite Maison de Bernadette is a religious-themed play area for kids, next to the Domaine's main square. In the first room, there's a polystyrene model of the grotto on a low children's table. Next to it, there's a box of special Lego. There are Lego volunteers in red-and-white uniforms, exactly like the ones outside. There are disabled Lego characters in Lego wheelchairs. There's a Lego basilica and a Playmobil Jesus in a Playmobil manger inside the Playmobil stable with Playmobil wise men, Playmobil sheep, Playmobil camels, Playmobil cows and a Playmobil Angel Gabriel holding a cross. The second room's about craft. On a large table in here, the kids colour in pictures of Mary and St Bernadette being blessed by her parish priest, Peyramale.

Outside here, across the Gave de Pau River, it's quiet and peaceful. We have a picnic on the lawns and I try to explain to Phoebe why, in her words, 'this whole town is all about Jesus'.

'So, over 100 years ago, a little girl called Bernadette was out collecting firewood when she walked inside that cave over there.'

'Bears live in caves,' says Charlie.

'They do, Charlie.'

'And dinosaurs.'

'Yes, they probably did as well. So, anyway, when Bernadette was inside the cave, she had a vision.'

'There was a picture in my animal book of a dinosaur in a cave,' says Charlie.

'Was there?'

'What's a vision?' asks Phoebe.

'It was a massive vermouth with tusks.'

'A mammoth, Charlie. Vermouth's a drink. And a vision is like a daydream, Phoebe.'

'Tusks are made of ivory,' says Charlie.

'They are, Charlie. They are. So, in the cave, Bernadette had a sort of daydream where she saw the Virgin Mary.'

'Jesus's mum?'

'Yeah, and Jesus's mum told Bernadette to build a church here.'

'Really?' says Phoebe.

'That's what some people think.'

'What people?'

'Catholics.'

'Whatolicks?'

'Catholics.'

Phoebe stares at me. 'Daddy?'

'What?'

'Are you joking me?'

'No.'

Phoebe holds out her little finger. 'Pinkie?'

I interlock my little finger with hers. 'Pinkie promise.'

'Double pinkie?' she says. 'Because you can keep your fingers crossed and then the pinkie doesn't count, but if you double pinkie you *have* to tell the truth.'

'Double pinkie.'

'So a little girl told everyone to build a church, a massive whole church, because she'd had a dream about it in a cave and they just did it, like that? Daddy, you have to tell the truth when it's a double pinkie.'

'I am.'

'That is so random, Daddy!'

'I know.'

'That is completely random. Isn't that random, Mummy?'

'I think you have a pretty good grasp of it, Pops,' says Dinah.

'Basically, Phoebe, the Catholic Church is a very old institution, a very powerful one too, and to sustain itself down the years in the face of scientific discoveries, like evolution, it needs, every now and again, for miracles to happen to—'

'Daddy?'

'Yes.'

'Look! When I grit my teeth like this,' she grits her teeth, 'my hairband moves.'

'Oh yes, so it does. So, as I was saying—'

'Mummy, look. When I grit my teeth, my hairband moves.'

I look at Dinah. She laughs. 'Nice try, Daddy. Guys, don't stare. It's rude,' she adds. Two blue chariots have pulled alongside us. In them are two children, aged about eleven and seven. Both have cerebral palsy. They're being pushed by a woman and a man. Seeing us, the older girl rises from her chariot and walks, in a bent-legged way, towards us. Her feet are turned over slightly and her arms are as rigid as tree branches. Her father gets up, wordlessly puts a reassuring arm around her shoulders and steers her back.

Dinah starts to read out from the guidebook about the village of Bugarach, near Couiza, where we're going next.

'It has recently been inundated with New Age travellers who believe that on 21 December 2012, when the Mayan Long Count Calendar ends, so will the world. Esoterics maintain that either a massive solar flare will extinguish us all or the planet Nibiru will collide with Earth, destroying all life. They have deemed Bugarach the safest place to be, as the local mountain is a gateway to alien beings who land their spaceships on a huge interior mountain lake. UFO sightings have encouraged "pilgrims" to believe the extraterrestrials are waiting for the apocalypse, at which time they'll emerge and whisk them to safety. Bugarach Mountain is said to have inspired the science-fiction writer Jules Verne's *Journey to the Centre of the Earth* and Steven Spielberg's movie *Close Encounters of the Third Kind*. Such has been the response, the mayor's brought in police to move along visitors who've been spotted climbing the mountain naked and ringing bells.'

Out of the corner of my eye, I watch the girl with cerebral palsy sit back down heavily in her chariot. Her eyes scan us for a second before she turns intently to the foil-wrapped lunch her father's placed in her lap.

'Daddy, what will the nutters be wearing?' asks Phoebe, as we approach Bugarach. 'How will we recognise them?'

'Good question. Nutters normally have bare feet, guys. That's the first sign. They might be ringing hand-bells as well. And if they're naked, then they're almost definitely nutters.'

'Are we warping their minds?' asks Dinah. 'Lourdes and the alien apocalypse in one day. And I'm not so sure about calling them nutters.'

'What then?'

'There!' exclaims Charlie.

'She's just someone on a bike, Charlie,' says Phoebe.

'She had a hat on,' he says.

'Good try, Charlie. A little more weird than that though.'

'That one?' he asks, a little further along. It's a man walking down the road pushing a wheelbarrow.

'Why?'

'Don't know,' he says.

'You're just pointing at anyone, Charlie,' says Phoebe. 'They've got to be weirdos, haven't they, Dad?'

'Weirdos?' I ask Dinah.

'That's sort of the same as nutters,' she says.

We park next to the sign for Bugarach and take a few pictures of us splaying our fingers like Spock in *Star Trek*. After this, we go for a wander. But not only are there no nutters about, there's nobody at all around. We walk along rue du Pont. It's the middle of the day and everyone's shutters are closed. It's baking hot and humid too. And there's nothing to see. We try rue du Baron, then Grande rue, and half an hour later, the weirdest thing we've found is still the mottled piece of bark from a plane tree shaped like the profile of an elephant that we saw when we got out of the car. That and a half-ripped poster for a spiritual conference in Montpellier. There's nothing in the town apart from a closed library flying the Tricolour, a cemetery and a very ordinary cat asleep on a doorstep that's not even black.

'Where are the weirdos, Daddy?'

'I don't know, sweetheart.'

'You said there'd be weirdos.'

'I thought there would be weirdos. I don't understand it.'

Heading back to the car, I spot something. 'Is that a picture of an alien?' I ask Dinah.

'It's of a fisherman, Ben. It's a sign for a bait shop.'

'What does that say?' I ask of another French sign.

'No crossing at this point.'

'Why is Daddy saying all this?' asks Phoebe.

'Because he wants it to be true,' says Dinah.

At the *Bucks Herald*, I always wrote the weirdo stories. The people who came into reception in ripped clothes claiming to be Jesus or to say they'd been abducted by aliens. I'm drawn to weirdos. Secretly, a little bit of me always half believes them. It's only by meeting weirdos and talking to them and realising they really *are* weirdos that I stop believing what the weirdos have to say.

We're in the car and I'm about to go for one final drive round the foot of the mountain when a dilapidated estate car passes us. The couple in the front have grungy, plaited hair, while the car's back seats have been folded forward and are covered with blankets.

'Bingo.' I put the car in gear.

'Why?' asks Dinah. I'm now following the car back into the village.

'They're obviously sleeping in their car.'

'We've done that,' says Dinah. 'And you did that the other night.'

'That's different. They have matted hair.'

'Oh, well, if they haven't brushed their hair . . .'

'And the woman had a tie-dye headscarf on.'

'Then they must be in a death cult.'

'Trust me, I know my weirdos.'

The estate car heads out of town on the D14. A few miles outside Bugarach, it's clear they're nothing to do with the place. Dinah looks smug and I turn round. But as we're heading back in, I see a little shop with picnic tables outside.

'Aye aye,' I say, as we pull in. Sat outside the shop is a misty-eyed man with wild ginger hair and a shapeless smock. He's talking to a woman in a green, hippy-style, tie-dye dress. On another table, there are two middle-aged women with Celtic sun pendants round their necks.

'Guys!' And, as I point, Phoebe sucks in her breath with excitement.

'Daddy! Look! Charlie! Bare feet. We've found them.'

'Well, we don't really know for sure. But it's a good sign. Let's look for more clues inside.'

'Charlie, we don't know for sure,' repeats Phoebe. 'Because they still have *some* clothes on, haven't they, Dad?'

In the shop, there's a glass counter. Underneath it are various goat's cheeses and loaves of homemade bread and, on the left of this, shelves of jam and rustic-looking honey. I approach the till woman. On shelves behind her are whale song CDs, but also a copy of a book entitled *The Secrets of Bugarach*. I'm about to ask if they sell bottled water when Charlie shouts, 'Look!' He tugs my trousers. Below the till, at his height, is a postcard pinned up for sale. It's of Bugarach Mountain, with a blue alien superimposed on it.

'They're *definitely* weirdos!' says Phoebe.

The barefoot woman and the smock man now follow us into the shop.

'Daddy!' says Phoebe, pointing at them, and I bend down and whisper, 'Don't frighten them. Weirdos are like cats. No sudden movements or they'll scamper away on their hard little feet.'

The till woman is waspishly thin and around 55, with long, beaded auburn hair tied up at the back. When I tell her we're interested in the secrets of the mountain, she smiles.

I do a little laugh. 'We have heard stories of naked people climbing the mountain, but I suppose the village is sick of it.'

'Some people are. Some people are not.' Pulling an enigmatic smile, she looks away at a spot close to a fridge stocked with fruit drinks.

'And which one are you?'

'My daughter, she has seen things,' she says.

'What has she seen?'

'She saw somefing with her camera with . . .' She turns her right hand into what looks like a sock puppet, then opens and closes its mouth rapidly.

'Fast shutter speed?'

'Yes, and when she slow it down . . .'

'What was on it?'

'This thing, it move faster than the 'uman eye, but slow it down and . . .'

'What did it look like?'

'Cigarette. It disappear into the . . .' She waves her arm.

'The mountain?'

'Yes.'

'So do you think aliens live in the mountain? And what about the date, 21 December?'

'The journaliste, he hide things, like a tree in the forest, you know? A bug in the mattress. It is lies. The news. The games on the television. It is about more than this, you understan'?'

'What is it about? What will happen on 21 December?'

'Before,' she says, and smiles knowingly.

'Before?' I ask. 'What will happen before?'

'I am 'ere to serve,' she says.

'I'm sorry. I'm holding your queue up.' I look round at smock man. He smiles.

'They are not here to buy,' she says. 'They are here to listen.'

'Oh, so when you said you serve, you mean . . . you work for the aliens?'

'They own the freehold on the shop,' whispers Dinah.

I cough back a laugh. The woman opens her palms religiously.

'They pay her in goat's cheese and honey,' says Dinah, under her breath.

'So are you a prophet?' I ask. She smiles as if she's been asked this obvious question many times.

'Jules Verne, you know?' she asks, fetching down his book. 'In 'ere, he has a character, Captain Bugarach. Many things like this. Something else. Four year ago, there was a man, he work in Geneva. Very . . .' She straightens an imaginary tie.

'Sensible?'

'Yes, sens-ee-ble. He work 'igh in traffic management.'

'Now we're getting somewhere – there's someone in traffic management on the scene,' whispers Dinah.

'He was excavating under the château near from here. He find a vessel, he say. People say, what is this vessel? He doesn't say. Tomorrow, he say. Tomorrow never come. He go into the caverns.'

She makes the same gesture as a referee signalling no goal.

'He died?'

'He was never seen again. Lot of things. Mitterrand, he fly over the mountain. Mossad. The Germans in the war.'

'You're right. They're weirdos,' whispers Dinah. 'Let's go.'

'And what did they do here?'

Dinah leads the children out.

'Nobody know.'

I thank her and leave the shop too, but as I reach the car, Dinah says, 'The water?'

'Argh!'

I go back in. 'I forgot what I came in for,' I say. The till woman laughs, then everyone else in the shop creepily joins in after she translates for them. 'You have been through the black hole,' she says. 'You have been to another universe. In Bugarach, this 'appen all the time. It is normal. You have been gone a long time in another dimension. You 'ave learnt something.'

'The kids are boiling and thirsty. I've learnt that much.'

She turns back to the hippy women. I overhear her say that she exists in many universes at the same time. One of them buys a copy of the *Secrets* book. I buy my water – 3.40 euros, twice the price than in Lourdes, which was itself already double what it should be. I thank her. The woman ignores me. I thank her again. No response. I'm right in front of her, but she's either annoyed that I haven't bought the 18-euro *Secrets* book or is in another universe temporarily.

'Satisfied?' says Dinah, back at the car.

'Very. Phoebe?' She holds out her hand. I pass her a square of chocolate.

'Charlie?' He does the same.

'Good weirdo-spotting, guys.'

We're staying in a small, beautiful, old stone house near the village of Couiza. There's no garden, but there's a bench outside the front door. The kids are in bed and I'm sat here with Dinah. Beyond the road in front of us, that we've not seen a single car pass by on, after a low wall, there are olive trees and beyond that the land falls away into a valley. There's a folk concert going on at the bottom of it. The skyline's lilac and the music's occasionally interrupted by the rumble of thunder beyond the hills.

'Did you see that poor couple today?' says Dinah. She reaches down for her red wine.

'With the kids with cerebral palsy? I know. I've been thinking about them. They didn't say a word to each other the whole time.'

'Imagine how hard that must be,' says Dinah.

'And that's on a day out. Imagine the home environment.'

'And not one but both kids,' says Dinah. 'You do have to count your lucky stars sometimes.'

The crickets stop chirping and, a few moments later, fork lightning tears open the sky. Thunder rumbles and the crickets resume. It's a Rolling Stones song we can hear, I realise – *You Can't Always Get What You Want*. Someone's playing it beautifully on a mandolin.

'It's lovely here,' Dinah says.

'And this is just the sort of folk I like.'

'What, you don't say!? A tousled, probably very pretty, possibly shoeless woman playing the mandolin with an audience clapping and whooping between spirited songs involving metaphors about landscapes?' she says.

I laugh. 'You do know me quite well.'

We talk about tomorrow – we're heading east towards the Mediterranean – and laugh about the kids, who were talking about aliens and impersonating weirdos at bath time. But we're both still thinking about the family. That example of how things might have gone for us, might still go if we carry on having kids.

'Makes you think,' says Dinah.

'About having the third?'

'Imagine how it might change things.'

'And not just for us.'

'Hard for everyone,' she says. 'And if something went wrong, I'd go through with the pregnancy.'

'Would you?'

'You know I would. And the odds get worse the older you get.'

The concert's still playing when Dinah goes to bed alone. I stay outside for a while, watching the lightning. Every now and again, the sky lights up blue, then returns to pitch-black. I send texts to my brother, sister and to Mary. And on Facebook I find a photo my sister's posted. There's Happy Birthday bunting up in her kitchen and all her family and Mary are sat grinning around the dining-room table. The tag says simply: Takeaway pizza on the way! And it makes me sad. I wish I was with them, waiting for pizza to arrive. Also, for the first time in a while, I have an urge to stand on the other side of the door of this gite and speak to my dad.

'Glad you miss me,' Buster's text reads. 'You're my bungee.'

'And you're my snitch,' I reply. It's what we called each other when we fought as kids.

Dinah comes down a few stairs and cranes her head to look at me, 'Come on! You know I can't settle until you come to bed.'

Even with the shutters closed, we can hear the mandolin.

'It's funny,' Dinah says, in the crook of my arm. 'We worked alongside each other in that study every day at home and we had no idea what each other was thinking. Sometimes I think that isn't very healthy.'

'The proximity?'

'You get blasé,' she says. 'We never go out by ourselves at home.'

'I liked it when we used to have lunch together,' I tell her.

When we first shared a study, we'd sit outside to eat. We laid the table for a while.

'You always had toast and finished too quickly for me,' she says.

'You should have told me when you were halfway through making your mackerel salad, then I could've popped my toast down and come out of the study. I'm actually dreading it a bit. You becoming a teacher.'

'Really?'

'You've been my little work colleague.'

'Don't you get bored of me? I've never got anything to tell you. When I'm a teacher, I'll be able to come back and tell you things and you know what a good gossip I am.'

'That'll be nice.'

The rain starts, lightly at first, then gets much heavier.

'So have we made up our minds about kids?'

'I have,' says Dinah.

'You're right – let's not tempt fate. Can we go through more names for my plumbing van now? It helps me sleep.'

'Wet and Wild,' she says. 'Whatever Floats Your Boat; Bogs, Baths and Basins; Waterfight; Leaks and Tweaks; Ball-cock and Bits . . .'

CHAPTER 17

The ski chalet is all blonde pine. The balcony has rear views to Mont Blanc and overlooks Megève's main square from the front. I shout into the bathroom, 'Better pack jumpers for the kids.'

Dinah emerges. 'I'm still not happy, Ben.'

'Make up your mind when we're there. We have to leave now or we'll miss our slot.'

In the kids' room, I pull out Phoebe's thumb. She's so shocked and sleepy, it comes out leaving the round mouth that's been wrapped around it still perfectly in place.

It's three weeks since the Pyrenees and we're in mountain country again, the Alps now. We've eaten sandwiches at the railway station in Perpignan that Salvador Dalí considered the centre of the known universe. In Narbonne, we attended a liberation day festival, where Charlie was invited on stage to chase geese down a slide for a reason that eluded us.

We zigzagged east along the Mediterranean coast, spending days at water parks and on beaches, before we cut up north into Clermont-Ferrand, through the Auvergne region and into the bellybutton of France. Here, we walked inside the crater of the Strombolian volcano Lemptégy, where instead of exciting visitors about the awesome power of nature and fragility of our world, we were shown a video about *pouzzolane* – a porous volcanic rock useful in road surfacing.

We had a swordfight in the Roman amphitheatre of Arles and yacht-spotted in Antibes. We've been on Picasso walks, van Gogh trails and seen the wild horses of the Camargue. We sang 'Sur le Pont d'Avignon' on the Pont d'Avignon, rode the bubble cable car in Grenoble and swam in rivers at Bize-Minervois and Cessenon-sur-Orb. We've notched up our fiftieth château, our fourteenth Petit Train, and sneaked on to our seventh crazy golf course. We've been to so many aquariums, I'm on first-name terms with virtually every giant turtle in France. Claude, Kiki, Pierre, Yvette, Mo, Ghislaine. And I've eaten so much steak, more than 90 per cent of my French vocabulary now revolves around ways beef can be prepared and referred to. Dinah's filed four pieces for the *Telegraph*, we've now driven 8,000 miles, and France must finally be rubbing off on the kids because the other day Phoebe refused to eat her breakfast sausages until the waiter fetched Dijon mustard.

The squat toilet is pleasingly almost a thing of the past, it would seem, as I can also report that the other day we encountered our very first one of the trip. Charlie was not impressed.

'Where's the toilet?' he asked.

'That *is* the toilet.'

'What do I sit on?'

'You squat.'

He looked at me.

'I know, it's disgusting, but it's what they do.'

He shook his head. We left.

'I don't blame you,' I said. 'Go with Mummy to the ladies'.'

He nodded, still looking shocked.

It's a ten-minute drive to the altiport outside Megève. It's very small, with five or six red-and-white propeller-driven planes on the tarmac in front of two grey hangers, set against a backdrop of pine trees and, beyond them, mountains.

We park and Phoebe says, 'Is that the surprise? Are we going on a plane?'

I look at Dinah. 'Maybe,' I say. 'It's up to Mummy.'

'Let me watch for a while,' she says. 'I need to assess.'

'*Yessss!*' says Charlie, punching the air. 'We're going on a plane!'

'Maybe,' I repeat. 'Maybe, Charlie.'

There's one wooden chalet building. Most of it's given over to a café with a decked terrace. The rest is a small booking office. I give our names at the counter. The flight's at 9.30 a.m. We're given a map of the route, with the names of various glaciers on it. Sat outside the café, drinking tea, we watch the small planes taking off and landing. A family of four crosses the tarmac. Their kids aren't much older than ours. The father carries his son across the runway on his shoulders. They take off and immediately the next plane is readied.

'They go all the time – safe as houses,' I say.

'Perhaps they're overstretched,' says Dinah.

Men in overalls fiddle with the propeller of the next plane, preparing it.

'Lots of safety checks,' I say. 'That's good.'

'But what do they think might be wrong?' asks Dinah.

When this plane's airborne, the same men drag another out from the hangar.

'Look how light it is,' I say to the kids. 'One man can pull it along.'

'Flimsy,' Dinah says.

The family we saw take off when we arrived an hour ago now lands. We watch their plane taxi to a stop. They head for the booking hall. When they pass us, Dinah asks how it was. The father nods his approval.

'And the children?'

'OK,' he says, nodding again.

Our pilot has slicked-back black hair, pointed brown shoes and a pink polo shirt. We climb into the plane across its wing. The kids sit in the back, either side of Dinah. The pilot steers me into a seat next to him. We put headphones on, he starts the propeller and talks to the air control centre. A few seconds later, the engine grows louder and we're moving. It's a short, sloping runway, and soon we're in the air and clearing the trees. We rise over the green quilted hills and head towards Vallée Blanche. And when I turn round, Charlie's staring down in amazement, Phoebe's eating a Dora the Explorer biscuit and Dinah's grimly determined, licking her dry lips over and over again, like a lizard.

At 3,000 feet, I can see Mont Blanc through the blur of the propeller. The engine doesn't sound as if it has any more horsepower than a lawnmower. And it's like sitting on a feather – any gust of wind and we're swept left or right.

It's fine until the Green Needle, a massive shard of snow-covered rock. I'm no aviation expert, but one of the givens, I'd have thought, is to avoid the mountains. I don't know whether he's showing off, trying to scare us, or if it must be done this way, but the pilot heads straight for this column of rock. On and on we fly, closer and closer to it. I've seen *The Dam Busters* enough times to know what happens if a pilot doesn't pull back on the throttle quickly enough, and it reaches a point where I'm looking at him and actually wondering if something happened with his girlfriend the night before. When we're right on top of it, so I can pick out individual rocks, I ask, as calmly as I can, 'Are you flying above it?' The pilot doesn't reply. I look back at my family. Dinah's staring blindly at me, her face expressionless with fear. Phoebe's thumb's in her mouth and Charlie's gripping Dinah's underarm tightly. Then, suddenly, very sharply, we bank right.

'Too hard to fly over,' the pilot says, and we turn, turn, turn, turn. When we straighten up, we're in a large basin. It's like a giant arena. Enormous glaciers pour down the sides of the jagged slopes. But I can only relax for a moment because now we hit turbulence. It's like the way you can blow a soap bubble very far with a tiny puff of breath. The pilot keeps correcting the nose as we veer dramatically off course. Then, without warning, we drop 15 feet. My heart's in my mouth. The same thing happens again, except this time, we fall further. 'Everything alright?' I ask, and the pilot's silence speaks volumes. We're buffeted like a ping pong ball round the basin for another five minutes. To calm Charlie, Dinah reads snippets from our Disneyland guidebook. They start to sound like prayers.

'Alice's Curious Labyrinth is a maze of well-manicured hedges complemented by fountains and animatronic characters from the famous story, where children attempt to reach the Queen of Heart's castle.'

We drop another 20 feet.

'Quite often, large queues are the result of the long loading and unloading times and because of issues with traffic-engineering. This is the case at Dumbo the Flying Elephant.'

Now we drop 30 feet.

'It's funny,' says Phoebe. 'Because this is *like* a Disneyland ride.'

'That's right, Phoebe,' I say, looking at Dinah's green face. 'It's like being at a funfair.'

And Dinah passes the book to me and dry burps as I continue with the catechism.

'Woody's Roundup Village is basically a character-greeting zone incorporated within a replica of a Wild West homestead. Woody and Jessie from *Toy Story* are often on hand to meet visitors.'

Our first approach is cancelled. We land successfully on the second. On the ground, it's no surprise to learn that the rest of today's flights have been cancelled because of the wind. Dinah waits until we reach the car before she says, 'I am never letting you persuade me to do anything *ever* again.'

To which Phoebe adds: 'It was great. It was *so* bouncy.'

Charlie has the last word. 'Mummy,' he says, plaintively, as I start the engine, 'I feel a bit . . .' and he's sick in his lap.

To make it up to the kids, we take them on a horse and carriage ride. It leaves from the town's main square. The driver has a face the colour of rare steak, and the kids shout encouragement to Polka, our horse, when she goes up hills. We're driven out of Megève, past larger and larger chalets. Phoebe lies on the sheepskin-covered seat opposite us in the rear, pretending to be a princess waving to her subjects, while I'm soon standing up and dropping a fully recovered Charlie, to mimic the turbulence he now finds funny.

The summer luge is rained off, so after lunch we go to the Soviet-sounding Le Palais des Sports et des Congrès de Megève. It's an Olympic-sized pool with great mountain views and a 70-foot water slide. The daily swim routine has massively brought on the kids' abilities. Phoebe can now dive to the bottom of the pool, swim front crawl with her head under the water and do a beautiful clockwork backstroke. Today it's Charlie's turn. Each time we've swum, we've removed a float from his swimsuit. Today he's down to his last two. What he likes is to hang on to the pool side and bob up and down in the water before thrusting himself to the bottom, like a human depth charge. I try to persuade him to swim a width of breast-stroke.

'Come on, Charlie!'

He takes a huge, exaggerated lungful of air and does another depth charge.

'What about for Mummy?'

Another depth charge.

'Charlie, we'll have a swordfight later.'

Phoebe's beside him, doing the same thing in her pink goggles. They're pretending, as they often do, that we're not there.

'Charlie, you can have half my day's chocolate ration!'

They both do another depth charge.

'Charlie, half my chocolate allowance. Just to swim towards me.'

''K,' he says, and he's off, doing doggy paddle.

'Breaststroke,' I shout and he changes to breaststroke – tiny, anaemic strokes that he completes very quickly, panicked that he might sink, which are reminiscent of Tommy Cooper doing his 'Just Like That' action. Despite this, and no leg movement, he progresses. As he draws closer to me, I move backwards.

'Stand still!' he shouts.

'I'm not moving,' I say, smiling.

His neck's high out of the water, like he's a poodle.

'Stand still,' he says, more angrily.

Dinah's encouraging him. 'Come on, Charlie! That's amazing.'

When he's almost there, I move out of the way, so he can see the other side of the pool.

'See! You're nearly there. Half my chocolate ration, Charlie.'

His tongue sticks out with determination. He reaches for the side.

'Well done, Charlie!'

Dinah swims towards him. 'Charlie, did you just swim a width?' she says.

I hold him up out of the water. He smiles and punches the air.

'And guess how many floats you've got on?'

'Let me see.' He feels round his costume. His voice becomes the baby one he uses when the focus of attention is on him. 'Two?' he says.

'None,' I say. 'I took the last two out when you weren't watching.'

'None,' he repeats.

'You can swim, my son.'

'I can swiiim,' he shouts. Then, in a quieter voice, 'Can I have my choccy now?'

I smile at Dinah. 'No more drowning nightmares.'

On the way back to the chalet, we stop for a communal haircut at Sympa'tif on Route Nationale. We've been away so long now, several things have happened. Our fringes have grown so long, we all look like that bloke out of A Flock of Seagulls. Dinah dreams in French, Charlie's developed a Gallic shrug for when I ask him where his shoes are, and I add the word 'hor' to the start of sentences whenever I speak to a French person. ('Hor, medium-rare, please.' 'Hor, do you have Béarnaise sauce?' 'Hor, *je ne parle pas Français*. But I do want *frites*.')

Even my iPhone's been affected. It keeps misfiling apps under new and confusing categories. 'It's turning French,' Dinah reckons. 'It's putting everything into dossiers. It's undermining you with needless bureaucracy.'

'Daddy!' says Phoebe, glancing over at me every now and again from the booster seat balanced on top of the barber's reclining chair she's in, so she can see herself in the mirror. 'Not *too* much.' Weirdly, but sweetly too, Phoebe hates it when I have a haircut. All four of us are sat in a line, being worked on simultaneously with scissors, when Jake's text bleeps in.

He's sorry he can't use my Pamplona idea on the website, but is wondering about something else. He's met a woman called Jennifer Barclay who works at a small travel publisher based in Chichester. He told her about our journey around England for *Britain with Your Family* and she wants to meet for a chat about possibly commissioning a travelogue about writing that guidebook. I give my phone to Phoebe, who passes it to Dinah. Dinah smiles as she hands it back along the chain.

'And so the roller coaster continues . . .' she says.

After we've fed and bathed the kids, I move the small table and chairs from the dark kitchenette area into the main body of the living room, beneath the window that overlooks the road into Megève. The table's round and heavy, and Dinah watches as I bear-hug it across the room.

'What do you think?' I ask.

'I don't know why we never thought of it ourselves.'

'I know. All those crap ideas, and this one was staring me in the face.'

I pour us some wine.

'This reminds me of the flat a bit,' she says. Before and immediately following Phoebe's birth, soon after we'd moved into our flat in Brighton, because we could no longer go out, it became a custom to pretend instead that we were *already* out. We ate off a little square pine Ikea table under the sash window that overlooked Lansdowne Square and Hove Lawns. I'd cook a curry, pour us wine and make sure Dinah couldn't see the TV, or the rest of the messy flat, by hemming us in with large pot plants I'd skid across the laminate floor to seal us in. We'd make out we were in a restaurant called Number 8, the number of our flat block. Phoebe would be next door, asleep in a Moses basket. We'd worry about cot rub, talk about Dinah's sore nipples, and the more we drank, the more we'd marvel about how magical the world suddenly felt now that we'd added someone to it.

'I think that's the happiest I've ever been.'

'Me too,' she says. 'And I loved that flat too. The sea breeze through the sash window which used to rock the Chinese lantern.'

'I just remember we played Scrabble the whole time.'

'It was harder work than that,' she says.

'It was like a static buzz around my head the whole time. I've never felt more contented. I know there were your breastfeeding troubles, but apart from the cracked nipples . . .'

Dinah smiles. 'And all those little arguments about what was wrong with Phoebe – she's too hot, too cold. She's tired, she's hungry. What was her nickname?'

'Mrs Hoskins.'

'That's right,' she says.

It was Mrs Hoskins because, suddenly, we had this baby to look after, whom we felt incapable of caring for properly, and somehow giving her the name of a demanding matriarch hid this inadequacy. 'Mrs Hoskins wants her bath.' 'Mrs Hoskins, if you will bang your head on your basket it *will* hurt.' 'Mrs Hoskins has a touch of wind. Shall I see to her?'

There's an eyebrow of cloud illuminated by the full moon. Occasional planes traverse the blue-black sky. And, as we go through the various nicknames the kids have had down the years, it becomes apparent that we're not only remembering how idyllic life was after Phoebe was born, we're also mourning the fact that it will never be like this again. But at the same time, it feels right too – like we've caught up with each other at last.

For the first time since home, we can't think of anything to debate, so in the end we watch English telly – Mary Beard on BBC Two, discussing life in Pompeii, telling us that, contrary to popular myth, slaves led a good life. We sit on the sofa afterwards, joking about what a slave could do for us.

'Right now he'd be finding my phone charger.'

'He'd come in with it after an hour of scouring the chalet,' Dinah says.

'Well done, Tiberius,' I say. 'You may go to bed now.'

'After you've washed up,' says Dinah.

'And vacuumed the car.'

'He'd be in his early 30s,' she says.

'And very loyal.'

'With a fearful respect for us,' Dinah adds.

'And a soft spot for the kids.'

'And he'd boast about our sense of justice to other slaves he bumped into in Tesco doing our weekly shop,' she says.

'Tiberius, what do you dream of?' I say.

'Only serving you, master,' says Dinah.

'Come, come Tiberius,' I say, 'we know each other better than that. How many years Tiberius?'

'Ten, master,' says Dinah.

'And in recognition of that loyal service, I have something for you, Tiberius. Something every man wants. Tiberius, look at me, Tiberius! That's better. But first, tell me what it is you want. I want to hear you say it.'

'My freedom, master,' says Dinah.

'Freedom! Oh! Right . . . Well, erm, we've bought you a new potato peeler that shaves spuds much, much quicker.'

'Thank you, master.'

'You sound disappointed, Tiberius.'

'No, master,' says Dinah.

'That will help inordinately when we have sausages and mash.'

'Thank you, master.'

'Get a spud out of the veg tray and I'll show you.'

Dinah laughs. 'I still have the most fun with you,' she says.

'And me.'

We change for bed and, under the covers, Dinah says, 'We're going to be busy when we get back.'

'I know. Are you worried?'

'A bit,' she says.

She's forgotten the name of her mentor and talks about the GTP course leader she doesn't really like.

'It will be great for you. You'll be learning new things. I'm quite jealous in fact.'

'But what if I'm no good?'

'You quit and I lure you back into the study.'

'And there'll be work in the evenings and weekends sometimes. The onus of childcare will be back on you,' says Dinah. 'Pick-ups and drop-offs. I'll have to teach you how to cook something other than fish fingers.'

'I'm looking forward to it.'

'And what if the travel book comes off?'

'I'll work it around you and the kids.'

'You are quite devoted to me, aren't you?'

'I told you I was.'

'Good. I'm glad you said that.' And Dinah holds up her empty water glass, waggles it and points to the door. I take it from her and fling back the covers.

'And, Tiberius, bring me in my book? It's on the coffee table.'

'Yes, master.'

CHAPTER 18

The first time I came to Paris, I was 19. It was the end of an InterRail holiday and I was visiting my girlfriend, Laura, who was studying French at Manchester University and spending her summer in the city. Laura was my first love and I fell for her during a Spandau Ballet slow dance at a village hall disco in Old Amersham. She had a face so white it looked plastic, wore multicoloured laces in her shoes and dyed her hair pink. She laughed at my jokes, a great, rumbling laugh that sounded like a tide rolling in, and she had pale, empty blue eyes that were like looking through a keyhole into an empty room. She refused to have sex out of wedlock, as she was a born-again Christian, although after lengthy dialectical arguments where I'd invoke Bertrand Russell and deconstruct the whole foundation of Western theology, she sometimes wanked me off.

I was studying at Sheffield University and I'd take the National Express coach across the Pennines to see her every weekend and join her in the extramural activities my presence never encouraged her to abandon – canoeing in the Manchester Ship Canal with her outdoorsy friends, vegan evenings with her VegSoc pals. I even accompanied her on a Methodist retreat to Bangor in Wales.

When she announced she was spending the first summer of university in Paris, I was crestfallen, convinced she'd run off with some Gauloise-smoking Frenchman. My visit to the city that summer was an attempt to forestall this. I romantically surprised her by wrapping myself up in a large Samsung cardboard box I'd found in a skip outside the Crédit Lyonnais office across the road from her apartment block in the 8th arrondissement. The porter, whom I'd convinced to apply the last length of duct tape, rang her doorbell, at which point I leapt up, clutching a bunch of flowers. She wasn't that thrilled to see me and we exchanged parting love gifts outside Notre Dame Cathedral a few days later. I gave her a Style Council album and a silver necklace with a 'B for Ben' pendant on it. She handed me a neatly wrapped package that contained a bottle of Kouros scent for men by Yves St Laurent. She'd never given me a present or a card before, as she thought Christmas and birthdays were 'commercial bullshit'. It was a heavy bottle, so it wasn't until I unscrewed the lid that I discovered it was empty. Much like when she used to ring me up in my halls in the first term and say, 'I'm down at the porter's lodge. I've come over to surprise you . . . Kidding! I'm still in Manchester, having a tofu bhuna with Clive and Andy,' it was one of her 'jokes'.

She finished with me shortly after my return to England, and I didn't hear from her again for two years, when she rang up for a chat just before my finals, and told me, while laughing (I think expecting me to now find it funny too), that throughout our time together, she'd been getting off with half the students in her year and every male in VegSoc.

The kids have been looking out for the Eiffel Tower while I've been telling Dinah this story.

'There, Daddy!'

'No, that's a pylon.'

'Daddy!'

'What?'

'The Eiffel Tower! Look!'

'Another pylon, Charlie.'

'Daddy, look! LOOK! There it is!'

'Guess what?'

'Pylon?'

Phoebe laughs.

'Correct.'

It's one road all the way into central Paris. We keep the Seine to our left and, as we get closer to the centre, the industrial barges loaded with sand and tyres are replaced with glass-roofed cruise ships. Then the Haussmann buildings start. The bridges become ornate, the traffic thickens. And, suddenly, there it is – the top of the Eiffel Tower.

'Wow!' says Charlie.

'It's massive!' says Phoebe.

A mile further in, we're right beside it.

'This would make the perfect picture.'

'No!' says Dinah.

'It sums up the whole trip. The car right in front of the Eiffel Tower!'

'Please don't get out and take a picture. I'm asking you, as your wife you are devoted to.'

The lights turn red. We stop. I take my seatbelt off.

'I'll be one second.'

'Ben!'

I open the car door.

'BEN!'

I jump out and, leaving the engine running, I run round the car to a traffic island.

Dinah winds down her window. 'You total shit! The lights are going to change now.'

I remove the camera from its case. The lights turn green.

'Wind the back window down, so I can see Charlie and Phoebe.'

Dinah's hooted from behind. A man swerves round and shouts into the passenger window at Dinah.

'Just take it!' she shouts.

'Smile, everyone.'

Dinah snaps on a smile. Phoebe grins and Charlie leans across from his seat, so I can see him too. But I don't crouch down far enough, so I clip off the top of the Eiffel Tower.

'Sorry. One more.'

'No! You're being a knob.'

More cars jerk around the Passat and Dinah can't stand it any longer. She shuffles across into the driver's seat and pulls away. I run alongside the car. I open the door, jump into the moving vehicle and put up a hand for her to give me five, but Dinah's already concentrating too hard to see it. Her face is pressed up against the windscreen. She's leaning forward, perched on the edge of the seat, with a perfectly straight back, like she's Princess Anne riding a dressage horse.

'You do realise this is my worst nightmare?' she says, her eyes not leaving the road for a moment.

'It's a straight road – you'll be fine. It's only five minutes, then we're there.'

'Love, I have not driven in France the whole time we've been here. And now I'm driving in *central Paris*.'

And although the road's been straight for several miles, it now forks right. The traffic layout changes, we shimmy through a square and, before we know it, we're on the rumbling cobblestones of the place de la Concorde.

'BEN!' barks Dinah. 'What have you done?'

Motorbikes zip in and out of gaps in the traffic. Horns sound around us.

'Just follow the sat nav. You're doing fine.'

The kids now start swordfighting in the back.

'Tell them!' orders Dinah.

'Guys, Mummy's driving through a scary city centre with no experience of ever driving on the right. Please put those down.'

The sat nav now indicates a sharp right in 200 metres.

'You need to go right almost immediately, love.'

'Right!'

To go right Dinah must cross five lanes of traffic.

'I know, it's given you very little warning.'

'It's given me *no* warning. What's wrong with it?'

'It's panicking. It always does in cities.'

'It's not the only one. I am *not* changing lanes, Ben.'

Then things get worse. I see it ahead of us, marked on the sat nav screen: the Arc de Triomphe. I've read horrific stories about this famous roundabout, and my Adam's apple feels dry at the prospect of Dinah driving round it. Apparently, 50 per cent of all drivers' insurance claims are invalid on the Arc de Triomphe because it's so dangerous. Accidents happen so frequently and it's so difficult to determine blame that most insurance companies specifically exclude the roundabout on policies. And these are normal drivers. *French* drivers, who drive on the right every day. These drivers are not my wife.

Dinah edges forward. 'Love,' I say, pointing at the sat nav screen, 'just to warn you.'

'What?' she says to the windscreen, and it's like slowly approaching the edge of a giant waterfall in a flimsy raft, as we inch towards the precipice.

'That's the Arc de Triomphe.'

'So?'

'Do you know what that is?'

'It's a monument?'

'Yes,' I tell her. 'It's just a monument. It's a monument Napoleon had built. Think of it as that.' I haven't the heart to tell my wife, who's scared of merging on motorways, who won't even drive in England if she thinks there's one, that she's about to merge on to the most dangerous round-about in Western Europe, maybe the world. As we draw nearer, it reminds me of that moment on nature docu-mentaries when an enormous herd of frightened, migrating cattle must cross a deep, fast-flowing river.

At the junction, some cars leap into the chaos, others hang back. Dinah simply yanks on the handbrake. Survey-ing the chaos before her eyes, she holds her heart with her right hand and looks at me with the sort of fear in her eyes I last saw at 3 a.m. in the Royal Sussex Hospital, after she was told she was too far gone for an epidural and that the only thing left to do was push.

She's beeped from behind. A car swerves round us, and

Dinah stares at me in disbelief. Ten lanes of traffic are circulating the monument, though to call them lanes is something of an exaggeration because there *are* no lanes. In fact, there are no road markings at all. It's a free-for-all. To add to the jumble of danger, there are also 12 junctions – 12 junctions of heavy traffic feeding into this roundabout with *no* road markings. And what's more, 12 junctions of traffic that all have priority on the right. If you were to design a way of killing the maximum number of people by road, this is close to what you'd come up with. Horns sound, tyres screech, people shout. But now my ears are numb to the sounds outside our car. The world's shrunk. All I'm aware of is the flicking sound of Dinah's hair as she twists it with her right hand round her little finger and releases it, time and time again, in a nervous tic.

'I know it looks dangerous, but you have priority. They *will* get out of your way.'

Two more cars twist past. Dinah breathes in, then out, and finally releases the handbrake. She pulls out slowly. A Citroën swerves out of our way. A Mondeo does an emergency stop. Even the kids are quiet now. In a similar way to how fish in a giant shoal suddenly and beautifully change direction to avoid an obstacle, a gap opens in the traffic and we're in the current. We're swept round the monument and complete two full circuits before either of us says a word.

At the start of the third rotation, I say, 'Love, we need to leave this roundabout.'

'I am aware of that,' she says to the windscreen.

'I'm going to tell you when to move right. We'll do one lane at a time. One lane per revolution of the roundabout. Do you want to chant something?'

My wife chants when she's nervous.

'Don't take the piss out of me.'

'I'm not. Do you want to chant something?'

'Concentrate, Dinah. Concentrate, Dinah,' she starts to say.

'Good. OK, wait for it. Wait for it. Now *go*!'

She jerks into the next lane.

'Concentrate, Dinah, concentrate,' she says.

'Well done. By the way, that bus is stopping.'

'I can see.'

'And that guy's pulling out.'

'I know.'

'Ready to go again?'

She nods. 'Concentrate, Dinah. Concentrate. One thing,' she says to the windscreen.

'What?'

'This time, don't put your arms in front of your face.'

'OK.'

'It affects my confidence,' she says.

'I'm sorry.'

Dinah's phone rings. I answer it. It's her mum. 'Can she call you back, Marian? She's driving round the Arc de Triomphe.' There's a pause. I hear her mum shout, 'Oh my God!' and the phone goes dead. I check the road again. 'OK, go now! Go! Then exit the roundabout straightaway. GO!'

Dinah changes lane. The junction approaches. Dinah's so keen not to miss it, she goes early. We mount the kerb and knock over a keep right sign, but we make it. We're off the roundabout. There are two left turns then another right and we're in front of the Opera House. And there it is – the Intercontinental Paris Le Grand.

'You've done it! This is it.'

Dinah double-parks outside the hotel and slumps over the wheel. I take my seatbelt off and drape myself around her.

'Well done, love! WELL DONE! I'll get the bags and kids out, you get the porter.'

'Give me a second,' she says.

A liveried porter arrives with a gold luggage trolley. I start unpacking the boot.

'Let's see the picture then,' Dinah says, coming round to help.

'Ah.'

'What?'

'I deleted it.'

'You what?'

'It was a bit crap. I cut the top of the tower off.'

Dinah slaps me round the back of the head.

At the main reception, something strange yet wonderful happens. Dinah, who's been commissioned to write about the hotel for another national newspaper, is suddenly engulfed by floor managers. In fact, it's like Lady Gaga just walked in. At least four of them fuss around her. The porter wants our keys, to park the car. Our room's not ready, but in the meantime, a manager would like to offer us a complimentary glass of Champagne, or how about wine in the winter gardens? Yet another manager wants to know how old the children are, so the presents in our suite can be made age-appropriate. A female guest-relations manager tells us a babysitter's arranged for tonight and asks that we let the front desk know what time we'd like her to come. We're handed maps of Paris and a glossy bag of gifts, including two Rubik's cubes whose sides are adorned with night-time views of the hotel.

We walk through the thick-carpeted lobby into the glass-domed winter gardens, which are full of exotic plants, wicker chairs and rich-looking Arabs. There's a clench-jawed guy with pale blue eyes, designer stubble and a cap and scarf who we recognise from a Brit-flick but can't place.

We're sipping Chablis, while the kids are having hot chocolate from silver teapots, when Dinah remembers: 'Shit!'

'What?'

'The glove box!'

Valerie, the media attaché, comes to deliver the latest news on our room.

'We have a little problem with the car,' I tell her. 'Could I explain it to you?'

'Of course,' she smiles.

'The glove box is broken. Do you understand glove box?'

'Yes.'

'It won't shut. And the trouble is, it has an interior light. Do you understand?'

'Yes.'

'Sorry, your English is wonderful. It's just that it's important. It means that if the glove box is not propped shut with the tea flask, the car battery goes flat. And we have to get away early tomorrow for Disneyland. The tea flask is in the footwell.'

'No problem.' She smiles again. 'I will have a word with the concierge,' she says, dipping her head.

'And please,' says Dinah, butting in, 'can I apologise for the cheese?'

Valerie looks at Dinah quizzically. 'The cheese?'

'My husband,' Dinah looks at me, 'bought a large wheel of Comté cheese in Les Rousses and . . .' She grips her nose with her thumb and forefinger.

Valerie smiles politely. 'No problem', and she turns to go.

'Oh, and when you open the boot, the hinges have rusted away and don't work,' I tell her. 'You have to prop it open with a golf putter. If you don't, it slams shut on your head.' I show her the bruise I have from this happening to me. 'The golf putters are also in the boot. They're underneath the cheese.'

Valerie's smile flickers, but it's still there.

'And thank you for the wine and hot chocolate,' says Dinah.

'And do you have WiFi?' I ask.

'I am coming back with the code now,' she says, sweeping away from us.

'And could we have a cloth?' I show her where the kids have spilt hot chocolate on the table.

A few minutes later, the table's cleaned and more hot chocolate and a plate of olives arrives, along with a platter of petits fours on a silver salver. I open three emails when Valerie returns with the code. Two of them are pictures of babies who've just been born. My university friend Dave's baby, Tom; my stepmum's nephew Matt's baby, Charlie. I show them to Dinah. We coo. They're all bent limbs and mottled, red skin and fleece blankets. They're the sort of pictures I dreaded receiving before we had kids, but that now turn me to slush. The third email's from the Parisian PR Stephane, who's planning to eat with us at lunch *and* dinner. It's a blow. We'd hoped to use the babysitter to have a romantic meal out.

Our room's still not ready when we've finished the wine, so we decide to go straight out. The Louvre is only a ten-minute walk away, down Avenue de l'Opéra. The pavements are lined with wicker chairs that have those distinctive red covers I remember from France as a child. Black-and-white-suited waiters buzz around. The women all seem to wear big sunglasses and expensive gold-strapped handbags over their slim, tanned shoulders. The men carry metrosexual satchels.

'Well, here we are in Paris,' I say, putting my arm around Dinah.

'Look at these buildings!' she says.

On all sides, we're surrounded by ornate Haussmann buildings. The classical Opera House is at one end of the street, the Louvre Palace at the other.

'I know. As good as any mountain view.'

We've spent the last two weeks in small French towns and villages, but it's almost reassuring to hear the blare of traffic again. After Megève, we drove north, via the ice caves of Chamonix. I accidentally bought the huge wheel of Comté at Europe's largest cheese cellar, in Les Rousses. I thought I was buying five ounces. It turns out it was actually five kilos. At the Musée de la Lunette in Morez, we tried on Marie de Medici's spyglasses. In Dole, we saw the home of Louis Pasteur, and we absorbed more information than we ever wanted to know about condiments at the Royal Saltworks at Arc-et-Senans.

Thoughts of home dominate now. Dinah's been trying to sort out a student for the attic room for when we're back. On the outskirts of Amiens, we bought the last of Charlie's school uniform in a huge hypermarket. On the same day, Dinah splashed out on a new business suit for her teacher-training. Phoebe, meanwhile, has been asking about her friends for the first time, and in Reims yesterday, Charlie, finally weary of chocolate cereal, had a craving for Scottish porridge oats.

'Well, who'd have thought it back then,' says Dinah, in the courtyard outside the Louvre. We came to Paris once before. There's a photo on the wall at home of us standing right where we are now. In it, Dinah's pregnant with Phoebe. We were about to move to Brighton, living at my sister's in St Albans, waiting for the flat to go through. I was spending my time trying to buy washing machines and fridges on eBay, while Dinah was working at *Business Traveller* magazine in London. Two weeks before exchange, the vendor demanded another £5,000. The move almost fell through. Dinah was under stress. It wasn't good for the baby. So she took a week off and we caught the Eurostar to Paris. It was our last holiday before we had the kids.

A tour bus pulls in behind us. The sun beats down, glinting off the glass pyramid, and I look across at the children, now playing in the sunshine, and it rears up at me, that sense of time rushing on.

'It makes me want to . . .' and Dinah's chin wobbles.

It's very unexpected. 'Oh, love, you alright?' I hold her shoulder. 'Stop it! You're making me want to go now.'

'Sorry,' she says. A man's photographing the Louvre in front of us.

'Careful, you'll be crying in his photo.'

Dinah laughs. We sit down in the courtyard.

'Is it because we made it here in one piece?'

'It's come to an end so quickly,' she says. We sail from Caen to Portsmouth the day after tomorrow. Dinah dries her eyes on her sleeve. I pull her towards me.

'The other day, I was on the phone to my mum, telling her I was homesick. I was counting the days down. I wanted to be back in my kitchen, padding about. Now I don't want to go home.'

'Neither do I. It's been up and down, but overall . . .'

'It's been great,' she says, putting her head on my shoulder. 'A real adventure.'

The kids are leaning on bollards in front of us, drawing pictures of French aristocrats being guillotined.

'I also think it's being here,' says Dinah. She looks around the square.

'I know what you mean.'

'Last time we were here, we had no idea what was going to happen,' she says. 'How our lives were going to change. Now look at them! I think that's why I'm so delighted whenever a baby's born.'

'Matt and Dave's pictures?'

She nods.

'Because you know how great it is.'

'Yeah.'

Phoebe holds up her picture of Louis XVI. She tells us he's crying because he can't have a filled roll. At his trial, the insufferable glutton was more upset that he couldn't eat anything than he was about the verdict. It was something we read to her earlier.

'Very good, Pops.'

'He's thinking about chicken nuggets,' she says, turning back to her picture.

'These have been the best eight years of my life,' says Dinah.

'Mine too, although I also enjoyed it when it was just us. Do you remember The Authorities?'

276

She laughs.

We were so broke when we came here last time, we spent less than £100 the entire week. There was a running joke that 'The Authorities' were always trying to trick us into paying over the odds for things. When we baulked at buying bottled water, or passed an expensive restaurant to find a much cheaper one, we'd tell each other, 'The Authorities will be furious. They thought they had us there.' If we paid for anything, 'They're rubbing their hands together,' Dinah would say. We walked everywhere, rather than take the Metro, to save on fares.

'Remember my plates of meat,' says Dinah. That's how she described her feet the whole time.

'And all those plate stops,' I say. Every 200 metres, Dinah would have to sit down, to rest her plates of meat.

'Not much has changed,' says Dinah. She has her inferior Birkies off and is now rubbing her feet, while I hunt in my bumbag for the entrance tickets.

Phoebe comes up. 'What's the special thing about the moaning woman again?'

'The *Mona Lisa*?'

'Yes.'

'Her smile.'

'And why is she smiling, Daddy?'

'Some people say she's smiling because the artist, Leonardo da Vinci, actually painted himself as a woman, and that he's laughing at us because of this joke. Other people say she's smiling secretively because she's pregnant.'

'She might be pregnant?'

'Yes.'

Inside, we head straight for the *Mona Lisa*. She's on the first floor in Denon Italian painters. There's a scrum around the portrait. Opposite, Veronese's *The Wedding at Cana* covers an entire wall. Surrounded by noblemen, Christ's sat at the centre of a table groaning with food, with a Ready Brek glow round his head. It's just after he's turned the water into wine, and while everyone else is eating or engrossed in conversation, Jesus looks alone, still and unhappy, 'Because his *steak avec frites* hasn't arrived yet,' says Dinah. 'I think he's also a bit worried about his sauces. Are you taking them in?'

'Resting your plates?' She nods.

The *Mona Lisa*'s flanked by signs warning about pickpockets. People at the back hold up cameras and take pictures over their heads, like photographers outside Scotland Yard trying to snatch shots of serial killers being taken by vans to court. Guards with walkie-talkies stop people from using their flashes. I ask one if it's always like this.

'There is a joke – how was your 'oliday?' the guard says. 'You ask a Japanese man. And 'e say, "I dun't know. I 'aven't seen my photos yet." Yes, always the same.'

The kids and I start at the back and slowly pour into holes in front of us, until we're in front of the painting. It takes ten minutes, but it's worth the wait because the painting is extraordinary. It seems almost liquid, as if it's changing before our eyes. One side of Mona Lisa's lips are raised coyly and the other side of her mouth seems flat, but when I look again, it seems to rise slightly, as though she's smiling, pleased but embarrassed by the attention. When the cameras flash, her eyes change. They shift leftwards, then move back into the middle, as if somehow the attention's overwhelming her. The mobility of her features makes her look incredibly beautiful, so that I can well imagine Napoleon, as the legend goes, hanging the picture in his bedroom and Josephine jealously forcing him to remove it.

'What do you think, guys? Is she smiling?'

'She looks sarcastic,' says Phoebe.

'Really?'

'Yeah, she looks likes she's going, "Whatevs."'

'Whatevs, by Leonardo da Vinci!'

The Egyptology rooms are where things go wrong. It's a long schlep, to the outer reaches of what is the biggest museum in the world, to find them in the Sully section. Phoebe sometimes becomes a little obsessive. In Lyon's Lumière museum, she insisted on pressing every single numbered display on her audio guide. The tour took three hours as a result. Here, we sit on various benches as she attempts to read each laminated information board about the Pharaonic city of Tanis, in the north-east area of the Nile Delta, which was the capital of Egypt during the third intermediate period, which lasted three centuries from 1080 to 729 BC.

'Phoebe, it cannot *all* be interesting.'

'We're doing the Egyptians at school, Daddy.'

Thousands of exhibits are spread over two floors, but Phoebe won't skip a single one.

'Sweetheart, this whole room's about the type of grain milled in Alexandria 3,000 years ago.'

'But I like it.'

She's finally defeated by a room devoted to the papyrus leaf, but even then, that's only after I promise we'll look for a café. This is easier said than done. Like Harrison Ford found in *Raiders of the Lost Ark*, the curse of the mummy is strong, and we soon become caught in a sapping

Egyptology circuit. Even with our 3D map, we're hopelessly lost. What's more, nobody's able to give us directions. We wander downstairs, upstairs, then down a flight of steps to a mezzanine floor that doesn't exist on the map. Time and again, we find ourselves on a narrow gantry, beside a mocked-up pyramid. Phoebe keeps stopping to read about hieroglyphics or Rameses II. It's hot and busy, and with zombie-like groups of visitors filing this way and that in thin, hopeless crocodiles, it almost feels like the atmosphere's computer-generated and we're doomed avatars in a video game (*Louvre* for Nintendo) where the sole object is to find Vittel mineral water at the Le Comptoir Café before everyone dies of dehydration and is dissected and decanted into Canopic jars.

We chance upon another security man, but he gives rogue instructions, or else we're too tired to follow them correctly – we go left, right, then up, then down, then left, then down, then up, and finally, by accident, emerge from the maze of Sully, out under the boiling glass of the pyramid. At the main information desk, we're directed up another escalator and there it is – the Richelieu Takeaway counter.

'Remember The Authorities,' jokes Dinah, as I queue to buy water.

'The Authorities want to help us,' I say robotically. 'We were wrong about them. They were only trying to give us a nice time.'

'Ben!'

'I'm going to buy a bottle of water *each* and also a glossy copy of *Veronese: A Master and His Workshop in Renaissance Venice.*'

She laughs. 'Stop that.'

'It's only 34 euros,' I say, glazing my eyes. 'And look at

these lovely bookmarks for 10 euros a pop, with a picture of the *Mona Lisa* on them.'

Dinah slaps my wrist. I drop the book. 'Stop being silly.'

'*Bonjour*,' I say to the lady, snapping out of it. 'Just . . .' and I hold up a 25cl bottle of water.

We meet Stephane in a restaurant which is down a side street near the Eiffel Tower. He has dyed blond hair that's balding on top and wears the sort of wide, mirrored sunglasses that Poncherello used to wear in *CHiPs*, the 80s cop show. He's in an artist-style blue smock, looks a bit like an anxious Robin Williams and claims he learnt his English from listening to Madonna. He shakes our hands like his fingers are tongs and our hands are lumps of dirty coal. He's immediately conspiratorial. We've just been up the Eiffel Tower, for which he apologises profusely – 'It is awful. Queuing for hours to see some rooftops in zis freezing cold' – although we quite enjoyed it. His phone keeps ringing. It's his birthday, it turns out, and most of his friends must be Spanish because he answers with a restrained, '*Hola*,' before he moves away from our table with a little apologetic wave.

Unlike most PRs we've met, there's no professional gloss. We share a bottle of wine before the food arrives because 'I am 43 today and I need to 'ave some wine', and he's soon informing us of the reason why the French consume as much medication as the Japanese and more than anyone else in Europe. It's because they're unhappy in their jobs, as the country's not a meritocracy. It's all about the school you went to. Your experience counts for nothing. 'You get confined in a job. And you cannot leave. So to make it better, you have a pill to sleep. I haf this pill.'

In a great torrent, Stephane tells us about his job and the difficulties. 'For the functionary, like me, is terr-ee-ball. It is awful. To depart the city, two autographs.'

'Signatures?'

'Yes.'

'My boss and my boss's boss.'

'Really?'

'Yes, and to leave the department, three. The third: the may-yor.'

'The mayor?'

'Yes.'

Café la Maison Bleue is chic, but the meal's not what the kids are used to. There's no *steak haché* and the least offensive option to their palettes is a chicken quiche with lettuce. Phoebe pulls a face as it arrives.

'And what's this leaf? Do I have to eat it?'

'Yes. It's lettuce.'

'But it's straggly.'

'It's a type of lettuce.'

'Do we get pudding?'

'Don't keep asking about pudding, or praying about it.' Phoebe has been putting her hands together, closing her eyes and quietly mantra-ing: 'Please, God, pudding. Please, God, pudding.'

'Pudding is outside of our control.'

When Stephane returns from another phone call, the kids wrap up their cutlery in napkins and hand it to him as birthday presents. He laughs and gives us a map of the Père Lachaise Cemetery and tickets for a boat trip on the Seine.

Before we leave, Brighton comes up. He watched the Julie Burchill TV drama *Sugar Rush*, based in the city, and visited once. It's the first time we've heard the word 'Brighton' on a stranger's lips since we left England, and we can't contain ourselves. Stéphane's thinking of moving to Spain with his partner, but they're regressive about gay marriage, so Dinah and I persuade him to consider Brighton. We tell him about Gay Pride, the fact that we have the country's first Green MP.

When we first moved to Brighton, we were evangelists for the city and wanted everyone we knew and liked to live there too. We bored visitors senseless about how it was Britain's San Francisco. The beautiful Hove Lawns, set against the Regency cream of Brunswick Square, where on a sunny day, you could watch a carload of troublemakers arrive on a Bank Holiday but become so instantly suffused with the tolerant vibe, they become part of it themselves within half an hour. That walk from pier to pier, past the basketball hoops and the volleyball sandpits. The murmuration of starlings over the West Pier at dusk. Wandering through the Lanes. The open-air top floor of the Lion and Lobster pub.

There's a poster on the café wall of a red London callbox. It lifts my heart to see it, but when I look down at the table mat, it's full of French words and, as Dinah continues the Brighton sales pitch, I suddenly feel tired of not understanding anything, of being the oaf who needs every word not related to beef translated for him. We must bore Stéphane half to death because it's *his* idea, in the end, that we dine without him tonight.

'In fact, shall we skip tea?' he suggests. 'You can visit the city and I 'ave a birfday.' He pays the bill. 'And I fink,' and he points to his head, 'here, you are almost 'ome now.'

After the boat trip, where The Authorities persuaded me to buy the kids Eiffel Tower models for 2 euros each when Dinah was in the ladies' loo, we take the Metro to Père Lachaise, to ghoul around the tombs. Oscar Wilde's grave has a sandstone male angel sculpted from an unwieldy utilitarian block of what looks like mottled stone, until we realise that the red smudges up the angel's legs are lipstick kisses. Proust's marble grave has fresh flowers on it. Jim Morrison's is fenced off. There are cigarette packets on it, dying flowers and magazines – tributes, according to our guidebook. Something for Jim to read and smoke in the afterlife.

'OK, Daddy, only A-listers from now on,' says Dinah, when the kids start to flag.

'No more *chanteuses*?'

'No, and I sacrificed Max Ernst, so you'll have to do the same with Edith Piaf,' she says.

'Sarah Bernhardt?'

'What did she do again?'

'Er . . .'

'Exactly,' says Dinah.

'Marshal Ney?'

'If you let me have Molière.'

'Scrub them both,' I say. 'I'm tired. We'll get the kids something to eat on the way home. Let's go.'

'Racine?' she suggests.

'Only if he's on the way out.'

Outside the cemetery, we walk up and down boulevard de Ménilmontant, looking for a restaurant. Weakened by the fact that my bum feels greasy and is chafing in the heat, The Authorities try to persuade me to feed the kids in the Café Ménilmontant for 25 euros a head so I can attend to it here.

'Your bum, that's another brainwave of The Authorities,' says Dinah.

'They did it in the cemetery when I was bending down to look at the Jim Morrison tributes.'

'They greased it with something,' says Dinah.

'A nerdy guy put his hand up in the control room and said he knew this trick with arseholes. This is his bum beforehand . . .' I pretend to spread out a picture of my bum on a table.

'And this is it afterwards.' Dinah lays out another.

Now I unroll a make-believe map and tap it with my forefinger. 'And here's where I calculate he'll be when the greasiness becomes intolerable.'

'The 20th arrondissement,' says Dinah, stroking her chin.

'Precisely. If my calculations are correct, he will be able to go no further. They will have to stop.'

'And where he wipes his bum . . .'

'They pay 25 euros a head in a café, not counting the glass of wine his wife always insists on at this time.'

'What is your name?' Dinah asks.

'Jean, sir.'

'And how long have you been with The Authorities, Jean?'

'A week, sir.'

'And the Sully gallery was your idea?'

'I got lost in Egyptology once myself, sir.'

'Very good, Jean. You have my authority to deploy the

20-euro *enfant* menu. Let's reel in this greasy-arsed fucker who didn't wipe his bum properly in the Eiffel Tower toilets.'

Back at the hotel, it's been worth the wait for the room. The kids have presents wrapped in neat bows on their beds – a cuddly seal for Phoebe and a white and black tiger for Charlie. They've been given Disney-logoed dressing gowns – Minnie (her) and Mickey (him). In a metal ice-bucket on the coffee table, there's Champagne, plus a chocolate jigsaw of the hotel and a plate of cookies.

'And have you seen this?' says Dinah.

Through the net curtains, double doors lead to a full-length balcony overlooking the Opera House. The acoustic changes as Dinah pushes them open. Traffic sounds fill the room.

'Wow!'

We open the Champagne and clink glasses.

'This is the best hotel I have *ever* stayed in,' announces Phoebe, joining us. She has chocolate all round her mouth and is still shovelling in more. Charlie nods his agreement. He can't talk. His mouth's too full of biscuits.

'Kids, have you enjoyed this holiday?'

'Yes,' shouts Phoebe.

'How much?' I ask.

'It's the best holiday *ever*,' splutters Charlie, showering us with biscuit crumbs.

'And with Disneyland still to come,' I say.

Dinah draws a bath in the palatial marble en suite and fills it with Molton Brown products. I find English CBeebies for the kids, but when the babysitter arrives at 8 p.m., Charlie doesn't want us to go. He hides behind the bathroom door as we try to say goodnight.

'Charlie!'

'Stay!' he says.

I pick him up. He squashes my face with his hands, moulding it like Plasticine.

'Elodie will read you a nice story, and Phoebe's with you.'

'I don't want you to go.'

'You have Disneyland tomorrow. Let Mummy and Daddy go out.'

He wriggles and jumps down. 'Okaaay,' he says, unhappily. 'But I'll cry.'

'Please don't.'

'Okaaay, I won't cry.'

'And, Phoebe, don't be boring Elodie, telling her about Moshi Monsters all night.'

She smiles sheepishly. It's what she does with babysitters.

'And not too late. Disneyland tomorrow, guys.'

Guy Savoy Paris has three Michelin stars and is a half-mile walk away in rue Troyon in the 17th arrondissement. We're dressed up. The concierge has drawn us a map, and it's strange to be out in the dark without the kids.

'No one to chivvy,' she says.

'Nothing to carry.'

We hold hands and it feels strange. 'Your hand feels so big,' I say. 'I'm used to Phoebe's.'

'I know what you mean.'

'Make-up?'

'But of course. We're in Paris,' she says.

'You look lovely.'

'Thank you.'

Outside the Opera House, people are congregating on the steps. A few are eating baguette and cheese.

'How parochial,' sniffs Dinah.

'Have the decency to hide your dirty cheese box!' I say.

There's nothing apart from a number outside Guy Savoy to indicate it's the right address. Inside it's modern art, wood and leather. Black-jacketed waiters remove my leather coat and fuss us to a table. The maitre d' approaches. We're having a seven-course tasting menu that includes several amuse-bouches, the first of which is a small disk of pastry. The atmosphere's of the sort that ensues when diners are so pleased to be somewhere, they can't resist clandestinely looking around to see if everyone else seems as pleased to be there as they are.

When the first course arrives, they're the tastiest vegetables I've ever eaten. In fact, they're so tasty, they don't actually taste of vegetables. During the second course, Guy Savoy enters the restaurant and an ever greater hush descends. What happens next takes me a few moments to comprehend. From across the floor, it becomes apparent that Guy is pointing at me. He's raising his voice to one of the waitresses, a young woman in square spectacles, and nodding at our table. I look at Dinah.

'What's happening?'

'I don't know, but I think you've upset Guy.'

'I've upset Guy!'

'Guy's angry with you,' she says.

'What have I done?'

'I don't know. She's coming over,' says Dinah.

The waitress approaches. Did I eat some crudités with the wrong fork? I left one baby carrot suffused with cinnamon. Is that what it is? When she reaches the table, the waitress says to me, 'I'm sorry, but have you a jacket?'

The next course is crab in liquorice and I creak as I spoon in each mouthful. I've been made to wear my leather coat and it's hard to bend my right arm sufficiently to reach my mouth with the spoon. In fact, it can't be done at all, unless I bend forward *towards* my spoon. It's also hot, and I'm sweating under the spotlighting.

'We should leave in a huff,' Dinah suggests.

'We really should.'

'You've been humiliated.'

'I have. He shouted at me.'

'Although this crab's very nice,' she says.

'The crab's delicious. What's next?'

'Lamb and thyme,' she says.

'That sounds good as well.'

'Maybe storm out after that,' says Dinah.

'But then it's the cheese.'

'That's true. And I want a coffee at the end,' she says. 'How humiliated do you feel?'

'Quite humiliated.'

'Hmmm.'

'Do you want to stay?'

'You do seem to be getting on better with the spoon.' Dinah looks at me imploringly.

'OK, but the price is, we go through tomorrow's touring plan.' I've been studying our Disneyland guidebook quite closely.

'We have a touring plan?' she asks

'Of course.'

I unfold a piece of paper. Dinah picks it up and reads from it.

'Commence in Discoveryland and ride Space Mountain: Mission 2. Then turn left to Buzz Lightyear and right to

Star Tours. After this, return to the entrance of Discovery-land, ensuring we cross the central plaza to Frontierland. We must pass the log stockade without stopping and go straight to Big Thunder Mountain. Turn left from here and proceed along the waterfront and, after passing Fuente del Oro Restaurante, we will enter Adventureland. Turn left prior to the bridge and make a beeline for Indiana Jones and the Temple of Peril. Bypass the Swiss Family Robinson Tree House (important) and cross a second bridge to Adventure Isle, then we head for Fantasyland. In Fantasy-land, check the wait time for Peter Pan's Flight. It's a fast-pass ride. If the wait is under 25 minutes, then join the queue. If longer, secure a fast-pass to return later.' She puts it down.

'Love!'

'What?'

'Please don't make this into a military campaign. That reads like the brief they gave the US Navy Seals who stormed Bin Laden's compound. Is that from the book?'

'Yeah. It's brilliant. It was written by two guys who studied queue theory. Their touring plans are based on . . . Hang on.' I take the book out of my jacket pocket and find the page. 'Theme-park traffic flow, attraction capacity, baulking constraints—'

'What?'

'Baulking constraints. The maximum time a visitor is willing to wait. As well as strolling distances between rides and queuing time data amassed at regular daily intervals and at episodic times of year. The combinatorial model combines the well-documented assignment difficulties of linear programming with queuing theory.' I close the book. 'Are you going to argue with a combinatorial model?'

'I don't even know what a combinatorial model is.'

'And I did agree to your uniforms,' I remind her.

'True,' she says.

'And the name disks you bought from Paws and Claws pet shop.'

'You said that was a good idea.'

'I was humouring you.'

'What else does it say in your silly book?'

'To avoid character encounters with fur heads.'

'Fur heads?'

'Mickey Mouse, Donald Duck, Minnie Mouse.'

Dinah laughs.

'That's what they call them. There are two types of Disney character. Face characters. They're cast members in costume but with real faces. Cast members just means members of staff.'

'Ben, you've read way too much about this.'

'And fur heads, who don't speak but sign autographs. Character encounters cause chaos and can destroy a touring plan.'

'So the kids can't meet Mickey Mouse?'

'And no parades.'

'Anything else?'

'One more thing. This is my idea. Do you know how much a burger is in there?'

'£7?'

'Higher.'

'£10?'

'More than £12. It's given me an idea.'

'If this is about smuggling in sandwiches, I know for a fact they search bags.'

'But what if I had a way round that?'

'Which is?'

'Don't put them in the bags.'

'What, swallow a baggie of goat's cheese and shit it out the other end?'

'Better. Tape baguettes to their legs.'

'Whose legs?'

I look at her.

'The children's legs?! You want to tape baguettes to the children's legs?'

I lean forward. 'Inside their trousers. Two tubes of baguette. One tube behind each calf.'

'You're a monster!'

I lean back. 'It's the thinnest part of their legs.'

'You're actually serious!'

I lean forward again. 'Cheese in their shoes. Jarlsberg. A non-sweaty cheese. Cut thin. Wrapped in cellophane. And in their pacamacs – yoghurts.'

I lean back again and Dinah laughs. 'So, let's get this straight, you want to turn our kids into sandwich mules?'

'You're making sandwiches sound bad. We're smuggling in healthy food for our kids. We're being good parents.'

'NO!' she says.

'Plus, if we take our own sandwiches in, we avoid bottleneck lunch queues. That equals more rides, which equals more fun. It's a win-win.'

'NO!' she says. 'We'll follow your bonkers touring plan. I don't mind that. But we're buying lunch. And if they want to stop to talk to a *fur head*, you'll have to stop them because I'm not.'

The waitress places a small silver plate beside each of us, bearing halved peas, then moves theatrically away after an explanation.

'What did she say?' I ask Dinah.

'Guy's apparently done something to the peas,' she says.

'Nothing dirty, I hope.'

It's been a tense meal, what with the mental dexterity required to use the correct implements (Dinah ate her lamb with a pâté knife) and the worry that Guy might emerge at any moment to bark at us. Over time, without us being fully aware of it, it's created a suppressed bubble of anxiety that now explodes into hilarity. Dinah has to keep putting her hand up to her mouth. She can't look at me. She breathes in deeply. 'Nothing dirty,' she repeats, coughing on a half-chewed pea, and after she's seemingly recovered from this, she cries with laughter, the strength of her resistance to the out-of-place amusement only reinforcing it, so that eventually I lose control as well. We try to rein ourselves in by focusing separately on the menu, but it makes it worse. The menu appears to have been written by some random word generator which is only allowed to pick ones from a Paulo Coelho novel or a self-help manual for depression.

'Cuisine is the art of instantaneously turning produce suffused with history into happiness. But is it art?' reads Dinah. 'No. Just serious craftsmanship. At Guy Savoy, a meal is a celebration of life. Dining at Guy Savoy means weaving your own personal, intangible pathway between flavours engaged in dialogue with one another. If you respect and worship the raw materials, you can do as you wish.'

'And your review?' I ask.

'Nice peas, but get over yourself, Guy.'

In a bar behind the Opera House afterwards, Dinah

tells me the disastrous story of her au pair year in Paris and how, after she quit, she moved in with Serious Pete. That same year, I resigned from Copenhagen Reinsurance. I'd had to work out the insurance cover for oil tankers, but hadn't listened when it was explained and didn't want to ask how to do it again, so I kept filing the forms and making up the cover. After a week, I decided I'd better leave before an under-insured tanker sank.

'So we were both quitting things at the same time,' Dinah says.

'Cutting our paths towards each other,' I tell her. 'It was after that I trained to be a journalist.'

'I like that thought,' she says.

We go through the best and worst moments of the trip, discuss what the kids enjoyed the most, and the waitress comes over. Dinah asks for the bill. The waitress smiles and they talk for a while in French. 'Thank you,' says Dinah, blushing when they've finished.

'What was that?' I ask when she's gone.

'She said I spoke French without an accent. That's the second person who's said that.'

'You love it.'

'I do.'

'You should be a French teacher.'

She laughs. 'That's what everyone who did French on my course became, what I'd have become if I hadn't quit my year out in France,' she says.

'So you've come full circle, and in a way I'm back where I was too, except now I've got a wife and two kids.'

We both look right. From where we're sitting, we can see our hotel balcony to the right of Café de la Paix. There's still a light on in the room.

'She's telling Elodie about her Moshi Monsters,' says Dinah.

I laugh.

'Funny to think that the last time we were in Paris, we were crossing from being the people we were then to who we are now.'

'Come on, let's go and rescue Elodie.'

I slip a ten euro note under the clip with the bill. We stand.

'Can we talk about the Bureaucracy Biscuit on the way back?'

'OK, what would the adverts be like?' she says, linking arms with me.

For the last few nights, Dinah and I have been discussing the perfect chocolate bar for France. In England we have the Double Decker, which references both our love for red London buses and our interest in nougat and Rice Krispies. We've devised a comparable French chocolate bar – the Bureaucracy Biscuit – that combines two important French passions: chocolate and pointless administration.

'I think the ads would feature a civil servant eating a Bureaucracy Biscuit. He'd be sat in front of a huge pile of unnecessary forms.'

She laughs. 'The implication being that the biscuit will give him the necessary energy he needs to complete this bureaucratic toil.'

'Exactly. The chocolate bar that helps you work, rest *and* inconvenience members of the public.'

The Opera House is lit up inside and looks like a giant gold lantern. Traffic is still pouring round it. I press the button on the pelican crossing. 'Or the consumption of the biscuit *itself* could involve bureaucracy,' I say.

'You have to apply in writing to buy a Bureaucracy Biscuit?' says Dinah.

'No, in person, at the post office.'

'With a passport-sized photo and two separate forms of ID,' she says.

'And references from two previous biscuit companies whose snacks you have eaten in the past, including the wrappers of those biscuits.'

'Countersigned by the shopkeeper who sold you the biscuits,' she says.

Dinah's slow crossing the road. '*Marche*, Taquin,' I say, and I tap her on the bum.

'Actually, that was probably my funniest moment – you thrashing Taquin when he was stood on your toe.' We're still laughing as we enter the hotel via Café de la Paix. The American pensioners eating here when we left have been replaced with parties of Spaniards.

We take the lift up and, outside our room, through our door, we can hear a familiar monotone: 'And Lady Goo Goo's an ultra rare Moshi. She's from series two. And this one's called Dustbin Beaver, although actually Blingo is my favourite . . .'

CHAPTER 19

'What are you talking about?' says Phoebe, over the top of her Coco Pops at breakfast.

'It's Daddy's silly idea,' says Dinah.

'I want to smuggle sandwiches into Disneyland,' I tell Phoebe, 'strapped to your legs.' Dinah leans across to cut open Charlie's croissant and fill it with orange marmalade.

'Imagine the thrill of getting through security.'

'No!' says Dinah.

'Untaping the baguettes from their legs in a public toilet.'

'Disgusting!'

'How pleased you'll be, eating your smuggled lunch, watching everyone else shelling out for chicken nuggets.'

'Chicken nuggets!' says Phoebe, her eyes lighting up.

'That's blown your chances,' says Dinah.

'Why do we have to wear this?' asks Charlie.

I look at the kids in their Postman Pat uniforms. They have brass pet disks with their names punched into them hanging from their wrists on flea collars. Their feet have been dusted with talc because the book advised it to avoid blisters. And it comes at me in a wave, the utter ridiculousness of today, and this whole trip, which, in three months, has made me so feral and so inured me to common decency, I can have a serious conversation about taping cheese sandwiches to my children's legs to save a few quid in Disneyland. Despite her tiredness, it catches Dinah too. She sees me laughing and, as I try to explain myself, tears begin running from her eyes as she folds herself around the table and the rolled napkin containing a Jarlsberg-filled baguette I've just passed her.

'What are you laughing at now?' Phoebe demands. 'You're always laughing.'

'They're being silly again,' says Charlie, so dismissively it makes us laugh even more.

And as we leave the dining room to approach the front desk to check out, vestiges of the laughter remain in the pit of my stomach as a sort of tingle of excitement. It feels like a distant echo of that thrill I remember when Dinah and I first fell in love. The expectation that around the corner there might be another shared laugh like this, or perhaps an even better one.

And for a little while, waiting for the car to be driven round to the front of the hotel, all the laughs we've had like this over the years seem to join up and Mexican-wave around us. The celebrity homes tour in Hollywood in 2001. With a $1 map, we'd bombed around Rodeo Drive, seeing as many of the famous homes as we could before our flight back. We were eating a mini sandwich – a slice of Monterey Jack cheese between two Ritz biscuits – outside Angela Lansbury's house, which we couldn't even see because of the huge hedge, and we'd looked at each other at the same moment and had laughed so hard at the manic absurdity of what we were doing that Dinah had wet her knickers.

Another time, in Amsterdam, the year after we'd married, after smoking coffee-shop skunk, Dinah became convinced we'd be mown down by a tram and I had to explain to her, very seriously and over and over again, as we ricocheted from laughter to fear, that 'They only operate on rails, Dinah. They cannot come into this bar even if they wanted to.'

When the bellboy says the boot's too full for all the bags, I smile. '*Regardez!*' I say.

The four liveried bellboys stand back. It's so early in the morning, they've nothing else to do but watch me. And there's a perky, fun atmosphere, inspired, I think, by the unconventional nature of our departure. I'm parked next to an Aston Martin and a Porsche, stuffing squishy bags into our stinky, roof-boxed Passat, whose boot is propped open with a golf putter and whose glove box is wedged shut with a tea flask. Inside, our two children look like prisoners on community service, about to go and paint bus shelters.

'*Voilà!*' I say, when it's packed, and the bellboys clap. I bow.

'Where to?' asks one.

'*Disneyland!*' shout the kids through their open windows, and one of the bellboys opens the passenger door and pretends to climb in. They wish us bon voyage and, in a rush of affection for the hotel, Paris and these guys, I momentarily forget we aren't the high rollers our presence here indicates and fold a ten-euro tip into one of their hands.

Out of Paris, we take the Metz road. The kids sit bolt upright, looking for the small blue Disney signs featuring Mickey in his sorcerer's hat, and an hour later, taking the Bailly-Romainvilliers exit, we see the pink turret of Sleeping Beauty's castle for the first time, and the kids go crazy.

The car park's the size of a town and is bisected by a canopied airport-style travelator. We prepare ourselves in Goofy D Row 234.

'Phoebe, come here!' I roll up her trouser legs and fix two baguette halves to each of her calves. 'Walk around.'

She takes a few steps. 'It's itchy.'

'You'll get used to it.'

'It feels funny.'

'It's only for a few minutes. Charlie, come and get yours.'

He wanders over. I strap him up. He fiddles with his trouser legs.

'And don't keep adjusting them,' I tell him. 'Just pretend they're not there.'

We stand by and survey them.

'That one's slipped a bit,' says Dinah.

'Come here, Charlie.'

I reaffix the baguette, pulling it higher up. 'Is that OK? Not too close to your knee?'

'It feels *weird*.'

'It's only until we get in, Charlie,' says Phoebe. 'We're buying souvenirs with the money we save, aren't we, Dad?'

'Small ones, yeah.'

'Right, cheese slices, then we're off. Shoes off please. Dinah, inside or outside the socks?'

'I can't believe you've made me do this. Outside.'

I've already loaded up our coat pockets with apples and bananas wrapped, to hide their shape, in gloves and hats. The pacamacs contain the Petits Filous yoghurts.

We join the travelator. On it, the kids discuss what they'll see. 'Scooby Doo isn't Disney, Charlie, is he, Dad?' And all around us, families and young couples are arriving. They move purposefully, like commuters, except with small day-bags instead of laptops. We pass three armed soldiers in green berets with snub-nosed automatic weapons slung across their chests. They study everyone in turn on the travelator. Tannoys next to the Welcome to Disneyland signs pump out the marching music from *Fantasia*, 'Pink Elephants on Parade'. It tallies with the military feel of the day, so that we find ourselves falling into a trooping step.

Before we leave the travelator, we pass beneath a black and white sign. It depicts a uniformed man in a peaked cap searching through a bag, beside the words: 'Thank you for not bringing in food. There are picnic areas outside the park.'

Dinah looks at me.

'We'll be fine. They won't strafe us with machine-gun fire for taking in sandwiches.'

Off the travelator, we pass Planet Hollywood, and outside Annette's Diner, beside the huge, full-size Cadillac on a tilted stand, Phoebe says, 'I'm having to walk like this.' She's walking with bow legs, like a cowboy. 'Or the baguette rubs.'

'You're doing well, guys. Just remember those souvenirs.'

We walk 400 metres, past more restaurants, and join the bag-check queue.

'Move right,' I tell Dinah, when I notice we're in the

only line that has an airport scanning machine. 'But don't make it obvious.'

She shuffles right. I follow her. This new line's headed by a table on which visitors are placing handbags and rucksacks, already unzipped, ready for inspection.

'I'll go first with the kids,' I say.

Dinah balances Phoebe's coat on top of her handbag. 'Keep it in your hand,' I say, out of the corner of my mouth. 'He might feel the apple. And keep talking and smiling.'

The nerves increase as we get closer, more so when I notice Charlie's baguette's slipped again. Crust is poking out of the bottom of his trouser leg. Dinah bends forward.

'Leave it!' I spit. 'It's too late.'

She straightens and sniffs.

'What?'

'Cheese,' she says.

'Really? How bad?'

'Noticeable,' she says.

'I *knew* we should have brought Philadelphia.'

'Just say it's your socks,' says Dinah.

At the table, the security man takes the water bottle from Charlie and puts it to his lips. It takes me a moment to realise he's joking, pretending to drink from it, rather than confiscating it. I've already opened the rucksack and he peers inside it, pushing aside one of the pacamacs.

'Parlez-vous anglais?'

'Yes.'

'Any food in here?' he asks.

'No,' I lie, as Dinah distracts the kids so they don't hear this. The man invites me to enjoy my day, and I'm through.

I identify the Donald Duck window of the Disneyland Hotel, where we're supposed to pick up our tickets. Dinah draws alongside me.

'Alright?' I say, staring straight ahead.

'Yeah,' she says, under her breath.

'Sort his baguette out,' I say, still not looking at her. 'But only when we reach the Donald Duck window.'

I wait until we're at the window round the corner before I ferret around in Dinah's handbag and pull out a bag of Naturele crisps.

'Where did *they* come from?' she asks.

I pull out two more, one for her and one for the kids to share. 'The best mules don't even know they're mules.'

'You hid them in my bag?'

'For the good of the family.'

'Without *telling* me?'

'I knew he'd check my rucksack more thoroughly than your handbag. I drew the fire.'

'You're outrageous,' she says.

By lunchtime, we've been on Big Thunder Mountain, Snow White and the Seven Dwarves, Phantom Manor, Autopia, the Buzz Lightyear Laser Blast and the Pirates of the Caribbean ship. We've narrowly missed fur head encounters with the Chipmunks, Donald Duck and Minnie Mouse and have avoided two parades, and now we're eating our muled lunch on a concrete bench outside Studio One in Walt Disney Studios.

'What you don't see is people smiling. Have you noticed?' I ask Dinah. There are two parks. Disneyland and Walt Disney Studios, and each of these is sub-divided into zones called things like Frontierland and Discoveryland.

It's spread out, and everyone's either queuing, heading across the park to queue or looking at the park plan to decide where to queue next. Nobody, unless they're in a queue, is still. The crowds are vast, and it's like permanently attempting to find the correct Tube platform at Oxford Circus a few days before Christmas, except it's also very hot.

We've marched along, swallowing mouthfuls of other people's cigarette smoke, bellowing 'Charlie, stay with us please', as he's refused to hold mine or Dinah's hand and has slipped into a dream world, staring at a Lightning McQueen bag for £30 or a Goofy lolly the size of a human face. The kids' low fascination threshold means a man dressed as a clown selling helium balloons with pictures of Mickey Mouse on them from a trolley is just as likely to snag their interest as any of the must-see rides people are spending up to two hours queuing for.

We hear a distant scream.

'In fact,' I tell Dinah, 'I don't even think that's excitement. Those are suppressed screams of frustration from all the queuing. That's how people release their anger and shame at wasting two hours in the queue for Crush's Coaster.'

'You're not the right person to come to Disneyland, are you?'

'What I don't understand is, thanks to me, we've been on double the rides a normal person would manage and yet we've still spent less than 30 minutes actually *on* rides.'

'It's about the experience.'

'OK, delete the background of the park. Imagine you've whited out everything but the people. All the rides. Look at the people. Look at their faces. Then imagine having to try to guess where they are.'

Dinah stares at the crowd in front of us and laughs. 'They look lost and dazed,' she says.

'Exactly. It's like the aftermath of a terrible crash. Nobody's having fun. They've just been told Disneyland's fun, so they assume that's what they're having: fun.'

'Daddy, it *is* fun,' says Phoebe.

'Yes, it is, sorry, Pops. The peculiar thing is, I am actually having fun. I'm not sure why though.'

'It's because you're getting to boss us around in a way that is hitherto, even for you, almost unknown.'

'That reminds me. Blimey, look at the time! Right, give Mummy back what you haven't eaten, guys.'

Charlie says he's thirsty.

'Water when we get to Slinky Dog Zigzag Spin,' I tell him.

'But I'm thirsty,' he protests.

'Ben?' says Dinah.

'OK, OK.'

I turn round and Dinah reaches into my rucksack, just as people start to arrange themselves along a series of brass-embossed images of Mickey Mouse in the pavement. Two face characters appear round the corner, holding a rope at either end. They're walking towards us, ahead of a convoy of vehicles. Other cast members, acting like motorcycle outriders, clear the path where we're standing.

'Oh no! It's a parade!' I say, but we're already too late.

'Do You Believe in Magic' begins playing through 100 different speakers, at an ear-piercing, almost mind-altering volume. This Stars in their Cars parade is like a cross between a royal cavalcade entering a medieval village and a heavily marshalled, almost North Korean, display of Disney might. It's the Walt Disney equivalent of Kim

Jong-il parading military hardware through Pyongyang, only it's Mickey Mouse and Goofy waving from brightly coloured cars, instead of surface-to-air missiles.

'GOOFY!' shouts Charlie, as the cars snake past us.

'MINNIE MOUSE!' shouts Phoebe, and the crowd goes crazy. We're buffeted from behind and banged on the head with Disney flags. People shout out to their favourite characters. And there's almost a fight when a man in a Stitch Live! T-shirt accidentally dislodges the Mickey Mouse ears of another man's wife.

When Gordon Brown was prime minister, he did a 'spontaneous' walkabout at a seafront play park in Hove. I was there with a diehard Tory mother at the time, who practically threw her baby at him to be kissed, she was so swept up in the intoxicating proximity of fame. Although it seemed absurd, Brown did at least, in theory, have his finger on the nuclear button. These are people dressed as characters from Disney movies, with their fingers in outsized latex hands.

After the parade, the fur heads go on a walkabout. Daisy Duck's with two minders in blue shirts. They're needed because fur heads are effectively blind. Daisy holds autograph books very close to her face to sign them, like a short-sighted old lady checking a shopping list in the Co-op. Fifty people have swarmed around her. Daisy blindly touches the heads of random toddlers, like a priest offering a blessing. This benediction signifies whose turn it is next, and the minders step forward and pluck that lucky child from the crowd, so they can get their photograph or autograph.

'Daisy doesn't hug people who push,' I hear a minder say, and I look round. Charlie, who was beside me, is gone. There's a moment's panic before I see his boiler suit reappear. Utilising all his knowledge of Laurel and Hardy, he's crawled through the legs of the crowd in front of him and has popped up in front of Daisy, who's now tapping his shoulder.

Signs above the travelator say 'À Bientôt'. The sun's going down. In the back of the car, the kids clutch their Minnie and Mickey soft toys to their faces. Dinah's leaning back in her seat, her eyes closed with exhaustion. We added the Rustler Roundup Shootin' Gallery, the Thunder Mesa Riverboat Landing, Pocahontas's Indian Village, Star Tours and Les Voyages de Pinocchio to our tally. The kids have had their picture taken with Daisy Duck and Harold the Seahorse, and we have Chicken Little's autograph.

'So, guys, the big question – was it better than the onion museum?'

'It was the best thing *ever*,' says Phoebe.

It's our last big drive, and we're on the road to Rouen, heading for Caen, on the Normandy autoroute, when we hit our final tollbooth in France. Tollbooths are Charlie's favourite bit of any journey, in particular that moment when we exit the pay barrier and the ten lanes of traffic narrow to two. As always, Charlie demands I do my Lightning McQueen Chip and Chuck commentary.

'Daddy, do the voices.'

'And who is this rookie, Chuck? I don't know, Chip, but I'd sure like to have what he's got in his tank. Would you look at him go! In his first Piston Cup nobody had heard of this fella. They know him now. He's in the lead. The VW diesel-engined hatchback with the roof-box and the footwells full of chocolate wrappers and banana skins and the wheel of smelly Comté cheese in the boot is In. The. Lead.'

''Gain,' says Charlie. ''Gain.'

We talk about the rides, take it in turns to play our favourite records, and when it gets dark, the kids grow excited. They love being in the car at night and take it in turns to point at each other in the now sepia light of the car and tell each other:

'You look old-fashioned.'

'*You* look old-fashioned.'

'No, you look old-fashioned.'

'No, YOU look old-fashioned.'

Three hours later, at 11 p.m., we arrive at the Best Western. We meant to stop for dinner, but in the end we drove on, the hunger keeping us awake. The hotel's on place Maréchal-Foch. We park under a canopy of plane trees. It's become accepted that if we arrive at a destination and a good song is on – 'The Promise' by Bruce Springsteen, a Sundays track, Bob Dylan, Lloyd Cole – nobody takes their seatbelt off until it's over. In fact, whenever the chorus to 'The Promise' comes on – and this applies equally to 'Take the Long Way Home' by Supertramp and '1979' by the Smashing Pumpkins – it takes precedence over everything else that's happening in the car. It doesn't matter what it is – the sat nav issuing instructions, Dinah reading the *Rough Guide* to me, Charlie playing with his big Lightning, Phoebe reading *Harry Potter* – everything stops when the refrain begins: 'Thundeeerrr Roaaaaaaaaad'.

It's playing now. It's warm outside. It's our last night away and, as I stare into the rear-view mirror, the music vibrating from the speakers through me and Dinah and through the kids, tuning our hearts almost like strings, it seems, to the same pitch. For a moment, watching them strum imaginary guitars with their plectrums of baguette crust, mouthing inappropriately along: 'Thunder Road, for the lost lovers and all the fixed games. Thunder Road, for the tires rushing by in the rain', I know we're as solid and together as we'll ever be as a family.

The receptionist makes us plastic swipe passes while we check out room service. Except it's 11 euros for an omelette.

'Eleven euros for an egg!'

'Love, we have to eat,' says Dinah.

I ask for the number of a takeaway. The man doesn't understand. I look at Dinah.

'*Un emporter?*' she asks.

He gives us the number for Pizza Hut. He says the word 'pizza' with a frightened wince, as though we've just suggested dining on the entrails of a dead dog.

We struggle up in the tiny lift. It's like a game of Twister, as we flop forward over the bags to get far enough away from the lift doors to allow them to close.

'Further back, Charlie.'

'Phoebe, you'll have to take that rucksack off and sit on it.'

'Stop pushing me, Charlie.'

'Phoebe's standing on my toe.'

On the third swish, the room-key works.

'Clothes off, jammies on, ready for pizza.'

The pizza takes half an hour to arrive. The fact that it's on its way, that food and sleep are on the horizon, that the manhandling of bursting bags of dirty clothes is almost over, that tomorrow I'll be in my own bed, is enough to make me delirious with happiness. I flop on to the bed and Charlie jumps on me. I thrust my chin into his chest and press down. He laughs crazily. I carry on until he cries out, 'Stop, stop.' He rolls away, exhausted, then back towards me. ''Gain,' he says. ''Gain.'

'My turn,' says Phoebe. She bites her tongue.

'The tongue's out. She means business,' says Dinah.

I pin her down and lift my chin high in the air, like a Mayan executioner with a sacrificial knife, about to dispatch a human offering. Phoebe cries out 'Noooo!' as I bury my chin into her chest. She laughs uncontrollably and sighs with exhaustion, like an idling machine, beside me, as Charlie has another go.

The phone rings.

'The pizza, guys!'

Dinah answers it. She replaces the receiver. 'Your pizza,' she pushes back her nose, imitating the snobbish man downstairs, 'is here.' She puts her shoes on.

'Get him to bring them up. To *handle* them.'

Dinah laughs and calls the man. 'Could you send them up?' Then she has an idea. 'With a corkscrew?'

A few minutes later, we eat the pizzas like a pack of hyenas. Our faces are stained with tomato and pepperoni after we've finished.

'Full?'

Charlie burps long and hard in reply.

'Probably quite nice to eat something that hasn't previously been strapped to your legs, hey, Pops?' asks Dinah. 'Teeth, then bed, guys.'

They're on the sofa bed adjacent to us. I tuck them in.

'Do the Mickey voice,' says Charlie, passing his toy to me. The Mickey voice is basically Ray Winstone's.

'Well, you tarts. It's been a proper nice day. And a proper nice 'oliday. Have you enjoyed yourselves?'

They both nod.

'And 'as your baguette rash gawn down on your legs, my darlin'?'

Phoebe shows Mickey her leg.

'Good.'

'Ben,' says Dinah. She waggles her glass.

'OK, that's it now, guys. Night, night. Home tomorrow.'

I go to the bathroom to top up their glasses of water. Dinah raises her eyebrows when I return. They're already fast asleep. In the end, we can't face wine tonight and, ten minutes later, we've joined them.

CHAPTER 20

'Look at that picture of Charlie. Look at his hair!'
We're at breakfast. It's 6.15 a.m. We're the only ones here. Dinah's looking at photos from the start of the trip on my camera. Charlie's hair was brown when we left. Now it's blond. His feet have also grown so much, his toes poke over the top of the soles of his sandals, and Phoebe's shirt sleeves are all now too short for her.

The breakfast's all laid out. There are no waitresses watching us. It's fill your boots time. We take half a baguette, three types of cheese, saucisson, fruit yoghurts, croissants, teabags and bottles of water.

But I'm twitchy about missing the ferry. I keep checking my watch. I'm so nervous that when we return to the room, I make us walk the three flights of stairs, in case we get stuck in the lift. We do a sweep of the room for the last time. I pack the boot for the last time.

At the ferry port, we show our passports and glide to a stop in Row Nine. We hang our boarding card over the rear-view mirror. It's cold. I have the car-seat warmer on for the first time. And it's drizzling.

'Well, would we do it again right now, if we could?' I say to the windscreen.

Dinah stares ahead in a sleepy daze. 'No,' she says.

'If someone gave you another three months, I mean? And if we went to new places?'

'I need to recharge my batteries,' says Dinah.

The kids spot British cars. It's a game we've often played on autoroutes. But they've all got British yellow and black number plates here. It's like the ferry's a giant magnet sucking British cars out of France. I think about home, of the New Church Road in Hove, the kids' school and Tesco, our small, uneventful daily tramlines. I picture weekends on the seafront, at National Trust properties, and I feel a jolt that's almost fear at the routine round the corner.

'I'd carry on,' I say.

'I know you would.'

The brake lights come on in the row of cars to our left. It starts to move forward.

We find our cabin on Deck Nine. Dinah flops onto a bunk. The porthole window is partially obscured by the rain. On the floor, Charlie makes the Big Thunder Mountain roller coaster by propping up sections of his rail track with Lego. While he hated the ride, he now draws it, makes replicas of it and talks about it as though trying to understand it.

'We almost went upside down.'

'We didn't, Charlie.'

'We did. Look!'

'Is that a loop?'

He nods.

'But there was no loop. Did you worry there'd be a loop?'

He nods.

Phoebe won't come to the top deck with me to watch the land recede – she's too busy pretending to be a Brittany Ferries operative, staring at herself in the vanity mirror and saying to us, when she's perfected her posh face, with a puckered mouth and supercilious smile, 'I will not allow pets, bananas and smelly cheese on board. I am sorry, but those are the rules, *madame*. Now, where are your passports, *monsieur*?'

Outside, the clouds are a smudgy grey, the same colour they were when we left England, so that it's like two pieces of a jigsaw have joined up. I lean over the rail and watch the red light of the Caen lighthouse until it's out of sight. It feels like the start of a new year. Years don't start in January when you're a parent. They begin in September, when the kids return to school. People peel away inside, to try to sleep under their coats or have breakfast in Les Romantiques, where the tables are being laid by red-coated ferry staff. I hear someone say 'mate' into his mobile phone. France is now a charcoal watercolour blur on the horizon, until the grey sky finally swallows it up.

We watch *The Muppet Movie* in Cinema One, eat the last of our baguette and cheese and finally finish the big Marmite pot. The kids enter a competition to draw the best Pierre the Bear, the ferry mascot. They lie on the floor of the Deck Nine entertainment area, as other kids hare around them, shouting in a reassuringly unruly British way. Meanwhile, Dinah and I feast on newspapers from the ferry shop. Back home, a man in Weymouth has set fire to his flat microwaving two pairs of his pants. I show Dinah the story. Heathrow's third runway's back on the cards, and there's still a recession.

It's half an hour before we dock. The kids are plucking up the courage to approach the grey-haired entertainments officer on stage, to ask if they can have one of the balloon animals he's twisting into shape.

'Go on, Phoebe!' I say, though she's too far away to hear me.

'She won't do it,' says Dinah.

'She will.'

Phoebe looks up. I wave her forward. In a way, it's a test of France. Of the holiday. Has it helped or hindered Phoebe's shyness, spending three months solely with her family? It feels like something is at stake. The future of these trips, my success in persuading Dinah to agree to another. Phoebe returns. She walks in her clockwork, shy way, the shyness that's like a reactive arthritis, a shyness that seizes muscles not just in her face and in her throat, preventing words and natural expressions, but throughout her entire body.

'Approach him from the front.'

'He's talking to someone else,' she whispers.

'He hasn't seen you. Approach him from the front and remember to say please. Go on.'

She 'Pinocchios' forward, shuffling to within his range of vision, but is gripped by fear.

'Come on,' I'm saying to Dinah. 'She's doing her best here, say something to her. I don't think he's very good with kids.'

'Love, it's not him.'

'He's nervous. He's sticking to kids that will talk to

him. He doesn't want to look a lemon. He must be able to see she's shy.'

'I can't bear to watch,' says Dinah. She turns away, but is drawn back to the spectacle.

'Go on, Phoebe!'

Phoebe looks up again. Her hand is playing with her face, as if it's not her own, and her fingers are tugging at her bottom lip. Then he's turned to her, is looking up, saying something. He picks out an orange balloon and starts to twist it.

'He's making her one.'

'Thank God for that!' says Dinah.

He hands Phoebe the balloon, then bends forward and cocks a hand to his ear. Phoebe's whispering her thank you. She turns to us afterwards, a little spring in her step now as she walks back.

'A lion,' she says. 'Look at his nose!'

'Well done, Pops!' I'm saying, when there's an announcement on the Tannoy: 'If you look to your left in a few minutes, you will see the Isle of Wight, ladies and gentlemen. Stay looking at that side and you will soon see the Spinnaker Tower. We will be arriving in Portsmouth shortly. Thank you for sailing with us.'

At the passport barrier, a young English guy says, 'Welcome home, Mr and Mrs Hatch.'

Phoebe looks stunned. 'How did he know that?'

'Magic powers,' he says to her. 'The same powers that will now open this barrier.' The barrier opens. He hands back our passports.

Almost immediately, on the M275, there's a blue and white Brighton sign.

'What will you do when you get home?' Dinah asks Charlie. 'Get your cars out?'

He nods.

'Phoebe?'

'Get my CD player out.'

'Are we going *home* home?' Charlie asks.

'Yes.'

'The home where we have the table downstairs?'

It's all our house means to him – the place with the table in the kitchen.

'And it has our toys,' says Phoebe.

'Thanks for making it a great holiday, guys. You've been such great company. Haven't they, Mummy?'

Dinah looks up. 'What?'

She's reading 'What I Know Now' by Kym Marsh, in *Closer* magazine.

'You've missed your tat, haven't you?'

She laughs.

'Mummy, what's for tea?' asks Phoebe. 'Fish fingers?'

'And beans?' asks Charlie.

'If you want.'

'English beans what are orange?'

'It's all English now, Charlie.'

As we bypass Shoreham-by-Sea on the A27, Dinah finds 'Homeward Bound' on my Ooh La La Mega French Holiday Compilation. It's the version on *Simon and Garfunkel's Greatest Hits* that starts with a live audience clapping and cheering. We clap and cheer too. I turn it up and open the window.

'Ready, guys?'

'Yes,' says Phoebe.

'Charlie?'

He nods.

And, as we sing along, I look in the rear-view mirror at the kids joining in.

'All together now, homeward bound,' I say, when the chorus starts. And we all sing now at the tops of our voices. 'I wiiiish I waaaas – Come on, guys, louder! – homeward boooound.'

We come the showbiz way into Brighton, down past the huge mansions on Dyke Road. Then Montpelier Road to the sea and along Hove Lawns. The beach huts shine in the sun. The sea glitters. There's a solitary yacht with a red sail, marooned on the perfectly still water. The sky's blue with fluffy clouds that look like the ones in *The Simpsons*.

'Recognise it now?' I ask the kids.

'The seafront!' says Phoebe. 'We're here, Charlie.'

We pass Hove Lagoon and I feel a weird excitement as we turn right up our road. But the house looks just the same. We find a space right outside. The milometer records 10,034 miles.

Inside, the pile of post on the mat includes my plumbing application form. The hall smells musty and the house seems darker than I remembered, and colder too.

'Because the summer's over,' says Dinah. 'It's September, my love.'

Phoebe and Charlie run upstairs to their rooms, forgetting all their things are still locked away in the study, while Dinah and I go room to room downstairs, checking things.

'Living room's OK,' I shout.

'The playroom's fine,' she shouts back.

We meet in the kitchen. Phoebe comes downstairs with Charlie.

'Where's my CD player?'

'My cars aren't there.'

'They're locked in the study, guys. Play outside.'

I open the back door. Sunshine pours in. 'The trampoline, Charlie!' They run towards it. The lawn's knee-height. The Montana creepers have covered a new section of trellis.

'How do you feel?' Dinah asks.

'OK. You?'

'OK,' she says. 'Cup of tea?'

'I'd love one.'

I bath the kids, while Dinah prepares their uniforms for tomorrow.

Afterwards, Dinah reads Charlie a story and Phoebe reads her *Harry Potter* to me. But, in bed, Phoebe can't sleep. Her room's different. It's echoey without her things in it and it's hot and her eczema that never bothered her in France itches. I bring her downstairs.

'Oh, hello,' says Dinah, coming into the living room with the post. 'Having a little game of chess, are we?'

'Cos I was itchy. Dad said I could.'

'And what are these ones again?' I ask.

'Prawns,' says Phoebe.

'Not prawns, pawns, remember? And what's this one?'

'Er . . .'

'What does it look like?'

'My bucket?'

'It looks like your bucket, but only because your bucket looks like . . .'

'A castle?'

'Exactly. Although, actually, I like buckets more. Let's call them buckets.'

'Mummy,' Phoebe says, 'we're calling them buckets.'

'Good,' says Dinah.

'And these?'

'Horses.'

'Yes, and you can also call them knights.'

'I want to call them horses.'

'Fair enough.'

'Mummy, we're calling these ones horses,' says Phoebe.

'Good,' says Dinah.

Ten minutes later, I tuck her into bed. Downstairs, we carry on unpacking until we're so exhausted we give up and watch telly. I'm sat on the sofa when Buster's text comes through: 'The Eagle has landed. Beckham's having breakfast in the cookhouse. Apparently he's really quiet. He doesn't laugh, he just smiles.'

I text back: 'Smile back. He smiles. You smile.'

Buster replies: 'Probably doesn't make for great radio though. I'm going to be on the 10 o'clock news tomorrow. Hope you got back safely. Good luck with the builder tomorrow. Love yer.'

I try to ring him, but it goes through to voicemail, so I leave a message.

Before I come to bed, I set the video camera up for tomorrow, after checking it's fully charged. I make a hole in the front of my Panama hat to poke the lens through, then I find the best place to position it. After this, I wander around the house. I walk from room to room, picking things up and putting them down again. It seems strange to have so much space, to own things. On one level, it's a relief being home because we don't have to plan anything, but at the same time, it's scary having no plans.

I text a few people, to say we're back and to ask what

they're doing at the weekend, then I go to bed. Outside Charlie's room, his crisp new uniform's draped on the radiator, ready for tomorrow, and I feel a stab of fear, an echo of all those first days back at school after summer holidays when I was a kid.

Dinah's in bed, reading some notes from the university that came in the post about her first day tomorrow.

'You set for it?'

She nods towards the wardrobe. Her own business suit is hanging there.

CHAPTER 21

I sit on the end of Charlie's bed. I say his name. He wakes and lifts his head. I kiss his cheek. He opens his eyes and puts his hand round my head. Lying next to him, in his headlock, I ask whether he slept well. He nods. I ask if he's ready for porridge. He nods. I ask whether he needs a wee. He shakes his head. I ask if we should wake Phoebe and he nods. We walk across the landing. He touches Phoebe's face. He uses only his palms. He pats her cheeks. She sits up and pushes him away. Charlie tells Phoebe he's a cat, she can be the dog. But Phoebe says she wants to be the cat.

'Nooooo!' shouts Charlie.

Phoebe says, 'Not playing then.'

'Okaaay,' shouts Charlie. '*You* can be the cat.'

She puts on her dressing gown and her Dora the Explorer slippers. She starts to meow. Charlie begins to bark.

Later, in the kitchen, Dinah's in her new suit and is dressing Charlie. Phoebe dresses herself, while I make their sandwiches. I take their photo on the front doorstep.

'My school shoes are funny,' Charlie says.

'Why?'

'They're tight.'

'It's because you've had sandals on for so long.'

'Where's my Mickey Mouse key ring?'

'I've attached him to your book bag.'

When it's time to leave, Charlie goes missing. I find him at the bottom of the garden, hiding behind the shed.

'What's the matter, sunbeam?' He won't look at me. 'Is it school?'

He wails, 'I don't want to go.'

'Charlie, it will be fine.' I lift him up. He flops on my shoulder like a sandbag. Dinah comes out.

'There you are!'

'He's a bit upset.'

'You'll see Philip from nursery,' she says. 'Don't you want to see Philip?'

I walk him round the garden. It's something my dad would do with me and it's what I did when Charlie was a baby and wouldn't stop crying. I show him a snail on a leaf.

'Shall we eat it, like the French?'

He doesn't say anything. There's a faint moon. 'What are you doing out, moon? It's daytime.'

He says something. I can't hear him. His voice is muffled in my shoulder. 'What was that?'

'I wish we were going to a château,' he says.

'And I know it seems hard,' I whisper in his ear. 'We've been together three months, but the next big thing is Christmas. That's what to look forward to now. We'll open our stockings on Mummy and Daddy's bed. Then it's turkey for lunch and presents. After Christmas is over, you look forward to Easter eggs, and then it's almost the summer again. And it goes on every year like that.'

'I want a dinosaur base for Christmas,' he says, into my shoulder. Then he looks up. 'Actually, a dinosaur set. What you put dinosaurs on, with rocks and trees and volcanoes. I don't like cars any more.'

I look into his serious brown eyes. 'Really?'

He thinks, double-checks this momentous statement, and backs away from it. 'Actually, I do.'

'And, for your birthday, would you like to go to the Natural History Museum and see dinosaur bones?'

'Yes.'

I suggest he brings something from France to school. 'Orange sword?' he suggests.

'Maybe not a sword on your first day.'

'A dinosaur?'

'OK.'

He wriggles from my arms, jumps down and runs through the long grass back into the house, to find his remote-controlled T-Rex with the flashing red eyes.

First, we drop Dinah at Brighton University. I pull over outside the School of Education. Dinah rests her head on my shoulder.

'Do *you* want to take something in from France?'

'All of you,' she says.

She opens the kids' doors and kisses them in turn. They try to hold on to her. She has to prise herself away. She disappears into the campus, head down, her bag over her shoulder. 'Good luck, Mummy,' the kids shout through their windows, at the tops of their voices. They carry on shouting it, and she doesn't look round, but raises an arm of acknowledgment. 'Good luck,' they shout, until we're over the brow of the hill and she's out of sight.

Driving down the New Church Road, it's strange with just the three of us in the car. Phoebe spots classmates walking to school. 'Open the window, Daddy! It's Maisy.' She waves and dangles her Minnie Mouse out of the window at them.

In the Tesco car park outside the school, when Charlie won't leave his seat, Phoebe plays the wiser, older sister. 'You'll see Philip, Charlie.' 'You have to learn things, Charlie.' 'You can show them your dinosaur, Charlie.'

But I have to carry him to the gate. Other parents look at me pityingly. 'It will be alright, Charlie,' one or two tell him.

At the gate, I put him down. I give him his water bottle and Phoebe hers. I hand over their gym bags, their book bags, Charlie's dinosaur, and I balance the hoods of their coats on the backs of their heads. I kiss Charlie's cheek. And Phoebe's. Another reception boy arrives. He clings to his mum's legs.

'See, Charlie, everyone's the same,' says Phoebe, and she takes his hand. He breaks away and presses himself into my legs for a second. He grips hard, then lets go. They walk in together. I watch them go. His gym bag slips off his shoulder. Phoebe puts it back on for him. Neither of them look round. Other parents arrive, including Steve, Philip's dad.

We walk back to the car park together. 'Good summer?' he asks.

'Yeah,' I say. 'What about you?'

He tells me about his fortnight lying around a pool in Turkey. When he asks what we did, I start to tell him about Disneyland and Bugarach, but it all seems less relevant now than the fact that there are new barriers in Tesco's car park.

Back home, I unpack more boxes. I fill out my plumbing application form and email Jake about meeting up to discuss the travelogue with his publisher friend. I do some food shopping, so the kids have something for tea tonight. I buy flowers to cheer Dinah up for when she gets home. At lunchtime, sat in front of my blank screen, I call her.

'Kids go alright?'

'He was very brave.'

'And how was his daddy?'

'I was very brave too. And guess what I've done? I've rigged up a dummy in your seat in the study to keep me company.'

She laughs.

'I've dressed it in your clothes. I'm going to serve it mackerel for lunch.'

'Missing me then?'

'Not at all. Dummy and I have been reading out funny tweets to each other.'

'Let me know how it goes with Nick. I'd better go, love.'

'Good, because Dummy's just brought me in a cup of tea and an orange Club biscuit and wants to show me a funny clip on YouTube of some unlikely objects that look like Hitler.'

She laughs. The doorbell rings. 'That's him.'

'Good luck,' she says.

'And you.' And, walking back through the kitchen, I notice Dinah's put their Pierre the Bear pictures up on the fridge. For some reason, the careful way Charlie's drawn the crease either side of Pierre's mouth and the knot for his tied scarf makes me feel suddenly tearful. But Dinah predicted I'd get the blues today, and I said I wouldn't, and I don't want to prove her right, so I hold it together and, in the living room, I lift up my Panama, press record on the video camera, replace my hat and let Nick the builder in.

ACKNOWLEDGMENTS

Thanks to Richard Roper for his superb and incredibly patient edit, Sarah Emsley for her support and knowledge of how many tines there are on a household fork (4), Phil Patterson at Marjacq for his moustache jokes and hard work, Louise Page for her fiendish ideas, Caitlin Raynor for what will one day be revealed about panthers, Jo Liddiard, Frances Doyle and Tom Noble, Mary for her spot-on advice, my sister Penny because she's ace, @Rob_Shirt_Anon for his Bugarach help, Bev and Wozza for their hospitality, Bert and Marian for their forgiving natures and being prepared to accept for better or worse that their daughter married an oaf, Phoebe and Charlie for when they're old enough to read this and want to retrace in therapy where it all went wrong, and my brother Buster because he gets touchy if he's not mentioned in these things. I'd also like to thank all my Twitter pals for their help along the way. And Liz Hyder, Sophie Norris and KC, as well as Jenny, Lisa, Mike, Maddy, JoJo, Chris, the Matts and the rest of The Board. Many thanks to Fran Kellett for all her help, support and for suggesting the travelogue in the first place and also to Dominic Minghella, the only man who actually maintains a real life snake pit on his property. Final thanks to Kirk Jones, who, as well as directing fantastic movies, can fashion his beard trimmings into very realistic animals.